YOUR MOST COMPREHENSIVE AND REVEALING INDIVIDUAL FORECAST

SUPER HOROSCOPE

SAGITTARIUS 19 97

November 23 - December 20

BERKLEY BOOKS, NEW YORK

CONTENTS

The publishers regret that they cannot answer individual
letters requesting personal horoscope information.

The Putnam Berkley World Wide Web address is
http://www.berkley.com

ISBN: 0-425-15356-8

BERKLEY®
Berkley Books are published by The Berkley Publishing Group,
200 Madison Avenue, New York, New York 10016.
The Name "BERKLEY" and the "B" logo
are trademarks belonging to Berkley Publishing Corporation.

PRINTED IN THE UNITED STATES OF AMERICA
10   9   8   7   6   5   4   3   2   1

NOTE TO THE CUSP-BORN

First find the year of your birth, and then find the sign under which you were born according to your day of birth. Thus, you can determine if you are a true Sagittarius (or Scorpio or Capricorn), according to the variations of the dates of the Zodiac. (See also page7.)

Are you *really* a Sagittarius? If your birthday falls around the fourth week in November, at the very beginning of Sagittarius, will you still retain the traits of Scorpio, the sign of the Zodiac before Sagittarius? And what if you were born near Christmas—are you more Capricorn than Sagittarius? Many people born at the edge, or cusp, of a sign have great difficulty determining exactly what sign they are. If you are one of these people, here's how you can figure it out once and for all.

Consult the following table. It will tell you the precise days on which the Sun entered and left your sign. If you were born at the beginning or end of Sagittarius, yours is a lifetime reflecting a process of subtle transformation. Your life on Earth will symbolize a significant change in consciousness, for you are about to enter a whole new way of living or are leaving one behind.

If you were born at the beginning of Sagittarius, you may want to read the horoscope for Scorpio as well as Sagittarius, for Scorpio holds the key to many of your hidden weaknesses, sexual uncertainties, wishes, fantasies, and spiritual potentials. You are the symbol of the human mind awakening to its higher capabilities. You are preparing the way for the liberation of your soul into the realms of wisdom and truth. You leave behind greed, blind desire and shallow lust, as you learn to create and understand yourself. You travel, see new places, see how people live, figure yourself out, acquire knowledge.

You may hide a stubborn and dangerous extremism and you may rely too much on luck, but at some crisis point in your life, a change of consciousness will occur to shift your behavior patterns. New worlds open up, as you become aware of immortality and the infinite possiblities of your own mind.

iii

If you were born at the end of Sagittarius, you may want to read the horoscope book for Capricorn as well as Sagittarius, for Capricorn is a deep part of your materialistic values. You were born with the need to bring your dreams into reality and put your talents and ambitions to practical use.

You need to find a balance between believing nothing and believing too much—between cynicism and blind idealism.

DATES SUN ENTERS SAGITTARIUS (LEAVES SCORPIO)

November 22 every year from 1900 to 2000, except for the following:

November 21:		November 23:		
1976	1992	1902	1915	1931
80	93	03	19	35
84	96	07	23	39
88		10	27	43
		11		

DATES SUN LEAVES SAGITTARIUS (ENTERS CAPRICORN)

December 22 every year from 1900 to 2000, except for the following:

December 21:				
1912	1944	1964	1977	1989
16	48	65	80	92
20	52	68	81	93
23	53	69	84	94
28	56	72	85	96
32	57	73	86	97
36	60	76	88	98
40	61			

HISTORY AND USES
OF ASTROLOGY

Does astrology have a place in the fast-moving, ultra-scientific world we live in today? Can it be justified in a sophisticated society whose outriders are already preparing to step off the moon into the deep space of the planets themselves? Or is it just a hangover of ancient superstition, a psychological dummy for neurotics and dreamers of every historical age?

These are the kind of questions that any inquiring person can be expected to ask when they approach a subject like astrology which goes beyond, but never excludes, the materialistic side of life.

The simple, single answer is that astrology works. It works for tens of millions of people in the western world alone. In the United States there are 10 million followers and in Europe, an estimated 25 million. America has more than 4000 practicing astrologers, Europe nearly three times as many. Even down-under Australia has its hundreds of thousands of adherents. The importance of such vast numbers of people from diverse backgrounds and cultures is recognized by the world's biggest newspapers and magazines who probably devote more of their space to this subject in a year than to any other. In the eastern countries, astrology has enormous followings, again, because it has been proved to work. In countries like India, brides and grooms for centuries have been chosen on the basis of astrological compatibility. The low divorce rate there, despite today's heavy westernizing influence, is attributed largely to this practice.

In the western world, astrology today is more vital than ever before; more practicable because it needs a sophisticated society like ours to understand and develop its contribution to the full; more valid because science itself is confirming the precepts of astrological knowledge with every new exciting step. The ordinary person who daily applies astrology intelligently does not have to wonder whether it is true nor believe in it blindly. He can see it working for himself. And, if he can use it—and this book is designed to help the reader to do just that—he can make living a far richer experience, and become a more developed personality and a better person.

Astrology is the science of relationships. It is not just a study of planetary influences on man and his environment. It is the study of man himself.

We are at the center of our personal universe, of all our rela-

1

tionships. And our happiness or sadness depends on how we act, how we relate to the people and things that surround us. The emotions that we generate have a distinct affect—for better or worse—on the world around us. Our friends and our enemies will confirm this. Just look in the mirror the next time you are angry. In other words, each of us is a kind of sun or planet or star and our influence on our personal universe, whether loving, helpful or destructive, varies with our changing moods, expressed through our individual character.

And to an extent that includes the entire galaxy, this is true of the planetary bodies. Their radiations affect each other, including the earth and all the things on it. And in comparatively recent years, giant constellations called "quasars" have been discovered. These exist far beyond the night stars that we can observe, and science says these quasars are emitting radiating influences more powerful and different than ever recorded on earth. Their effect on man from an astrological point of view is under deep study. Compared with these inter-stellar forces, our personal "radiations" are negligible on the planetary scale. But ours are just as potent in the way they affect our moods, and our ability to control them. To this extent they determine much of the happiness and satisfaction in our lives. For instance, if we were bound and gagged and had to hold some strong emotion within us without being able to move, we would soon start to feel very uncomfortable. We are obviously pretty powerful radiators inside, in our own way. But usually, we are able to throw off our emotion in some sort of action—we have a good cry, walk it off, or tell someone our troubles—before it can build up too far and make us physically ill. Astrology helps us to understand the universal forces working on us, and through this understanding, we can become more properly adjusted to our surroundings and find ourselves coping where others may flounder.

Closely related to our emotions is the "other side" of our personal universe, our physical welfare. Our body, of course, is largely influenced by things around us over which we have very little control. The phone rings, we hear it. The train runs late. We snag our stocking or cut our face shaving. Our body is under a constant bombardment of events that influence our lives to varying degrees.

The question that arises from all this is, what makes each of us act so that we have to involve other people and keep the ball of activity and evolution rolling? This is the question that both science and astrology are involved with. The scientists have attacked it from different angles: anthropology, the study of human evolution as body, mind and response to environment; anatomy, the study of bodily structure; psychology, the science of the human mind; and so on. These studies have produced very impressive classifications and valuable information, but because the approach to the problem is fragmented, so is the result. They remain "branches" of science. Science generally studies effects. It keeps turning up wonderful answers but no lasting solutions. Astrology, on the other hand approaches the question from the broader viewpoint. Astrology began its inquiry with the totality of human experience and saw it as an effect. It then looked to find the cause, or at least the prime movers, and during thousands of years of observation of man and his *universal* environment, came up with the extraordinary principle of planetary influence—or astrology, which, from the Greek, means the science of the stars.

Modern science, as we shall see, has confirmed much of astrology's foundations—most of it unintentionally, some of it reluctantly, but still, indisputably.

It is not difficult to imagine that there must be a connection between outer space and the earth. Even today, scientists are not too sure how our earth was created, but it is generally agreed that it is only a tiny part of the universe. And as a part of the universe, people on earth see and feel the influence of heavenly bodies in almost every aspect of our existence. There is no doubt that the sun has the greatest influence on life on this planet. Without it there would be no life, for without it there would be no warmth, no division into day and night, no cycles of time or season at all. This is clear and easy to see. The influence of the moon, on the other hand, is more subtle, though no less definite.

There are many ways in which the influence of the moon manifests itself here on earth, both on human and animal life. It is a well-known fact, for instance, that the large movements of water on our planet—that is the ebb and flow of the tides—are caused by the moon's gravitational pull. Since this is so, it follows that these water movements do not occur only in the oceans, but that all bodies of water are affected, even down to the tiniest puddle.

The human body, too, which consists of about 70 percent water, falls within the scope of this lunar influence. For example the menstrual cycle of most women corresponds to the lunar month; the period of pregnancy in humans is 273 days, or equal to nine lunar months. Similarly, many illnesses reach a crisis at the change of the moon, and statistics in many countries have shown that the crime rate is highest at the time of the full moon. Even human sexual desire has been associated with the phases of the moon. But, it is in the movement of the tides that we get the clearest demonstration of planetary influence, and the irresistible correspondence between the so-called metaphysical and the physical.

Tide tables are prepared years in advance by calculating the future positions of the moon. Science has known for a long time that the moon is the main cause of tidal action. But only in the last few years has it begun to realize the possible extent of this influence on mankind. To begin with, the ocean tides do not rise and fall as we might imagine from our personal observations of them. The moon as it orbits around the earth, sets up a circular wave of attraction which pulls the oceans of the world after it, broadly in an east to west direction. This influence is like a phantom wave crest, a loop of power stretching from pole to pole which passes over and around the earth like an invisible shadow. It travels with equal effect across the land masses and, as scientists were recently amazed to observe, caused oysters placed in the dark in the middle of the United States where there is no sea, to open their shells to receive the non-existent tide. If the land-locked oysters react to this invisible signal, what effect does it have on us who not so long ago in evolutionary time, came out of the sea and still have its salt in our blood and sweat?

Less well known is the fact that the moon is also the primary force behind the circulation of blood in human beings and animals, and the movement of sap in trees and plants. Agriculturists have established that the moon has a distinct influence on crops, which explains why for centuries people have planted according to moon cycles. The habits of many animals, too, are directed by the movement of the moon. Migratory birds, for instance, depart only at or near the time of the full moon. Just as certain fish, eels in particular, move only in accordance with certain phases of the moon.

Know Thyself—Why?

In today's fast-changing world, everyone still longs to know what the future holds. It is the one thing that everyone has in common: rich and poor, famous and infamous, all are deeply concerned about tomorrow.

But the key to the future, as every historian knows, lies in the past. This is as true of individual people as it is of nations. You cannot understand your future without first understanding your past, which is simply another way of saying that you must first of all know yourself.

The motto "know thyself" seems obvious enough nowadays, but it was originally put forward as the foundation of wisdom by the ancient Greek philosophers. It was then adopted by the "mystery religions" of the ancient Middle East, Greece and Rome, and is still used in all genuine schools of mind training or mystical discipline, both in those of the East, based on yoga, and those of the West. So it is universally accepted now, and has been through the ages.

But how do you go about discovering what sort of person you are? The first step is usually classification into some sort of system of types. Astrology did this long before the birth of Christ. Psychology has also done it. So has modern medicine, in its way.

One system classifies men according to the source of the impulses they respond to most readily: the muscles, leading to direct bodily action; the digestive organs, resulting in emotion, or the brain and nerves. Another such system says that character is determined by the endocrine glands, and gives us labels like "pituitary," "thyroid" and "hyperthyroid" types. These different systems are neither contradictory nor mutually exclusive. In fact, they are very often different ways of saying the same thing.

Very popular and useful classifications were devised by Dr. C. G. Jung, the eminent disciple of Freud. Jung observed among the different faculties of the mind, four which have a predominant influence on character. These four faculties exist in all of us without exception, but not in perfect balance. So when we say, for instance, that a man is a "thinking type," it means that in any situation he tries to be rational. It follows that emotion, which some say is the opposite of thinking, will be his weakest function. This type can be sensible and reasonable, or calculating and unsympathetic. The emotional type, on the other hand, can often be recognized by exaggerated language—everything is either marvelous or terrible—and in extreme cases they even invent dramas and quarrels out of nothing just to make life more interesting.

The other two faculties are intuition and physical sensation. The sensation type does not only care for food and drink, nice clothes and furniture; he is also interested in all forms of physical experience. Many scientists are sensation types as are athletes and nature-lovers. Like sensation, intuition is a form of perception and we all possess it. But it works through that part of the mind which is not under conscious control—consequently it sees meanings and connections which are not obvious to thought or emotion. Inventors and original thinkers are always intuitive, but so, too, are superstitious people who see meanings where none exist.

Thus, sensation tells us what is going on in the world, feeling (that is, emotion) tells us how important it is to ourselves, thinking enables us to interpret it and work out what we should do about it, and intuition tells us what it means to ourselves and others. All four faculties are essential, and all are present in every one of us. But some people are guided chiefly by one, others by another.

Besides these four types, Jung observed a division into extrovert and introvert, which cuts across them. By and large, the introvert is one who finds truth inside himself rather than outside. He is not, therefore, ideally suited to a religion or a political party which tells him what to believe. Original thinkers are almost necessarily introverts. The extrovert, on the other hand, finds truth coming to him from outside. He believes in experts and authorities, and wants to think that nature and the laws of nature really exists, that they are what they appear to be and not just generalities made by men.

A disadvantage of all these systems of classification, is that one cannot tell very easily where to place oneself. Some people are reluctant to admit that they act to please their emotions. So they deceive themselves for years by trying to belong to whichever type they think is the "best." Of course, there is no best; each has its faults and each has its good points.

The advantage of the signs of the Zodiac is that they simplify classification. Not only that, but your date of birth is personal—it is unarguably yours. What better way to know yourself than by going back as far as possible to the very moment of your birth? And this is precisely what your horoscope is all about.

What Is a Horoscope?

If you had been able to take a picture of the heavens at the moment of your birth, that photograph would be your horoscope. Lacking such a snapshot, it is still possible to recreate the picture—and this is at the basis of the astrologer's art. In other words, your horoscope is a representation of the skies with the planets in the exact positions they occupied at the time you were born.

This information, of course, is not enough for the astrologer. He has to have a background of significance to put the photograph on. You will get the idea if you imagine two balls—one inside the other. The inner one is transparent. In the center of both is the astrologer, able to look up, down and around in all directions. The outer sphere is the Zodiac which is divided into twelve approximately equal segments, like the segments of an orange. The inner ball is our photograph. It is transparent except for the images of the planets. Looking out from the center, the astrologer sees the planets in various segments of the Zodiac. These twelve segments are known as the signs or houses.

The position of the planets when each of us is born is always different. So the photograph is always different. But the Zodiac and its signs are fixed.

Now, where in all this are you, the subject of the horoscope?

Your character is largely determined by the sign the sun is in. So that is where the astrologer looks first in your horoscope.

There are twelve signs in the Zodiac and the sun spends approximately one month in each. As the sun's motion is almost perfectly regular, the astrologers have been able to fix the dates governing each sign. There are not many people who do not know which sign of the Zodiac they were born under or who have not been amazed at some time or other at the accuracy of the description of their own character. Here are the twelve signs, the ancient zodiacal symbol, and their dates for the year 1997.*

ARIES	Ram	March 20–April 19
TAURUS	Bull	April 19–May 20
GEMINI	Twins	May 20–June 21
CANCER	Crab	June 21–July 22
LEO	Lion	July 22–August 22
VIRGO	Virgin	August 22–September 22
LIBRA	Scales	September 22–October 23
SCORPIO	Scorpion	October 23–November 22
SAGITTARIUS	Archer	November 22–December 21
CAPRICORN	Sea-Goat	December 21–January 19
AQUARIUS	Water-Bearer	January 19–February 18
PISCES	Fish	February 18–March 20

The time of birth—part from the date—is important in advanced astrology because the planets travel at such great speed that the patterns they form change from minute to minute. For this reason, each person's horoscope is his and his alone. Further on we will see that the practicing astrologer has ways of determining and reading these minute time changes which dictate the finer character differences in us all.

However, it is still possible to draw significant conclusions and make meaningful predictions based simply on the sign of the Zodiac a person is born under. In a horoscope, the signs do not necessarily correspond with the divisions of the houses. It could be that a house begins halfway across a sign. It is the interpretation of such combinations of different influences that distinguishes the professional astrologer from the student and the follower.

However, to gain a workable understanding of astrology, it is not necessary to go into great detail. In fact, the beginner is likely to find himself confused if he attempts to absorb too much too quickly. It should be remembered that this is a science and to become proficient at it, and especially to grasp the tremendous scope of possibilities in man and his affairs and direct them into a worthwhile reading, takes a great deal of study and experience.

*These dates are fluid and change with the motion of the Earth from year to year.

If you do intend to pursue it seriously you will have to learn to figure the exact moment of birth against the degrees of longitude and latitude of the planets at that precise time. This involves adapting local time to Greenwich Mean Time (G.M.T.), reference to tables of houses to establish the Ascendant, as well as making calculations from Ephemeris—the tables of the planets' positions.

After reading this introduction, try drawing up a rough horoscope to get the "feel" of reading some elementary characteristics and natal influences.

Draw a circle with twelve equal segments. Write in counterclockwise the names of the signs—Aries, Taurus, Gemini etc.—one for each segment. Look up an ephemeris for the year of the person's birth and note down the sign each planet was in on the birthday. Do not worry about the number of degrees (although if a planet is on the edge of a sign its position obviously should be considered). Write the name of the planet in the segment/sign on your chart. Write the number 1 in the sign where the sun is. This is the first house. Number the rest of the houses, counterclockwise till you finish at 12. Now you can investigate the probable basic expectation of experience of the person concerned. This is done first of all by seeing what planet or planets is/are in what sign and house. (See also page 72.)

The 12 houses control these functions:

1st.	Individuality, body appearance, general outlook on life	(Personality house)
2nd.	Finance, business	(Money house)
3rd.	Relatives, education, correspondence	(Relatives house)
4th.	Family, neighbors	(Home house)
5th.	Pleasure, children, attempts, entertainment	(Pleasure house)
6th.	Health, employees	(Health house)
7th.	Marriage, partnerships	(Marriage house)
8th.	Death, secret deals, difficulties	(Death house)
9th.	Travel, intellectual affairs	(Travel house)
10th.	Ambition, social standing	(Business and Honor house)
11th.	Friendship, social life, luck	(Friends house)
12th.	Troubles, illness, loss	(Trouble house)

The characteristics of the planets modify the influence of the Sun according to their natures and strengths.

Sun: Source of life. Basic temperament according to sun sign. The will.
Moon: Superficial nature. Moods. Changeable. Adaptive. Mother.
Mercury: Communication. Intellect. Reasoning power. Curiosity. Short travels.
Venus: Love. Delight. Art. Beautiful possessions.
Mars: Energy. Initiative. War. Anger. Destruction. Impulse.
Jupiter: Good. Generous. Expansive. Opportunities. Protection.
Saturn: Jupiter's opposite. Contraction. Servant. Delay. Hardwork. Cold. Privation. Research. Lasting rewards after long struggle.
Uranus: Fashion. Electricity. Revolution. Sudden changes. Modern science.
Neptune: Sensationalism. Mass emotion. Devastation. Delusion.
Pluto: Creates and destroys. Lust for power. Strong obsessions.

Superimpose the characteristics of the planets on the functions of the house in which they appear. Express the result through the character of the birth (sun) sign, and you will get the basic idea of how astrology works.

Of course, many other considerations have been taken into account in producing the carefully worked out predictions in this book: The aspects of the planets to each other; their strength according to position and sign; whether they are in a house of exaltation or decline; whether they are natural enemies or not; whether a planet occupies his own sign; the position of a planet in relation to its own house or sign; whether the planet is male, female or neuter; whether the sign is a fire, earth, water or air sign. These are only a few of the colors on the astrologer's pallet which he must mix with the inspiration of the artist and the accuracy of the mathematician.

The Problem of Love

Love, of course, is never a problem. The problem lies in recognizing the difference between infatuation, emotion, sex and, sometimes, the downright deceit of the other person. Mankind, with its record of broken marriages, despair and disillusionment, is obviously not very good at making these distinctions.

Can astrology help?

Yes. In the same way that advance knowledge can usually help in any human situation. And there is probably no situation as human, as poignant, as pathetic and universal, as the failure of man's love.

Love, of course, is not just between man and woman. It involves love of children, parents, home and so on. But the big problems usually involve the choice of partner.

Astrology has established degrees of compatibility that exist between people born under the various signs of the Zodiac. Because people are individuals, there are numerous variations and modifications and the astrologer, when approached on mate and marriage matters makes allowances for them. But the fact remains that some groups of people are suited for each other and some are not and astrology has expressed this in terms of characteristics which all can study and use as a personal guide.

No matter how much enjoyment and pleasure we find in the different aspects of each other's character, if it is not an overall compatibility, the chances of our finding fulfillment or enduring happiness in each other are pretty hopeless. And astrology can help us to find someone compatible.

History of Astrology

The origins of astrology have been lost far back in history, but we do know that reference is made to it as far back as the first written records of the human race. It is not hard to see why. Even in primitive times, people must have looked for an explanation for the various happenings in their lives. They must have wanted to know why people were different from one to another. And in their search they turned to the regular movements of the sun, moon and stars to see if they could provide an answer.

It is interesting to note that as soon as man learned to use his tools in any type of design, or his mind in any kind of calculation, he turned his attention to the heavens. Ancient cave dwellings reveal dim crescents and circles representative of the sun and moon, rulers of day and night. Mesopotamia and the civilization of Chaldea, in itself the foundation of those of Babylonia and Assyria, show a complete picture of astronomical observation and well-developed astrological interpretation.

Humanity has a natural instinct for order. The study of anthropology reveals that primitive people—even as far back as prehistoric times—were striving to achieve a certain order in their lives. They tried to organize the apparent chaos of the universe. They had the desire to attach meaning to things. This demand for order has persisted throughout the history of man. So that observing the regularity of the heavenly bodies made it logical that primitive peoples should turn heavenwards in their search for an understanding of the world in which they found themselves so random and alone.

And they did find a significance in the movements of the stars. Shepherds tending their flocks, for instance, observed that when the cluster of stars now known as the constellation Aries was in sight, it was the time of fertility and they associated it with the Ram. And they noticed that the growth of plants and plant life corresponded with different phases of the moon, so that certain times were favorable for the planting of crops, and other times were not. In this way, there grew up a tradition of seasons and causes connected with the passage of the sun through the twelve signs of the Zodiac.

Astrology was valued so highly that the king was kept informed of the daily and monthly changes in the heavenly bodies, and the results of astrological studies regarding events of the future. Head astrologers were clearly men of great rank and position, and the office was said to be a hereditary one.

Omens were taken, not only from eclipses and conjunctions of the moon or sun with one of the planets, but also from storms and earthquakes. In the eastern civilizations, particularly, the reverence inspired by astrology appears to have remained unbroken since the very earliest days. In ancient China, astrology, astronomy and religion went hand in hand. The astrologer, who was also an astronomer, was part of the official government service and had his own corner in the Imperial Palace. The duties of the Imperial astrologer, whose office was one of the most important in the land, were clearly defined, as this extract from early records shows:

"This exalted gentleman must concern himself with the stars in the heavens, keeping a record of the changes and movements of the Planets, the Sun and the Moon, in order to examine the movements of the terrestial world with the object of prognosticating good and bad fortune. He divides the territories of the nine regions of the empire in accordance with their dependence on particular celestial bodies. All the fiefs and principalities are connected with the stars and from this their prosperity or misfortune should be ascertained. He makes prognostications according to the twelve years of the Jupiter cycle of good and evil of the terrestial world. From the colors of the five kinds of clouds, he determines the coming of floods or droughts, abundance or famine. From the twelve winds, he draws conclusions about the state of harmony of heaven and earth, and takes note of good and bad signs that result from their accord or disaccord. In general, he concerns himself with five kinds of phenomena so as to warn the Emperor to come to the aid of the government and to allow for variations in the ceremonies according to their circumstances."

The Chinese were also keen observers of the fixed stars, giving them such unusual names as Ghost Vehicle, Sun of Imperial Concubine, Imperial Prince, Pivot of Heaven, Twinkling Brilliance or Weaving Girl. But, great astrologers though they may have been, the Chinese lacked one aspect of mathematics that the Greeks applied to astrology—deductive geometry. Deductive geometry was the basis of much classical astrology in and after the time of the Greeks, and this explains the different methods of prognostication used in the East and West.

Down through the ages the astrologer's art has depended, not so much on the uncovering of new facts, though this is important, as on the interpretation of the facts already known. This is the essence of his skill. Obviously one cannot always tell how people will react (and this underlines the very important difference between astrology and predestination which will be discussed later on) but one can be prepared, be forewarned, to know what to expect.

But why should the signs of the zodiac have any effect at all on the formation of human character? It is easy to see why people thought they did, and even now we constantly use astrological expressions in our everyday speech. The thoughts of "lucky star," "ill-fated," "star-crossed," "mooning around," are interwoven into the very structure of our language.

In the same way that the earth has been created by influences from outside, there remains an indisputable togetherness in the working of the universe. The world, after all, is a coherent structure, for if it were not, it would be quite without order and we would never know what to expect. A dog could turn into an apple, or an elephant sprout wings and fly at any moment without so much as a by your leave. But nature, as we know, functions according to laws, not whims, and the laws of nature are certainly not subject to capricious exceptions.

This means that no part of the universe is ever arbitrarily cut off from any other part. Everything is therefore to some extent linked with everything else. The moon draws an imperceptible tide on every puddle; tiny and trivial events can be effected by outside forces (such as the fall of a feather by the faintest puff of wind). And so it is fair to think that the local events at any moment reflect to a very small extent the evolution of the world as a whole.

From this principle follows the possibility of divination, and also knowledge of events at a distance, provided one's mind were always as perfectly undisturbed, as ideally smooth, as a mirror or unruffled lake. Provided, in other words, that one did not confuse the picture with hopes, guesses, and expectations. When people try to foretell the future by cards or crystal ball gazing they find it much easier to confuse the picture with expectations than to reflect it clearly.

But the present does contain a good deal of the future to which it leads—not all, but a good deal. The diver halfway between bridge and water is going to make a splash; the train whizzing towards the station will pass through it unless interfered with; the burglar breaking a pane of glass has exposed himself to the possibility of a prison sentence. Yet this is not a doctrine of determinism, as was emphasized earlier. Clearly, there are forces already at work in the present, and any one of them could alter the situation in some way. Equally, a change of decision could alter the whole situation as well. So the future depends, not on an irresistible force, but on a small act of free will.

An individual's age, physique, and position on the earth's surface are remote consequences of his birth. Birth counts as the original cause for all that happens subsequently. The horoscope, in this case, means "this person represents the further evolution of the state of the universe pictured in this chart." Such a chart can apply equally to man or woman, dog, ship or even limited company.

If the evolution of an idea, or of a person, is to be understood as a totality, it must continue to evolve from its own beginnings, which is to say, in the terms in which it began. The brown-eyed person will be faithful to brown eyes all his life; the traitor is being faithful to some complex of ideas which has long been evolving in him; and the person born at sunset will always express, as he evolves, the psychological implications or analogies of the moment when the sun sinks out of sight.

This is the doctrine that an idea must continue to evolve in terms of its origin. It is a completely non-materialist doctrine, though it never fails to apply to material objects. And it implies, too, that the individual will continue to evolve in terms of his moment of origin, and therefore possibly of the sign of the Zodiac rising on the eastern horizon at his birth. It also implies that the signs of the Zodiac themselves will evolve in the collective mind of the human race in the same terms that they were first devised and not in the terms in which modern astrologers consciously think they ought to work.

For the human race, like every other kind of animal, has a collective mind, as Professor Jung discovered in his investigation of dreams. If no such collective mind existed, no infant could ever learn anything, for communication would be impossible. Furthermore, it is absurd to suggest that the conscious mind could be older than the "unconscious," for an infant's nervous system functions correctly before it has discovered the difference between "myself" and "something else" or discovered what eyes and hands are for. Indeed, the involuntary muscles function correctly even before birth, and will never be under conscious control. They are part of what we call the "unconscious" which is not really "unconscious" at all. To the contrary, it is totally aware of itself and everything else; it is merely that part of the mind that cannot be controlled by conscious effort.

And human experience, though it varies in detail with every individual, is basically the same for each one of us, consisting of sky and earth, day and night, waking and sleeping, man and woman, birth and death. So there is bound to be in the mind of the human race a very large number of inescapable ideas, which are called our natural archetypes.

There are also, however, artificial or cultural archetypes which are not universal or applicable to everyone, but are nevertheless inescapable within the limits of a given culture. Examples of these are the cross in Christianity, and the notion of "escape from the wheel of rebirth" in India. There was a time when these ideas did not exist. And there was a time, too, when the scheme of the Zodiac did not exist. One would not expect the Zodiac to have any influence on remote and primitive peoples, for example, who have never heard of it. If the Zodiac is only an archetype, their horoscopes probably would not work and it would not matter which sign they were born under.

But where the Zodiac is known, and the idea of it has become worked into the collective mind, then there it could well appear to have an influence, even if it has no physical existence. For ideas do not have a physical existence, anyway. No physical basis has yet been discovered for the telepathy that controls an anthill; young swallows migrate before, not after, their parents; and the weaverbird builds its intricate nest without being taught. Materialists suppose, but cannot prove, that "instinct" (as it is called, for no one knows how it works) is controlled by nucleic acid in the chromosomes. This is not a genuine explanation, though, for it only pushes the mystery one stage further back.

Does this mean, then, that the human race, in whose civilization the idea of the twelve signs of the Zodiac has long been embedded, is divided into only twelve types? Can we honestly believe that it is really as simple as that? If so, there must be pretty wide ranges of variation within each type. And if, to explain the variation, we call in heredity and environment, experiences in early childhood, the thyroid and other glands, and also the four functions of the mind mentioned at the beginning of this introduction, and extroversion and introversion, then one begins to wonder if the original classification was worth making at all. No sensible person believes that his favorite system explains everything. But even so, he will not find it much use at all if it does not even save him the trouble of bothering with the others.

Under the Jungian system, everyone has not only a dominant or principal function, but also a secondary or subsidiary one, so that the four can be arranged in order of potency. In the intuitive type, sensation is always the most inefficient function, but the second most inefficient function can be either thinking (which tends to make original thinkers such as Jung himself) or else feeling (which tends to make artistic people). Therefore, allowing for introversion and extroversion, there are at least four kinds of intuitive types, and sixteen types in all. Furthermore, one can see how the sixteen types merge into each other, so that there are no unrealistic or unconvincingly rigid divisions.

In the same way, if we were to put every person under only one sign of the Zodiac, the system becomes too rigid and unlike life. Besides, it was never intended to be used like that. It may be convenient to have only twelve types, but we know that in practice there is every possible gradation between aggressiveness and timidity, or between conscientiousness and laziness. How, then, do we account for this?

The Tyrant and the Saint

Just as the thinking type of man is also influenced to some extent by sensation and intuition, but not very much by emotion, so a person born under Leo can be influenced to some extent by one or two (but not more) of the other signs. For instance, famous persons born under the sign of Gemini include Henry VIII, whom nothing and no-one could have induced to abdicate, and Edward VIII, who did just that. Obviously, then, the sign Gemini does not fully explain the complete character of either of them.

Again, under the opposite sign, Sagittarius, were both Stalin, who was totally consumed with the notion of power, and Charles V, who freely gave up an empire because he preferred to go into a monastery. And we find under Scorpio, many uncompromising characters such as Luther, de Gaulle, Indira Gandhi and Montgomery, but also Petain, a successful commander whose name later became synonymous with collaboration.

A single sign is therefore obviously inadequate to explain the differences between people; it can only explain resemblances, such as the combativeness of the Scorpio group, or the far-reaching devotion of Charles V and Stalin to their respective ideals—the Christian heaven and the Communist utopia.

But very few people are born under one sign only. As well as the month of birth, as was mentioned earlier, the day matters, and, even more, the hour, which ought, if possible, to be noted to the nearest minute. Without this, it is impossible to have an actual horoscope, for the word horoscope means literally, "a consideration of the hour."

The month of birth tells you only which sign of the Zodiac was occupied by the sun. The day and hour tell you what sign was occupied by the moon. And the minute tells you which sign was rising on the eastern horizon. This is called the Ascendant, and it is supposed to be the most important thing in the whole horoscope.

If you were born at midnight, the sun is then in an important position, although invisible. But at one o'clock in the morning the sun is not important, so the moment of birth will not matter much. The important thing then will be the Ascendant, and possibly one or two of the planets. At a given day and hour, say, dawn on January 1st, or 9:00 p.m. on the longest day, the Ascendant will always be the same at any given place. But the moon and planets alter from day to day, at different speeds and have to be looked up in an astronomical table.

The sun is said to signify one's heart, that is to say, one's deepest desires and inmost nature. This is quite different from the moon, which, as we have seen, signifies one's superficial way of behaving. When the ancient Romans referred to the Emperor Augustus as a Capricornian, they meant that he had the moon in Capricorn; they did not pay much attention to the sun, although he was born at sunrise. Or, to take another example, a modern astrologer would call Disraeli a Scorpion because he had Scorpio rising, but most people would call him Sagittarian because he had the sun there. The Romans would have called him Leo because his moon was in Leo.

The sun, as has already been pointed out, is important if one is born near sunrise, sunset, noon or midnight, but is otherwise not reckoned as the principal influence. So if one does not seem to fit one's birth month, it is always worthwhile reading the other signs, for one may have been born at a time when any of them were rising or occupied by the moon. It also seems to be the case that the influence of the sun develops as life goes on, so that the month of birth is easier to guess in people over the age of forty. The young are supposed to be influenced mainly by their Ascendant which characterizes the body and physical personality as a whole.

It should be clearly understood that it is nonsense to assume that all people born at a certain time will exhibit the same characteristics, or that they will even behave in the same manner. It is quite obvious that, from the very moment of its birth, a child is subject to the effects of its environment, and that this in turn will influence its character and heritage to a decisive extent. Also to be taken into account are education and economic conditions, which play a very important part in the formation of one's character as well.

However, it is clearly established that people born under one sign of the Zodiac do have certain basic traits in their character which are different from those born under other signs. It is obvious to every thinking person that certain events produce different reactions in various people. For instance, if a man slips on a banana skin and falls heavily on the pavement, one passer-by may laugh and find this extremely amusing, while another may just walk on, thinking: "What a fool falling down like that. He should look where he is going." A third might also walk away saying to himself: "It's none of my business—I'm glad it wasn't me." A fourth might walk past and think: "I'm sorry for that man, but I haven't the time to be bothered with helping him." And a fifth might stop to help the fallen man to his feet, comfort him and take him home. Here is just one event which could produce entirely different reactions in different people. And, obviously, there are many more. One that comes to mind immediately is the violently opposed views to events such as wars, industrial strikes, and so on. The fact that people have different attitudes to the same event is simply another way of saying that they have different characters. And this is not something that can be put down to background, for people of the same race, religion, or class, very often express quite different reactions to happenings or events. Similarly, it is often the case that members of the same family, where there is clearly uniform background of economic and social standing, education, race and religion, often argue bitterly among themselves over political and social issues.

People have, in general, certain character traits and qualities which, according to their environment, develop in either a positive or a negative manner. Therefore, selfishness (inherent selfishness, that is) might emerge as unselfishness; kindness and consideration as cruelty and lack of consideration towards others. In the same way, a naturally constructive person, may, through frustration, become destructive, and so on. The latent characteristics with which people are born can, therefore, through environment and good or bad training, become something that would appear to be its opposite, and so give the lie to the astrologer's description of their character. But this is not the case. The true character is still there, but it is buried deep beneath these external superficialities.

Careful study of the character traits of different signs can be immeasurable help, and can render beneficial service to the intelligent person. Undoubtedly, the reader will already have discovered that, while he is able to get on very well with some people, he just "cannot stand" others. The causes sometimes seem inexplicable. At times there is intense dislike, at other times immediate sympathy. And there is, too, the phenomenon of love at first sight, which is also apparently inexplicable. People appear to be either sympathetic or unsympathetic towards each other for no apparent reason.

Now if we look at this in the light of the Zodiac, we find that people born under different signs are either compatible or incompatible with each other. In other words, there are good and bad interrelating factors among the various signs. This does not, of course, mean that humanity can be divided into groups of hostile camps. It would be quite wrong to be hostile or indifferent toward people who happen to be born under an incompatible sign. There is no reason why everybody should not, or cannot, learn to control and adjust their feelings and actions, especially after they are aware of the positive qualities of other people by studying their character analyses, among other things.

Every person born under a certain sign has both positive and negative qualities, which are developed more or less according to his free will. Nobody is entirely good or entirely bad, and it is up to each one of us to learn to control himself on the one hand, and at the same time to endeavor to learn about himself and others.

It cannot be repeated often enough that, though the intrinsic nature of man and his basic character traits are born in him, nevertheless it is his own free will that determines whether he will make really good use of his talents and abilities—whether, in other words, he will overcome his vices or allow them to rule him. Most of us are born with at least a streak of laziness, irritability, or some other fault in our nature, and it is up to each one of us to see that we exert sufficient willpower to control our failings so that they do not harm ourselves or others.

Astrology can reveal our inclinations and tendencies. Our weaknesses should not be viewed as shortcomings that are impossible to change. The horoscope of a man may show him to have criminal leanings, for instance, but this does not mean he will definitely become a criminal.

The ordinary man usually finds it difficult to know himself. He is often bewildered. Astrology can frequently tell him more about himself than the different schools of psychology are able to do. Knowing his failings and shortcomings, he will do his best to overcome them, and make himself a better and more useful member of society and a helpmate to his family and friends. It can also save him a great deal of unhappiness and remorse.

And yet it may seem absurd that an ancient philosophy, something that is known as a "pseudo-science," could be a prop to the men and women of the twentieth century. But below the materialistic surface of modern life, there are hidden streams of feeling and thought. Symbology is reappearing as a study worthy of the scholar; the psychosomatic factor in illness has passed from the writings of the crank to those of the specialist; spiritual healing in all its forms is no longer a pious hope but an accepted phenomenon. And it is into this context that we consider astrology, in the sense that it is an analysis of human types.

Astrology and medicine had a long journey together, and only parted company a couple of centuries ago. There still remain in medical language such astrological terms as "saturnine," "choleric," and "mercurial," used in the diagnosis of physical tendencies. The herbalist, for long the handyman of the medical profession, has been dominated by astrology since the days of the Greeks. Certain herbs traditionally respond to certain planetary influences, and diseases must therefore be treated to ensure harmony between the medicine and the disease.

No one expects the most eccentric of modern doctors to go back to the practices of his predecessors. We have come a long way since the time when phases of the moon were studied in illness. Those days were a medical nightmare, with epidemics that were beyond control, and an explanation of the Black Death sought in conjunction with the planets. Nowadays, astrological diagnosis of disease has literally no parallel in modern life. And yet, age-old symbols of types and of the vulnerability of, say, the Saturnian to chronic diseases or the choleric to apoplexy and blood pressure and so on, are still applicable.

But the stars are expected to foretell and not only to diagnose. The astrological forecaster has a counterpart on a highly conventional level in the shape of the weather prophet, racing tipster and stock market forecaster, to name just three examples. All in their own way are aiming at the same result. They attempt to look a little further into the pattern of life and also try to determine future patterns accurately.

Astrological forecasting has been remarkably accurate, but often it is wide of the mark. The brave man who cares to predict world events takes dangerous chances. Individual forecasting is less clear cut; it can be a help or a disillusionment. Then welcome to the nagging question: if it is possible to foreknow, is it right to foretell? A complex point of ethics on which it is hard to pronounce judgment. The doctor faces the same dilemma if he finds that symptoms of a mortal disease are present in his patient and that he can only prognosticate a steady decline. How much to tell an individual in a crisis is a problem that has perplexed many distinguished scholars. Honest and conscientious astrologers in this modern world, where so many people are seeking guidance, face the same problem.

The ancient cults, the symbols of old religions, are eclipsed for the moment. They may return with their old force within a decade or two. But at present the outlook is dark. Human beings badly need assurance, as they did in the past, that all is not chaos. Somewhere, somehow, there is a pattern that must be worked out. As to the why and wherefore, the astrologer is not expected to give judgment. He is just someone who, by dint of talent and training, can gaze into the future.

Five hundred years ago it was customary to call in a learned man who was an astrologer who was probably also a doctor and a philosopher. By his knowledge of astrology, his study of planetary influences, he felt himself qualified to guide those in distress. The world has moved forward at a fantastic rate since then, and in this twentieth century speed has been the keyword everywhere. Tensions have increased, the spur of ambition has been applied indiscriminately. People are uncertain of themselves. At first sight it seems fantastic in the light of modern thinking that they turn to the most ancient of all studies, and get someone to calculate a horoscope for them. But is it *really* so fantastic if you take a second look? For astrology is concerned with tomorrow, with survival. And in a world such as ours, those two things are the keywords of the time in which we live.

HOW TO USE
THESE PREDICTIONS

A person reading the predictions in this book should understand that they are produced from the daily position of the planets for a group of people and are not, of course, individually specialized. To get the full benefit of them he should relate the predictions to his own character and circumstances, co-ordinate them, and draw his own conclusions from them.

If he is a serious observer of his own life he should find a definite pattern emerge that will be a helpful and reliable guide.

The point is that we always retain our free will. The stars indicate certain directional tendencies but we are not compelled to follow. We can do or not do, and wisdom must make the choice.

We all have our good and bad days. Sometimes they extend into cycles of weeks. It is therefore advisable to study daily predictions in a span ranging from the day before to several days ahead; also to re-read the monthly predictions for similar cycles.

Daily predictions should be taken very generally. The word "difficult" does not necessarily indicate a whole day of obstruction or inconvenience. It is a warning to you to be cautious. Your caution will often see you around the difficulty before you are involved. This is the correct use of astrology.

In another section, detailed information is given about the influence of the moon as it passes through the various signs of the Zodiac. It includes instructions on how to use the Moon Tables. This information should be used in conjunction with the daily forecasts to give a fuller picture of the astrological trends.

THE MOON

Moon is the nearest planet to the earth. It exerts more observable influence on us from day to day than any other planet. The effect is very personal, very intimate, and if we are not aware of how it works it can make us quite unstable in our ideas. And the annoying thing is that at these times we often see our own instability but can do nothing about it. A knowledge of what can be expected may help considerably. We can then be prepared to stand strong against the moon's negative influences and use its positive ones to help us to get ahead. Who has not heard of going with the tide?

Moon reflects, has no light of its own. It reflects the sun—the life giver—in the form of vital movement. Moon controls the tides, the blood rhythm, the movement of sap in trees and plants. Its nature is inconstancy and change so it signifies our moods, our superficial behavior—walking, talking and especially thinking. Being a true reflector of other forces, moon is cold, watery like the surface of a still lake, brilliant and scintillating at times, but easily ruffled and disturbed by the winds of change.

The moon takes 28½ days to circle the earth and the Zodiac. It spends just over 2¼ days in each sign. During that time it reflects the qualities, energies and characteristics of the sign and, to a degree, the planet which rules the sign. While the moon in its transit occupies a sign incompatible with our own birth sign, we can expect to feel a vague uneasiness, perhaps a touch of irritableness. We should not be discouraged nor let the feeling get us down, or, worse still, allow ourselves to take the discomfort out on others. Try to remember that the moon has to change signs within 55 hours and, provided you are not physically ill, your mood will probably change with it. It is amazing how frequently depression lifts with the shift in the moon's position. And, of course, when the moon is transiting a sign compatible or sympathetic to yours you will probably feel some sort of stimulation or just plain happy to be alive.

In the horoscope, the moon is such a powerful indicator that competent astrologers often use the sign it occupied at birth as the birth sign of the person. This is done particularly when the sun is on the cusp, or edge, of two signs. Most experienced astrologers, however, coordinate both sun and moon signs by reading and confirming from one to the other and secure a far more accurate and personalized analysis.

For these reasons, the moon tables which follow this section (see pages 28–35) are of great importance to the individual. They show the days and the exact times the moon will enter each sign of the Zodiac for the year. Remember, you have to adjust the indicated times to local time. The corrections, already calculated for most of the main cities, are at the beginning of the tables. What follows now is a guide to the influences that will be reflected to the earth by the moon while it transits each of the twelve signs. The influence is at its peak about 26 hours after the moon enters a sign.

MOON IN ARIES

This is a time for action, for reaching out beyond the usual self-imposed limitations and faint-hearted cautions. If you have plans in your head or on your desk, put them into practice. New ventures, applications, new jobs, new starts of any kind—all have a good chance of success. This is the period when original and dynamic impulses are being reflected onto the earth. The energies are extremely vital and favor the pursuit of pleasure and adventure in practically every form. Sick people should feel an improvement. Those who are well will probably find themselves exuding confidence and optimism. People fond of physical exercise should find their bodies growing with tone and well-being. Boldness, strength, determination should characterize most of your activities with a readiness to face up to old challenges. Yesterday's problems may seem petty and exaggerated—so deal with them. Strike out alone. Self-reliance will attract others to you. This is a good time for making friends. Business and marriage partners are more likely to be impressed with the man and woman of action. Opposition will be overcome or thrown aside with much less effort than usual. CAUTION: Be dominant but not domineering.

MOON IN TAURUS

The spontaneous, action-packed person of yesterday gives way to the cautious, diligent, hardworking "thinker." In this period ideas will probably be concentrated on ways of improving finances. A great deal of time may be spent figuring out and going over schemes and plans. It is the right time to be careful with detail. People will find themselves working longer than usual at their desks. Or devoting more time to serious thought about the future. A strong desire to put order into business and financial arrangements may cause extra work. Loved ones may complain of being neglected and may fail to appreciate that your efforts are for their ultimate benefit. Your desire for system may extend to criticism of arrangements in the home and lead to minor upsets. Health may be affected through overwork. Try to secure a reasonable amount of rest and relaxation, although the tendency will be to "keep going" despite good advice. Work done conscientiously in this period should result in a solid contribution to your future security. CAUTION: Try not to be as serious with people as the work you are engaged in.

MOON IN GEMINI

The humdrum of routine and too much work should suddenly end. You are likely to find yourself in an expansive, quicksilver world of change and self-expression. Urges to write, to paint, to experience the freedom of some sort of artistic outpouring, may be very strong. Take full advantage of them. You may find yourself finishing something you began and put aside long ago. Or embarking on something new which could easily be prompted by a chance meeting, a new acquaintance, or even an advertisement. There may be a yearning for a change of scenery, the feeling to visit another country (not too far away), or at least to get away for a few days. This may result in short, quick journeys. Or, if you are planning a single visit, there may be some unexpected changes or detours on the way. Familiar activities will seem to give little satisfaction unless they contain a fresh element of excitement or expectation. The inclination will be towards untried pursuits, particularly those that allow you to express your inner nature. The accent is on new faces, new places. CAUTION: Do not be too quick to commit yourself emotionally.

MOON IN CANCER

Feelings of uncertainty and vague insecurity are likely to cause problems while the moon is in Cancer. Thoughts may turn frequently to the warmth of the home and the comfort of loved ones. Nostalgic impulses could cause you to bring out old photographs and letters and reflect on the days when your life seemed to be much more rewarding and less demanding. The love and understanding of parents and family may be important, and, if it is not forthcoming you may have to fight against a bit of self-pity. The cordiality of friends and the thought of good times with them that are sure

24 / THE MOON

to be repeated will help to restore you to a happier frame of mind. The feeling to be alone may follow minor setbacks or rebuffs at this time, but solitude is unlikely to help. Better to get on the telephone or visit someone. This period often causes peculiar dreams and up-surges of imaginative thinking which can be very helpful to authors of occult and mystical works. Preoccupation with the more person-al world of simple human needs should overshadow any material strivings. CAUTION: Do not spend too much time thinking—seek the company of loved ones or close friends.

MOON IN LEO

New horizons of exciting and rather extravagant activity open up. This is the time for exhilarating entertainment, glamorous and lavish parties, and expensive shopping sprees. Any merrymaking that relies upon your generosity as a host has every chance of being a spectacular success. You should find yourself right in the center of the fun, either as the life of the party or simply as a person whom happy people like to be with. Romance thrives in this heady at-mosphere and friendships are likely to explode unexpectedly into serious attachments. Children and younger people should be at-tracted to you and you may find yourself organizing a picnic or a visit to a fun-fair, the cinema or the seaside. The sunny company and vitality of youthful companions should help you to find some unsuspected energy. In career, you could find an opening for pro-motion or advancement. This should be the time to make a direct approach. The period favors those engaged in original research. CAUTION: Bask in popularity but not in flattery.

MOON IN VIRGO

Off comes the party cap and out steps the busy, practical worker. He wants to get his personal affairs straight, to rearrange them, if necessary, for more efficiency, so he will have more time for more work. He clears up his correspondence, pays outstanding bills, makes numerous phone calls. He is likely to make inquiries, or sign up for some new insurance and put money into gilt-edged invest-ment. Thoughts probably revolve around the need for future secur-ity—to tie up loose ends and clear the decks. There may be a ten-dency to be "finicky," to interfere in the routine of others, particu-larly friends and family members. The motive may be a genuine desire to help with suggestions for updating or streamlining their affairs, but these will probably not be welcomed. Sympathy may be felt for less fortunate sections of the community and a flurry of some sort of voluntary service is likely. This may be accompanied by strong feelings of responsibility on several fronts and health may suffer from extra efforts made. CAUTION: Everyone may not want your help or advice.

MOON IN LIBRA

These are days of harmony and agreement and you should find yourself at peace with most others. Relationships tend to be smooth and sweet-flowing. Friends may become closer and bonds deepen in mutual understanding. Hopes will be shared. Progress by cooperation could be the secret of success in every sphere. In business, established partnerships may flourish and new ones get off to a good start. Acquaintances could discover similar interests that lead to congenial discussions and rewarding exchanges of some sort. Love, as a unifying force, reaches its optimum. Marriage partners should find accord. Those who wed at this time face the prospect of a happy union. Cooperation and tolerance are felt to be stronger than dissension and impatience. The argumentative are not quite so loud in their bellowings, nor as inflexible in their attitudes. In the home, there should be a greater recognition of the other point of view and a readiness to put the wishes of the group before selfish insistence. This is a favorable time to join an art group. CAUTION: Do not be too independent—let others help you if they want to.

MOON IN SCORPIO

Driving impulses to make money and to economize are likely to cause upsets all round. No area of expenditure is likely to be spared the axe, including the household budget. This is a time when the desire to cut down on extravagance can become near fanatical. Care must be exercised to try to keep the aim in reasonable perspective. Others may not feel the same urgent need to save and may retaliate. There is a danger that possessions of sentimental value will be sold to realize cash for investment. Buying and selling of stock for quick profit is also likely. The attention may turn to having a good clean up round the home and at the office. Neglected jobs could suddenly be done with great bursts of energy. The desire for solitude may intervene. Self-searching thoughts could disturb. The sense of invisible and mysterious energies at work could cause some excitability. The reassurance of loves ones may help. CAUTION: Be kind to the people you love.

MOON IN SAGITTARIUS

These are days when you are likely to be stirred and elevated by discussions and reflections of a religious and philosophical nature. Ideas of far-away places may cause unusual response and excitement. A decision may be made to visit someone overseas, perhaps a person whose influence was important to your earlier character development. There could be a strong resolution to get away from present intellectual patterns, to learn new subjects and to meet more interesting people. The superficial may be rejected in all its forms. An impatience with old ideas and unimaginative contacts could lead to a change of companions and interests. There may be an upsurge of religious feeling and metaphysical inquiry. Even a new insight into the significance of astrology and other occult studies is likely under the curious stimulus of the moon in Sagittarius. Physically, you may express this need for fundamental change by spending more time outdoors: sports, gardening or going for long walks. CAUTION: Try to channel any restlessness into worthwhile study.

MOON IN CAPRICORN

Life in these hours may seem to pivot around the importance of gaining prestige and honor in the career, as well as maintaining a spotless reputation. Ambitious urges may be excessive and could be accompanied by quite acquisitive drives for money. Effort should be directed along strictly ethical lines where there is no possibility of reproach or scandal. All endeavors are likely to be characterized by great earnestness, and an air of authority and purpose which should impress those who are looking for leadership or reliability. The desire to conform to accepted standards may extend to sharp criticism of family members. Frivolity and unconventional actions are unlikely to amuse while the moon is in Capricorn. Moderation and seriousness are the orders of the day. Achievement and recognition in this period could come through community work or organizing for the benefit of some amateur group. CAUTION: Dignity and esteem are not always self-awarded.

MOON IN AQUARIUS

Moon in Aquarius is in the second last sign of the Zodiac where ideas can become disturbingly fine and subtle. The result is often a mental "no-man's land" where imagination cannot be trusted with the same certitude as other times. The dangers for the individual are the extremes of optimism and pessimism. Unless the imgination is held in check, situations are likely to be misread, and rosy conclusions drawn where they do not exist. Consequences for the unwary can be costly in career and business. Best to think twice and not speak or act until you think again. Pessimism can be a cruel self-inflicted penalty for delusion at this time. Between the two extremes are strange areas of self-deception which, for example, can make the selfish person think he is actually being generous. Eerie dreams which resemble the reality and even seem to continue into the waking state are also possible. CAUTION: Look for the fact and not just for the image in your mind.

MOON IN PISCES

Everything seems to come to the surface now. Memory may be crystal clear, throwing up long-forgotten information which could be valuable in the career or business. Flashes of clairvoyance and intuition are possible along with sudden realizations of one's own nature, which may be used for self-improvement. A talent, never before suspected, may be discovered. Qualities not evident before in friends and marriage partners are likely to be noticed. As this is a period in which the truth seems to emerge, the discovery of false characteristics is likely to lead to disenchantment or a shift in attachments. However, where qualities are realized it should lead to happiness and deeper feeling. Surprise solutions could bob up for old problems. There may be a public announcement of the solving of a crime or mystery. People with secrets may find someone has "guessed" correctly. The secrets of the soul or the inner self also tend to reveal themselves. Religious and philosophical groups may make some interesting discoveries. CAUTION: Not a time for activities that depend on secrecy.

MOON TABLES

CORRECTION FOR NEW YORK TIME, FIVE HOURS WEST OF GREENWICH

Atlanta, Boston, Detroit, Miami, Washington, Montreal,
Ottawa, Quebec, Bogota, Havana, Lima, Santiago .... Same time

Chicago, New Orleans, Houston, Winnipeg, Churchill,
Mexico City .... Deduct 1 hour

Albuquerque, Denver, Phoenix, El Paso, Edmonton,
Helena .... Deduct 2 hours

Los Angeles, San Francisco, Reno, Portland,
Seattle, Vancouver .... Deduct 3 hours

Honolulu, Anchorage, Fairbanks, Kodiak .... Deduct 5 hours

Nome, Samoa, Tonga, Midway .... Deduct 6 hours

Halifax, Bermuda, San Juan, Caracas, La Paz,
Barbados .... Add 1 hour

St. John's, Brasilia, Rio de Janeiro, Sao Paulo,
Buenos Aires, Montevideo .... Add 2 hours

Azores, Cape Verde Islands .... Add 3 hours

Canary Islands, Madeira, Reykjavik .... Add 4 hours

London, Paris, Amsterdam, Madrid, Lisbon, Gibraltar,
Belfast, Rabat .... Add 5 hours

Frankfurt, Rome, Oslo, Stockholm, Prague,
Belgrade .... Add 6 hours

Bucharest, Beirut, Tel Aviv, Athens, Istanbul, Cairo,
Alexandria, Cape Town, Johannesburg................ Add 7 hours

Moscow, Leningrad, Baghdad, Dhahran, Addis Ababa,
Nairobi, Teheran, Zanzibar......................... Add 8 hours

Bombay, Calcutta, Sri Lanka........................ Add 10½ hours

Hong Kong, Shanghai, Manila, Peking, Perth .... Add 13 hours

Tokyo, Okinawa, Darwin, Pusan .... Add 14 hours

Sydney, Melbourne, Port Moresby, Guam .... Add 15 hours

Auckland, Wellington, Suva, Wake .... Add 17 hours

1997 MOON TABLES—NEW YORK TIME

JANUARY		FEBRUARY		MARCH	
Day Moon Enters		**Day Moon Enters**		**Day Moon Enters**	
1. Libra		1. Sagitt.	11:52 pm	1. Sagitt.	7:02 am
2. Libra		2. Sagitt.		2. Sagitt.	
3. Scorp.	8:03 am	3. Sagitt.		3. Capric.	12:39 pm
4. Scorp		4. Capric.	3:45 am	4. Capric.	
5. Sagitt.	2:28 pm	5. Capric.		5. Aquar.	2:55 pm
6. Sagitt.		6. Aquar.	4:22 am	6. Aquar.	
7. Capric.	4:56 pm	7. Aquar.		7. Pisces	2:58 pm
8. Capric.		8. Pisces	3:35 am	8. Pisces	
9. Aquar.	5:01 pm	9. Pisces		9. Aries	2:34 pm
10. Aquar.		10. Aries	3:30 am	10. Aries	
11. Pisces	4:52 pm	11. Aries		11. Taurus	3:38 pm
12. Pisces		12. Taurus	5:57 am	12. Taurus	
13. Aries	6:23 pm	13. Taurus		13. Gemini	7:49 pm
14. Aries		14. Gemini	11:54 am	14. Gemini	
15. Taurus	10:41 pm	15. Gemini		15. Gemini	
16. Taurus		16. Cancer	9:14 pm	16. Cancer	3:52 am
17. Taurus		17. Cancer		17. Cancer	
18. Gemini	5:54 am	18. Cancer		18. Leo	3:09 pm
19. Gemini		19. Leo	8:53 am	19. Leo	
20. Cancer	5:30 pm	20. Leo		20. Leo	
21. Cancer		21. Virgo	9:39 pm	21. Virgo	4:00 am
22. Cancer		22. Virgo		22. Virgo	
23. Leo	2:51 am	23. Virgo		23. Libra	4:36 pm
24. Leo		24. Libra	10:24 am	24. Libra	
25. Virgo	3:27 pm	25. Libra		25. Libra	
26. Virgo		26. Scorp.	9:58 pm	26. Scorp.	3:43 am
27. Virgo		27. Scorp.		27. Scorp.	
28. Libra	4:22 am	28. Scorp.		28. Sagitt.	12:41 pm
29. Libra				29. Sagitt.	
30. Scorp.	3:49 pm			30. Capric.	7:08 pm
31. Scorp.				31. Capric.	

Summer time to be considered where applicable.

1997 MOON TABLES—NEW YORK TIME

APRIL Day Moon Enters		MAY Day Moon Enters		JUNE Day Moon Enters	
1. Aquar	11:00 pm	1. Pisces	7:51 pm	1. Taurus	7:40 pm
2. Aquar.		2. Pisces		2. Taurus	
3. Aquar		3. Aries	10:00 am	3. Gemini	11:56 pm
4. Pisces	0:43 am	4. Aries		4. Gemini	
5. Pisces		5. Taurus	12:05 pm	5. Gemini	
6. Aries	1:20 am	6. Taurus		6. Cancer	6:03 pm
7. Aries		7. Gemini	3:22 pm	7. Cancer	
8. Taurus	2:21 am	8. Gemini		8. Leo	2:59 pm
9. Taurus		9. Cancer	9:14 pm	9. Leo	
10. Gemini	5:29 am	10. Cancer		10. Leo	
11. Gemini		11. Cancer		11. Virgo	2:44 am
12. Cancer	12:04 pm	12. Leo	6:34 pm	12. Virgo	
13. Cancer		13. Leo		13. Libra	3:36 pm
14. Leo	10:23 pm	14. Virgo	6:44 pm	14. Libra	
15. Leo		15. Virgo		15. Libra	
16. Leo		16. Virgo		16. Scorp.	2:52 am
17. Virgo	11:01 am	17. Libra	7:28 am	17. Scorp.	
18. Virgo		18. Libra		18. Sagitt.	10:40 am
19. Libra	11:37 pm	19. Scorp.	6:13 pm	19. Sagitt.	
20. Libra		20. Scorp.		20. Capric.	3:03 pm
21. Libra		21. Scorp.		21. Capric.	
22. Scorp.	10:20 am	22. Sagitt.	1:52 am	22. Aquar.	5:21 pm
23. Scorp.		23. Sagitt.		23. Aquar.	
24. Sagitt.	6:33 pm	24. Capric.	6:52 am	24. Pisces	7:10 pm
25. Sagitt.		25. Capric.		25. Pisces	
26. Sagitt.		26. Aquar.	10:21 am	26. Aries	9:40 pm
27. Capric.	0:33 am	27. Aquar.		27. Aries	
28. Capric.		28. Pisces	1:19 pm	28. Aries	
29. Aquar.	4:51 am	29. Pisces		29. Taurus	1:24 am
30. Aquar.		30. Aries	4:19 pm	30. Taurus	
		31. Aries			

Summer time to be considered where applicable.

1997 MOON TABLES—NEW YORK TIME

JULY		AUGUST		SEPTEMBER	
Day Moon Enters		**Day Moon Enters**		**Day Moon Enters**	
1. Gemini	6:36 am	1. Cancer		1. Virgo	
2. Gemini		2. Leo	5:28 am	2. Virgo	
3. Cancer	1:34 pm	3. Leo		3. Libra	12:31 pm
4. Cancer		4. Virgo	5:16 pm	4. Libra	
5. Leo	10:46 pm	5. Virgo		5. Libra	
6. Leo		6. Virgo		6. Scorp.	1:11 am
7. Leo		7. Libra	6:18 pm	7. Scorp.	
8. Virgo	10:23 am	8. Libra		8. Sagitt.	11:55 am
9. Virgo		9. Scorp.	6:51 pm	9. Sagitt.	
10. Libra	11:22 pm	10. Scorp.		10. Capric.	7:24 pm
11. Libra		11. Scorp.		11. Capric.	
12. Libra		12. Sagitt.	4:46 am	12. Aquar.	11:11 pm
13. Scorp.	11:21 am	13. Sagitt.		13. Aquar.	
14. Scorp.		14. Capric.	10:43 am	14. Aquar.	
15. Sagitt.	8:03 pm	15. Capric.		15. Pisces	0:00 am
16. Sagitt.		16. Aquar.	12:59 pm	16. Aries	11:26 pm
17. Sagitt.		17. Aquar.		17. Aries	
18. Capric.	0:46 am	18. Pisces	1:02 pm	18. Taurus	11:22 pm
19. Capric.		19. Pisces		19. Taurus	
20. Aquar.	2:30 am	20. Aries	12:46 pm	20. Taurus	
21. Aquar.		21. Aries		21. Gemini	1:40 am
22. Pisces	3:01 am	22. Taurus	1:58 pm	22. Gemini	
23. Pisces		23. Taurus		23. Cancer	7:34 am
24. Aries	4:04 am	24. Gemini	5:57 pm	24. Cancer	
25. Aries		25. Gemini		25. Leo	5:13 pm
26. Taurus	6:54 am	26. Gemini		26. Leo	
27. Taurus		27. Cancer	1:12 am	27. Leo	
28. Gemini	12:05 pm	28. Cancer		28. Virgo	5:28 am
29. Gemini		29. Leo	11:20 am	29. Virgo	
30. Cancer	7:39 pm	30. Leo		30. Libra	6:33 pm
31. Cancer		31. Virgo	11:28 pm		

Summer time to be considered where applicable.

1997 MOON TABLES—NEW YORK TIME

OCTOBER		NOVEMBER		DECEMBER	
Day Moon Enters		**Day Moon Enters**		**Day Moon Enters**	
1. Libra		1. Sagitt.	11:28 pm	1. Capric.	1:39 pm
2. Libra		2. Sagitt.		2. Capric.	
3. Scorp.	6:58 am	3. Sagitt.		3. Aquar.	6:59 pm
4. Scorp.		4. Capric.	7:32 am	4. Aquar.	
5. Sagitt.	5:44 pm	5. Capric.		5. Pisces	11:08 pm
6. Sagitt.		6. Aquar.	1:34 pm	6. Pisces	
7. Sagitt.		7. Aquar.		7. Pisces	
8. Capric.	2:05 am	8. Pisces	5:36 pm	8. Aries	2:25 am
9. Capric.		9. Pisces		9. Aries	
10. Aquar.	7:30 pm	10. Aries	7:45 pm	10. Taurus	5:01 am
11. Aquar.		11. Aries		11. Taurus	
12. Pisces	10:00 am	12. Taurus	8:46 pm	12. Gemini	7:36 am
13. Pisces		13. Taurus		13. Gemini	
14. Aries	10:26 am	14. Gemini	10:06 pm	14. Cancer	11:26 am
15. Aries		15. Gemini		15. Cancer	
16. Taurus	10:17 am	16. Gemini		16. Leo	5:59 pm
17. Taurus		17. Cancer	1:33 am	17. Leo	
18. Gemini	11:27 am	18. Cancer		18. Leo	
19. Gemini		19. Leo	8:39 am	19. Virgo	4:01 am
20. Cancer	3:46 pm	20. Leo		20. Virgo	
21. Cancer		21. Virgo	7:34 pm	21. Libra	4:36 pm
22. Cancer		22. Virgo		22. Libra	
23. Leo	0.11 am	23. Virgo		23. Libra	
24. Leo		24. Libra	8:30 am	24. Scorp.	5:08 am
25. Virgo	12:00 pm	25. Libra		25. Scorp.	
26. Virgo		26. Scorp.	8:44 pm	26. Sagitt.	3:08 pm
27. Virgo		27. Scorp.		27. Sagitt.	
28. Libra	1:06 am	28. Scorp.		28. Capric.	9:49 pm
29. Libra		29. Sagitt.	6:29 am	29. Capric.	
30. Scorp.	1:16 pm	30. Sagitt.		30. Capric.	
31. Scorp.				31. Aquar.	1:59 am

Summer time to be considered where applicable.

1997 PHASES OF THE MOON—NEW YORK TIME

New Moon	First Quarter	Full Moon	Last Quarter
Dec. 10 ('96)	Dec. 17 ('96)	Dec. 24 ('96)	Jan. 1
Jan. 8	Jan. 15	Jan. 23	Jan. 31
Feb. 7	Feb. 14	Feb. 22	Mar. 2
Mar. 8	Mar. 15	Mar. 23	Mar. 31
Apr. 7	Apr. 14	Apr. 22	Apr. 29
May 6	May 14	May 22	May 29
June 5	June 12	June 20	June 27
July 4	July 12	July 19	July 26
Aug. 3	Aug. 11	Aug. 18	Aug. 24
Sept. 1	Sept. 9	Sept. 16	Sept. 23
Oct. 1	Oct. 9	Oct. 15	Oct. 22
Oct. 31	Nov. 7	Nov. 14	Nov. 21
Nov. 29	Dec. 7	Dec. 13	Dec. 21
Dec. 29	Jan. 5 ('98)	Jan. 12 ('98)	Jan. 20 ('98)

Each phase of the Moon lasts approximately seven to eight days, during which the Moon's shape gradually changes as it comes out of one phase and goes into the next.

There will be a partial solar eclipse during the New Moon phase on March 8 and September 1. There will be a lunar eclipse during the Full Moon phase on March 23 and September 16.

1997 PLANTING GUIDE

	Aboveground Crops	Root Crops	Pruning	Weeds Pests
January	12-13-16-17-21-22	1-2-3-4-8-28-29-30-31	3-4-31	6-24-25-26-27
February	8-9-13-17-18	1-4-5-25-26-27-28	1-27-28	2-3-6-23
March	12-13-16-17	4-8-24-25-26-27-31	8-26-27	2-6-29-30
April	8-9-13-14-20-21	1-4-5-23-24-27-28	4-5-23-24	2-3-6-25-26-29-30
May	10-11-18-19-20-21	2-25-29	2-29	4-22-23-27-31
June	7-14-15-16-17	2-3-21-22-25-26-29-30	25-26	1-4-23-24-27-28
July	5-11-12-13-14-15-18-19	22-23-27-31	22-23-31	2-20-21-24-25-29-30
August	8-9-10-11-15	1-19-23-24-27-28	1-19-27-28	21-25-26-30-31
September	4-5-6-7-11-12-15	19-20-24-25	24-25	1-17-18-21-22-26-27-28-29-30
October	2-3-4-5-8-9-13	17-21-22-28-29-30	21-22	19-23-24-25-26-27
November	1-5-9-10-13	17-18-25-26-27-28	17-18-27-28	15-16-20-21-22-23
December	2-3-6-7-11-30	15-16-22-23-24-25	15-16-25	17-18-19-20-27-28

1997 FISHING GUIDE

	Good	Best
January	15-20-23-24-25-26	2-9-21-22-31
February	7-14-19-20-21-22-23-24	25
March	2-9-21-22-23	16-24-25-26-27-31
April	7-19-25-30	14-20-21-22-23-24
May	14-22-23-24	6-19-20-21-25-29
June	5-13-18-19-20-23-27	17-21-22
July	17-20-21-26	4-12-18-19-22-23
August	3-16-17-18-20-21-25	11-15-19
September	1-10-13-14-17-18-23	15-16-19
October	14-15-16-18-19-23	1-9-13-17-31
November	7-11-12-15-16-21-30	13-14-17
December	12-13-14-17-21	7-11-15-16-29

MOON'S INFLUENCE OVER DAILY AFFAIRS

The Moon makes a complete transit of the Zodiac every 27 days 7 hours and 43 minutes. In making this transit the Moon forms different aspects with the planets and consequently has favorable or unfavorable bearings on affairs and events for persons according to the sign of the Zodiac under which they were born. Whereas the Sun exclusively represents fire, the Moon rules water. The action of the Moon may be described as fluctuating, variable, absorbent and receptive.

When the Moon is in conjunction with the Sun it is called a New Moon; when the Moon and Sun are in opposition it is called a Full Moon. From New Moon to Full Moon, first and second quarter—which takes about two weeks—the Moon is increasing or waxing. From Full Moon to New Moon, third and fourth quarter, the Moon is decreasing or waning. The Moon Table indicates the New Moon and Full Moon and the quarters.

ACTIVITY	MOON IN
Business:	
buying and selling	Sagittarius, Aries, Gemini, Virgo
new, requiring public support	1st and 2nd quarter
meant to be kept quiet	3rd and 4th quarter
Investigation	3rd and 4th quarter
Signing documents	1st & 2nd quarter, Cancer, Scorpio, Pisces
Advertising	2nd quarter, Sagittarius
Journeys and trips	1st & 2nd quarter, Gemini, Virgo
Renting offices, etc.	Taurus, Leo, Scorpio, Aquarius
Painting of house/apartment	3rd & 4th quarter, Taurus, Scorpio, Aquarius
Decorating	Gemini, Libra, Aquarius
Buying clothes and accessories	Taurus, Virgo
Beauty salon or barber shop visit	1st & 2nd quarter, Taurus, Leo, Libra, Scorpio, Aquarius
Weddings	1st & 2nd quarter

MOON'S INFLUENCE OVER YOUR HEALTH

ARIES	Head, brain, face, upper jaw
TAURUS	Throat, neck, lower jaw
GEMINI	Hands, arms, lungs, shoulders, nervous system
CANCER	Esophagus, stomach, breasts, womb, liver
LEO	Heart, spine
VIRGO	Intestines, liver
LIBRA	Kidneys, lower back
SCORPIO	Sex and eliminative organs
SAGITTARIUS	Hips, thighs, liver
CAPRICORN	Skin, bones, teeth, knees
AQUARIUS	Circulatory system, lower legs
PISCES	Feet, tone of being

Try to avoid work being done on that part of the body when the Moon is in the sign governing that part.

MOON'S INFLUENCE OVER PLANTS

Centuries ago it was established that seeds planted when the Moon is in certain signs and phases called Fruitful will produce more growth than seeds planted when the Moon is in a Barren sign.

FRUITFUL SIGNS	BARREN SIGNS	DRY SIGNS
Taurus	Aries	Aries
Cancer	Gemini	Gemini
Libra	Leo	Sagittarius
Scorpio	Virgo	Aquarius
Capricorn	Sagittarius	
Pisces	Aquarius	

ACTIVITY	MOON IN
Mow lawn, trim plants	**Fruitful sign:** 1st & 2nd quarter
Plant flowers	**Fruitful sign:** 2nd quarter; best in Cancer and Libra
Prune	**Fruitful sign:** 3rd & 4th quarter
Destroy pests; spray	**Barren sign:** 4th quarter
Harvest potatoes, root crops	**Dry sign:** 3rd & 4th quarter; Taurus, Leo, and Aquarius

THE SIGNS: DOMINANT CHARACTERISTICS

March 21–April 20

The Positive Side of Aries

The Arien has many positive points to his character. People born under this first sign of the Zodiac are often quite strong and enthusiastic. On the whole, they are forward-looking people who are not easily discouraged by temporary setbacks. They know what they want out of life and they go out after it. Their personalities are strong. Others are usually quite impressed by the Arien's way of doing things. Quite often they are sources of inspiration for others traveling the same route. Aries men and women have a special zest for life that is often contagious; for others, they are often the example of how life should be lived.

The Aries person usually has a quick and active mind. He is imaginative and inventive. He enjoys keeping busy and active. He generally gets along well with all kinds of people. He is interested in mankind, as a whole. He likes to be challenged. Some would say he thrives on opposition, for it is when he is set against that he often does his best. Getting over or around obstacles is a challenge he generally enjoys. All in all, the Arien is quite positive and young-thinking. He likes to keep abreast of new things that are happening in the world. Ariens are often fond of speed. They like things to be done quickly and this sometimes aggravates their slower colleagues and associates.

The Aries man or woman always seems to remain young. Their whole approach to life is youthful and optimistic. They never say die, no matter what the odds. They may have an occasional setback, but it is not long before they are back on their feet again.

The Negative Side of Aries

Everybody has his less positive qualities—and Aries is no exception. Sometimes the Aries man or woman is not very tactful in communicating with others; in his hurry to get things done he is apt to

be a little callous or inconsiderate. Sensitive people are likely to find him somewhat sharp-tongued in some situations. Often in his eagerness to achieve his aims, he misses the mark altogether. At times the Arien is too impulsive. He can occasionally be stubborn and refuse to listen to reason. If things do not move quickly enough to suit the Aries man or woman, he or she is apt to become rather nervous or irritable. The uncultivated Arien is not unfamiliar with moments of doubt and fear. He is capable of being destructive if he does not get his way. He can overcome some of his emotional problems by steadily trying to express himself as he really is, but this requires effort.

April 21–May 20

The Positive Side of Taurus

The Taurus person is known for his ability to concentrate and for his tenacity. These are perhaps his strongest qualities. The Taurus man or woman generally has very little trouble in getting along with others; it's his nature to be helpful toward people in need. He can always be depended on by his friends, especially those in trouble.

The Taurean generally achieves what he wants through his ability to persevere. He never leaves anything unfinished but works on something until it has been completed. People can usually take him at his word; he is honest and forthright in most of his dealings. The Taurus person has a good chance to make a success of his life because of his many positive qualities. The Taurean who aims high seldom falls short of his mark. He learns well by experience. He is thorough and does not believe in short-cuts of any kind. The Taurean's thoroughness pays off in the end, for through his deliberateness he learns how to rely on himself and what he has learned. The Taurus person tries to get along with others, as a rule. He is not overly critical and likes people to be themselves. He is a tolerant person and enjoys peace and harmony—especially in his home life.

The Taurean is usually cautious in all that he does. He is not a person who believes in taking unnecessary risks. Before adopting any one line of action, he will weigh all of the pros and cons. The

Taurus person is steadfast. Once his mind is made up it seldom changes. The person born under this sign usually is a good family person—reliable and loving.

The Negative Side of Taurus

Sometimes the Taurus man or woman is a bit too stubborn. He won't listen to other points of view if his mind is set on something. To others, this can be quite annoying. The Taurean also does not like to be told what to do. He becomes rather angry if others think him not too bright. He does not like to be told he is wrong, even when he is. He dislikes being contradicted.

Some people who are born under this sign are very suspicious of others—even of those persons close to them. They find it difficult to trust people fully. They are often afraid of being deceived or taken advantage of. The Taurean often finds it difficult to forget or forgive. His love of material things sometimes makes him rather avaricious and petty.

May 21–June 20

The Positive Side of Gemini

The person born under this sign of the Heavenly Twins is usually quite bright and quick-witted. Some of them are capable of doing many different things. The Gemini person very often has many different interests. He keeps an open mind and is always anxious to learn new things.

The Geminian is often an analytical person. He is a person who enjoys making use of his intellect. He is governed more by his mind than by his emotions. He is a person who is not confined to one view; he can often understand both sides to a problem or question. He knows how to reason; how to make rapid decisions if need be.

He is an adaptable person and can make himself at home almost anywhere. There are all kinds of situations he can adapt to. He is a person who seldom doubts himself; he is sure of his talents and his

ability to think and reason. The Geminian is generally most satisfied when he is in a situation where he can make use of his intellect. Never short of imagination, he often has strong talents for invention. He is rather a modern person when it comes to life; the Geminian almost always moves along with the times—perhaps that is why he remains so youthful throughout most of his life.

Literature and art appeal to the person born under this sign. Creativity in almost any form will interest and intrigue the Gemini man or woman.

The Geminian is often quite charming. A good talker, he often is the center of attraction at any gathering. People find it easy to like a person born under this sign because he can appear easygoing and usually has a good sense of humor.

The Negative Side of Gemini

Sometimes the Gemini person tries to do too many things at one time—and as a result, winds up finishing nothing. Some Geminians are easily distracted and find it rather difficult to concentrate on one thing for too long a time. Sometimes they give in to trifling fancies and find it rather boring to become too serious about any one thing. Some of them are never dependable, no matter what they promise.

Although the Gemini man or woman often appears to be well-versed on many subjects, this is sometimes just a veneer. His knowledge may be only superficial, but because he speaks so well he gives people the impression of erudition. Some Geminians are sharp-tongued and inconsiderate; they think only of themselves and their own pleasure.

June 21–July 20

The Positive Side of Cancer

The Cancerians's most positive point is his understanding nature. On the whole, he is a loving and sympathetic person. He would never go out of his way to hurt anyone. The Cancer man or woman

is often very kind and tender; they give what they can to others. They hate to see others suffering and will do what they can to help someone in less fortunate circumstances than themselves. They are often very concerned about the world. Their interest in people generally goes beyond that of just their own families and close friends; they have a deep sense of brotherhood and respect humanitarian values. The Cancerian means what he says, as a rule; he is honest about his feelings.

The Cancer man or woman is a person who knows the art of patience. When something seems difficult, he is willing to wait until the situation becomes manageable again. He is a person who knows how to bide his time. The Cancerian knows how to concentrate on one thing at a time. When he has made his mind up he generally sticks with what he does, seeing it through to the end.

The Cancerian is a person who loves his home. He enjoys being surrounded by familiar things and the people he loves. Of all the signs, Cancer is the most maternal. Even the men born under this sign often have a motherly or protective quality about them. They like to take care of people in their family—to see that they are well loved and well provided for. They are usually loyal and faithful. Family ties mean a lot to the Cancer man or woman. Parents and in-laws are respected and loved. The Cancerian has a strong sense of tradition. He is very sensitive to the moods of others.

The Negative Side of Cancer

Sometimes the Cancerian finds it rather hard to face life. It becomes too much for him. He can be a little timid and retiring, when things don't go too well. When unfortunate things happen, he is apt to just shrug and say, "Whatever will be will be." He can be fatalistic to a fault. The uncultivated Cancerian is a bit lazy. He doesn't have very much ambition. Anything that seems a bit difficult he'll gladly leave to others. He may be lacking in initiative. Too sensitive, when he feels he's been injured, he'll crawl back into his shell and nurse his imaginary wounds. The Cancer woman often is given to crying when the smallest thing goes wrong.

Some Cancerians find it difficult to enjoy themselves in environments outside their homes. They make heavy demands on others, and need to be constantly reassured that they are loved.

July 21–August 21

The Positive Side of Leo

Often Leos make good leaders. They seem to be good organizers and administrators. Usually they are quite popular with others. Whatever group it is that he belongs to, the Leo man is almost sure to be or become the leader.

The Leo person is generous most of the time. It is his best characteristic. He or she likes to give gifts and presents. In making others happy, the Leo person becomes happy himself. He likes to splurge when spending money on others. In some instances it may seem that the Leo's generosity knows no boundaries. A hospitable person, the Leo man or woman is very fond of welcoming people to his house and entertaining them. He is never short of company.

The Leo person has plenty of energy and drive. He enjoys working toward some specific goal. When he applies himself correctly, he gets what he wants most often. The Leo person is almost never unsure of himself. He has plenty of confidence and aplomb. He is a person who is direct in almost everything he does. He has a quick mind and can make a decision in a very short time.

He usually sets a good example for others because of his ambitious manner and positive ways. He knows how to stick to something once he's started. Although the Leo person may be good at making a joke, he is not superficial or glib. He is a loving person, kind and thoughtful.

There is generally nothing small or petty about the Leo man or woman. He does what he can for those who are deserving. He is a person others can rely upon at all times. He means what he says. An honest person, generally speaking, he is a friend that others value.

The Negative Side of Leo

Leo, however, does have his faults. At times, he can be just a bit too arrogant. He thinks that no one deserves a leadership position except him. Only he is capable of doing things well. His opinion of himself is often much too high. Because of his conceit, he is sometimes rather unpopular with a good many people. Some Leos are too materialistic; they can only think in terms of money and profit.

Some Leos enjoy lording it over others—at home or at their place of business. What is more, they feel they have the right to. Egocentric to an impossible degree, this sort of Leo cares little about how others think or feel. He can be rude and cutting.

August 22–September 22

The Positive Side of Virgo

The person born under the sign of Virgo is generally a busy person. He knows how to arrange and organize things. He is a good planner. Above all, he is practical and is not afraid of hard work.

The person born under this sign, Virgo, knows how to attain what he desires. He sticks with something until it is finished. He never shirks his duties, and can always be depended upon. The Virgo person can be thoroughly trusted at all times.

The man or woman born under this sign tries to do everything to perfection. He doesn't believe in doing anything half-way. He always aims for the top. He is the sort of a person who is constantly striving to better himself—not because he wants more money or glory, but because it gives him a feeling of accomplishment.

The Virgo man or woman is a very observant person. He is sensitive to how others feel, and can see things below the surface of a situation. He usually puts this talent to constructive use.

It is not difficult for the Virgoan to be open and earnest. He believes in putting his cards on the table. He is never secretive or under-handed. He's as good as his word. The Virgo person is generally plain-spoken and down-to-earth. He has no trouble in expressing himself.

The Virgo person likes to keep up to date on new developments in his particular field. Well-informed, generally, he sometimes has a keen interest in the arts or literature. What he knows, he knows well. His ability to use his critical faculties is well-developed and sometimes startles others because of its accuracy.

The Virgoan adheres to a moderate way of life; he avoids excesses. He is a responsible person and enjoys being of service.

The Negative Side of Virgo

Sometimes a Virgo person is too critical. He thinks that only he can do something the way it should be done. Whatever anyone else does is inferior. He can be rather annoying in the way he quibbles over insignificant details. In telling others how things should be done, he can be rather tactless and mean.

Some Virgos seem rather emotionless and cool. They feel emo-

tional involvement is beneath them. They are sometimes too tidy, too neat. With money they can be rather miserly. Some try to force their opinions and ideas on others.

September 23–October 22

The Positive Side of Libra

Librans love harmony. It is one of their most outstanding character traits. They are interested in achieving balance; they admire beauty and grace in things as well as in people. Generally speaking, they are kind and considerate people. Librans are usually very sympathetic. They go out of their way not to hurt another person's feelings. They are outgoing and do what they can to help those in need.

People born under the sign of Libra almost always make good friends. They are loyal and amiable. They enjoy the company of others. Many of them are rather moderate in their views; they believe in keeping an open mind, however, and weighing both sides of an issue fairly before making a decision.

Alert and often intelligent, the Libran, always fair-minded, tries to put himself in the position of the other person. They are against injustice; quite often they take up for the underdog. In most of their social dealings, they try to be tactful and kind. They dislike discord and bickering, and most Libras strive for peace and harmony in all their relationships.

The Libra man or woman has a keen sense of beauty. They appreciate handsome furnishings and clothes. Many of them are artistically inclined. Their taste is usually impeccable. They know how to use color. Their homes are almost always attractively arranged and inviting. They enjoy entertaining people and see to it that their guests always feel at home and welcome.

The Libran gets along with almost everyone. He is well-liked and socially much in demand.

The Negative Side of Libra

Some people born under this sign tend to be rather insincere. So eager are they to achieve harmony in all relationships that they will even go so far as to lie. Many of them are escapists. They find facing

the truth an ordeal and prefer living in a world of make-believe.

In a serious argument, some Librans give in rather easily even when they know they are right. Arguing, even about something they believe in, is too unsettling for some of them.

Librans sometimes care too much for material things. They enjoy possessions and luxuries. Some are vain and tend to be jealous.

October 23–November 22

The Positive Side of Scorpio

The Scorpio man or woman generally knows what he or she wants out of life. He is a determined person. He sees something through to the end. The Scorpion is quite sincere, and seldom says anything he doesn't mean. When he sets a goal for himself he tries to go about achieving it in a very direct way.

The Scorpion is brave and courageous. They are not afraid of hard work. Obstacles do not frighten them. They forge ahead until they achieve what they set out for. The Scorpio man or woman has a strong will.

Although the Scorpion may seem rather fixed and determined, inside he is often quite tender and loving. He can care very much for others. He believes in sincerity in all relationships. His feelings about someone tend to last; they are profound and not superficial.

The Scorpio person is someone who adheres to his principles no matter what happens. He will not be deterred from a path he believes to be right.

Because of his many positive strengths, the Scorpion can often achieve happiness for himself and for those that he loves.

He is a constructive person by nature. He often has a deep understanding of people and of life, in general. He is perceptive and unafraid. Obstacles often seem to spur him on. He is a positive person who enjoys winning. He has many strengths and resources; challenge of any sort often brings out the best in him.

The Negative Side of Scorpio

The Scorpio person is sometimes hypersensitive. Often he imagines injury when there is none. He feels that others do not bother to

recognize him for his true worth. Sometimes he is given to excessive boasting in order to compensate for what he feels is neglect

The Scorpio person can be rather proud and arrogant. They can be rather sly when they put their minds to it and they enjoy outwitting persons or institutions noted for their cleverness.

Their tactics for getting what they want are sometimes devious and ruthless. They don't care too much about what others may think. If they feel others have done them an injustice, they will do their best to seek revenge. The Scorpion often has a sudden, violent temper; and this person's interest in sex is sometimes quite unbalanced or excessive.

November 23–December 20

The Positive Side of Sagittarius

People born under this sign are often honest and forthright. Their approach to life is earnest and open. The Sagittarian is often quite adult in his way of seeing things. They are broadminded and tolerant people. When dealing with others the person born under the sign of Sagittarius is almost always open and forthright. He doesn't believe in deceit or pretension. His standards are high. People who associate with the Sagittarian, generally admire and respect him.

The Sagittarian trusts others easily and expects them to trust him. He is never suspicious or envious and almost always thinks well of others. People always enjoy his company because he is so friendly and easy-going. The Sagittarius man or woman is often good-humored. He can always be depended upon by his friends, family, and co-workers.

The person born under this sign of the Zodiac likes a good joke every now and then; he is keen on fun and this makes him very popular with others.

A lively person, he enjoys sports and outdoor life. The Sagittarian is fond of animals. Intelligent and interesting, he can begin an animated conversation with ease. He likes exchanging ideas and discussing various views.

He is not selfish or proud. If someone proposes an idea or plan that is better than his, he will immediately adopt it. Imaginative yet practical, he knows how to put ideas into practice.

He enjoys sport and game, and it doesn't matter if he wins or loses. He is a forgiving person, and never sulks over something that has not worked out in his favor.

He is seldom critical, and is almost always generous.

The Negative Side of Sagittarius

Some Sagittarians are restless. They take foolish risks and seldom learn from the mistakes they make. They don't have heads for money and are often mismanaging their finances. Some of them devote much of their time to gambling.

Some are too outspoken and tactless, always putting their feet in their mouths. They hurt others carelessly by being honest at the wrong time. Sometimes they make promises which they don't keep. They don't stick close enough to their plans and go from one failure to another. They are undisciplined and waste a lot of energy.

December 21–January 19

The Positive Side of Capricorn

The person born under the sign of Capricorn is usually very stable and patient. He sticks to whatever tasks he has and sees them through. He can always be relied upon and he is not averse to work.

An honest person, the Capricornian is generally serious about whatever he does. He does not take his duties lightly. He is a practical person and believes in keeping his feet on the ground.

Quite often the person born under this sign is ambitious and knows how to get what he wants out of life. He forges ahead and never gives up his goal. When he is determined about something, he almost always wins. He is a good worker—a hard worker. Although things may not come easy to him, he will not complain, but continue working until his chores are finished.

He is usually good at business matters and knows the value of money. He is not a spendthrift and knows how to put something away for a rainy day; he dislikes waste and unnecessary loss.

The Capricornian knows how to make use of his self-control. He

can apply himself to almost anything once he puts his mind to it. His ability to concentrate sometimes astounds others. He is diligent and does well when involved in detail work.

The Capricorn man or woman is charitable, generally speaking, and will do what is possible to help others less fortunate. As a friend, he is loyal and trustworthy. He never shirks his duties or responsibilities. He is self-reliant and never expects too much of the other fellow. He does what he can on his own. If someone does him a good turn, then he will do his best to return the favor.

The Negative Side of Capricorn

Like everyone, the Capricornian, too, has his faults. At times, he can be over-critical of others. He expects others to live up to his own high standards. He thinks highly of himself and tends to look down on others.

His interest in material things may be exaggerated. The Capricorn man or woman thinks too much about getting on in the world and having something to show for it. He may even be a little greedy.

He sometimes thinks he knows what's best for everyone. He is too bossy. He is always trying to organize and correct others. He may be a little narrow in his thinking.

January 20–February 18

The Positive Side of Aquarius

The Aquarius man or woman is usually very honest and forthright. These are his two greatest qualities. His standards for himself are generally very high. He can always be relied upon by others. His word is his bond.

The Aquarian is perhaps the most tolerant of all the Zodiac personalities. He respects other people's beliefs and feels that everyone is entitled to his own approach to life.

He would never do anything to injure another's feelings. He is never unkind or cruel. Always considerate of others, the Aquarian is always willing to help a person in need. He feels a very strong tie between himself and all the other members of mankind.

The person born under this sign is almost always an individualist. He does not believe in teaming up with the masses, but prefers going his own way. His ideas about life and mankind are often quite advanced. There is a saying to the effect that the average Aquarian is fifty years ahead of his time.

He is broadminded. The problems of the world concern him greatly. He is interested in helping others no matter what part of the globe they live in. He is truly a humanitarian sort. He likes to be of service to others.

Giving, considerate, and without prejudice, Aquarians have no trouble getting along with others.

The Negative Side of Aquarius

The Aquarian may be too much of a dreamer. He makes plans but seldom carries them out. He is rather unrealistic. His imagination has a tendency to run away with him. Because many of his plans are impractical, he is always in some sort of a dither.

Others may not approve of him at all times because of his unconventional behavior. He may be a bit eccentric. Sometimes he is so busy with his own thoughts, that he loses touch with the realities of existence.

Some Aquarians feel they are more clever and intelligent than others. They seldom admit to their own faults, even when they are quite apparent. Some become rather fanatic in their views. Their criticism of others is sometimes destructive and negative.

February 19–March 20

The Positive Side of Pisces

The Piscean can often understand the problems of others quite easily. He has a sympathetic nature. Kindly, he is often dedicated in the way he goes about helping others. The sick and the troubled often turn to him for advice and assistance.

He is very broadminded and does not criticize others for their faults. He knows how to accept people for what they are. On the whole, he is a trustworthy and earnest person. He is loyal to his

friends and will do what he can to help them in time of need. Generous and good-natured, he is a lover of peace; he is often willing to help others solve their differences. People who have taken a wrong turn in life often interest him and he will do what he can to persuade them to rehabilitate themselves.

He has a strong intuitive sense and most of the time he knows how to make it work for him; the Piscean is unusually perceptive and often knows what is bothering someone before that person, himself, is aware of it. The Pisces man or woman is an idealistic person, basically, and is interested in making the world a better place in which to live. The Piscean believes that everyone should help each other. He is willing to do more than his share in order to achieve cooperation with others.

The person born under this sign often is talented in music or art. He is a receptive person; he is able to take the ups and downs of life with philosophic calm.

The Negative Side of Pisces

Some Pisceans are often depressed; their outlook on life is rather glum. They may feel that they have been given a bad deal in life and that others are always taking unfair advantage of them. The Piscean sometimes feel that the world is a cold and cruel place. He is easily discouraged. He may even withdraw from the harshness of reality into a secret shell of his own where he dreams and idles away a good deal of his time.

The Piscean can be rather lazy. He lets things happen without giving the least bit of resistance. He drifts along, whether on the high road or on the low. He is rather short on willpower.

Some Pisces people seek escape through drugs or alcohol. When temptation comes along they find it hard to resist. In matters of sex, they can be rather permissive.

THE SIGNS AND
THEIR KEY WORDS

		POSITIVE	NEGATIVE
ARIES	self	courage, initiative, pioneer instinct	brash rudeness, selfish impetuosity
TAURUS	money	endurance, loyalty, wealth	obstinacy, gluttony
GEMINI	mind	versatility	capriciousness, unreliability
CANCER	family	sympathy, homing instinct	clannishness, childishness
LEO	children	love, authority, integrity	egotism, force
VIRGO	work	purity, industry, analysis	fault-finding, cynicism
LIBRA	marriage	harmony, justice	vacillation, superficiality
SCORPIO	sex	survival, regeneration	vengeance, discord
SAGITTARIUS	travel	optimism, higher learning	lawlessness
CAPRICORN	career	depth	narrowness, gloom
AQUARIUS	friends	human fellowship, genius	perverse unpredictability
PISCES	confine-ment	spiritual love, universality	diffusion, escapism

THE ELEMENTS AND QUALITIES OF THE SIGNS

ELEMENT	SIGN	QUALITY	SIGN
FIRE	ARIES LEO SAGITTARIUS	CARDINAL	ARIES LIBRA CANCER CAPRICORN
EARTH	TAURUS VIRGO CAPRICORN	FIXED	TAURUS LEO SCORPIO AQUARIUS
AIR	GEMINI LIBRA AQUARIUS		
WATER	CANCER SCORPIO PISCES	MUTABLE	GEMINI VIRGO SAGITTARIUS PISCES

Every sign has both an element and a quality associated with it. The element indicates the basic makeup of the sign, and the quality describes the kind of activity associated with each.

Signs can be grouped together according to their *element* and *quality*. Signs of the same element share many basic traits in common. They tend to form stable configurations and ultimately harmonious relationships. Signs of the same quality are often less harmonious, but they share many dynamic potentials for growth as well as profound fulfillment.

THE FIRE SIGNS

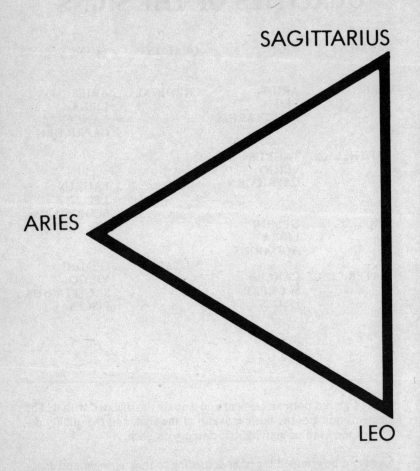

This is the fire group. On the whole these are emotional, volatile types, quick to anger, quick to forgive. They are adventurous, powerful people and.act as a source of inspiration for everyone. They spark into action with immediate exuberant impulses. They are intelligent, self-involved, creative and idealistic. They all share a certain vibrancy and glow that outwardly reflects an inner flame and passion for living.

THE EARTH SIGNS

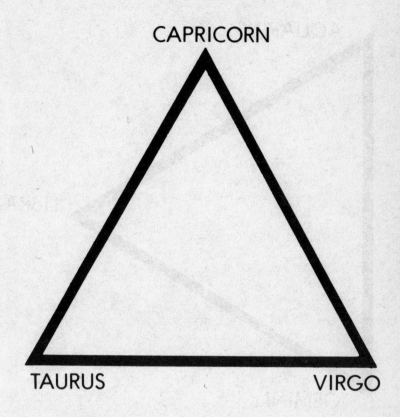

This is the earth group. They are in constant touch with the material world and tend to be conservative. Although they are all capable of spartan self-discipline, they are earthy, sensual people who are stimulated by the tangible, elegant and luxurious. The thread of their lives is always practical, but they do fantasize and are often attracted to dark, mysterious, emotional people. They are like great cliffs overhanging the sea, forever married to the ocean but always resisting erosion from the dark, emotional forces that thunder at their feet.

THE AIR SIGNS

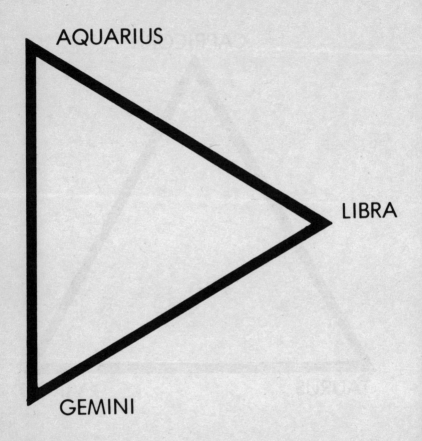

AQUARIUS

LIBRA

GEMINI

This is the air group. They are light, mental creatures desirous of contact, communication and relationship. They are involved with people and the forming of ties on many levels. Original thinkers, they are the bearers of human news. Their language is their sense of word, color, style and beauty. They provide an atmosphere suitable and pleasant for living. They add change and versatility to the scene, and it is through them that we can explore new territory of human intelligence and experience.

THE WATER SIGNS

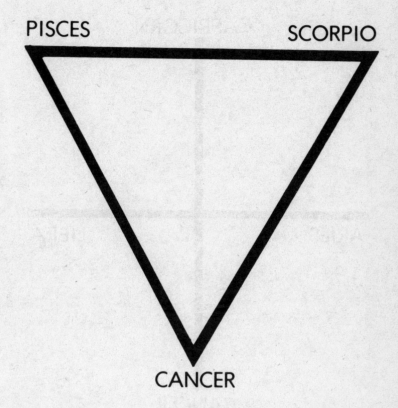

PISCES

SCORPIO

CANCER

This is the water group. Through the water people, we are all joined together on emotional, non-verbal levels. They are silent, mysterious types whose magic hypnotizes even the most determined realist. They have uncanny perceptions about people and are as rich as the oceans when it comes to feeling, emotion or imagination. They are sensitive, mystical creatures with memories that go back beyond time. Through water, life is sustained. These people have the potential for the depths of darkness or the heights of mysticism and art.

THE CARDINAL SIGNS

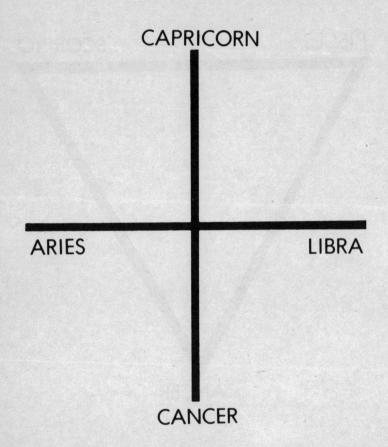

CAPRICORN

ARIES   LIBRA

CANCER

Put together, this is a clear-cut picture of dynamism, activity, tremendous stress and remarkable achievement. These people know
the meaning of great change since their lives are often characterized
by significant crises and major successes. This combination is like a
simultaneous storm of summer, fall, winter and spring. The danger
is chaotic diffusion of energy; the potential is irrepressible growth
and victory.

THE FIXED SIGNS

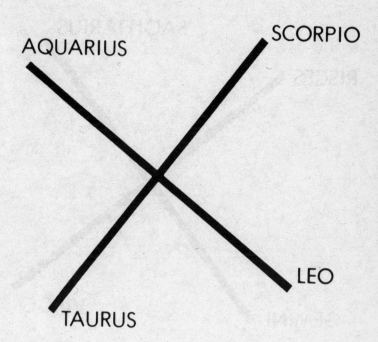

Fixed signs are always establishing themselves in a given place or area of experience. Like explorers who arrive and plant a flag, these people claim a position from which they do not enjoy being deposed. They are staunch, stalwart, upright, trusty, honorable people, although their obstinacy is well-known. Their contribution is fixity, and they are the angels who support our visible world.

THE MUTABLE SIGNS

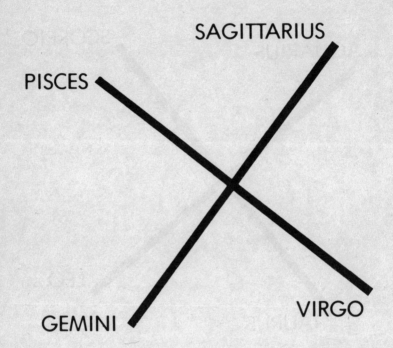

Mutable people are versatile, sensitive, intelligent, nervous and deeply curious about life. They are the translators of all energy. They often carry out or complete tasks initiated by others. Combinations of these signs have highly developed minds; they are imaginative and jumpy and think and talk a lot. At worst their lives are a Tower of Babel. At best they are adaptable and ready creatures who can assimilate one kind of experience and enjoy it while anticipating coming changes.

HOW TO APPROXIMATE YOUR RISING SIGN

Apart from the month and day of birth, the exact *time* of birth is another vital factor in the determination of an accurate horoscope. Not only do the planets move with great speed, but one must know how far the Earth has turned during the day. That way you can determine exactly where the planets are located with respect to the precise birthplace of an individual. This makes *your* horoscope *your* horoscope. In addition to these factors, another grid is laid upon that of the Zodiac and the planets: the houses. After all three have been considered, specific planetary relationships can be measured and analyzed in accordance with certain ordered procedures. It is the skillful translation of all this complex astrological language that a serious astrologer strives for in his attempt at coherent astrological synthesis. Keep this in mind.

The horoscope sets up a kind of framework around which the life of an individual grows like wild ivy, this way and that, weaving its way around the trellis of the natal positions of the planets. The year of birth tells us the positions of the distant, slow-moving planets like Jupiter, Saturn, Uranus and Pluto. The month of birth indicates the Sun sign, or birth sign as it is commonly called, as well as indicating the positions of the rapidly moving planets like Venus, Mercury and Mars. The day of birth locates the position of our Moon, and the moment of birth determines the houses through what is called the Ascendant, or Rising Sign.

As the Earth rotates on its axis once every 24 hours, each one of the twelve signs of the Zodiac appears to be "rising" on the horizon, with a new one appearing about every two hours. Actually it is the turning of the Earth that exposes each sign to view, but you will remember that in much of our astrological work we are discussing "apparent" motion. This *Rising Sign* marks the Ascendant and it colors the whole orientation of a horoscope. It indicates the sign governing the first house of the chart, and will thus determine which signs will govern all the other houses. The idea is a bit complicated at first, and we needn't dwell on complications in this introduction, but if you can imagine two color wheels with twelve divisions superimposed upon each other, one moving slowly and the other remaining still, you will have some idea of how the signs keep shifting the "color" of the houses as the Rising Sign continues to change every two hours.

The important point is that the birth chart, or horoscope, actually does define specific factors of a person's makeup. It contains a picture of being, much the way the nucleus of a tiny cell contains the potential for an entire elephant, or a packet of seeds contains a rosebush. If there were no order or continuity to the world, we could plant roses and get elephants. This same order that gives continuous flow to our lives often annoys people if it threatens to determine too much of their lives. We must grow from what we were planted, and there's no reason why we can't do that magnificently. It's all there in the horoscope. Where there is limitation, there is breakthrough; where there is crisis, there is transformation. Accurate analysis of a horoscope can help you find these points of breakthrough and transformation, and it requires knowledge of subtleties and distinctions that demand skillful judgment in order to solve even the simplest kind of personal question.

It is still quite possible, however, to draw some conclusions based upon the sign occupied by the Sun alone. In fact, if you're just being introduced to this vast subject, you're better off keeping it simple. Otherwise it seems like an impossible jumble, much like trying to read a novel in a foreign language without knowing the basic vocabulary. As with anything else, you can progress in your appreciation and understanding of astrology in direct proportion to your interest. To become really good at it requires study, experience, patience and above all—and maybe simplest of all—a fundamental understanding of what is actually going on right up there in the sky over your head. It is a vital living process you can observe, contemplate and ultimately understand. You can start by observing sunrise, or sunset, or even the full Moon.

In fact you can do a simple experiment after reading this introduction. You can erect a rough chart by following the simple procedure below:

1. Draw a circle with twelve equal segments.

2. Starting at what would be the nine o'clock position on a clock, number the segments, or houses, from 1 to 12 in a *counterclockwise direction*.

3. Label house number 1 in the following way: 4 A.M.-6 A.M.

4. In a counterclockwise direction, label the rest of the houses: 2 A.M.-4 A.M., MIDNIGHT-2 A.M., 10 P.M-MIDNIGHT, 8 P.M.-10 P.M., 6 P.M.-8 P.M., 4 P.M.-6 P.M., 2 P.M.-4 P.M., NOON-2 P.M., 10 A.M.-NOON, 8 A.M.-10 A.M., and 6 A.M.-8 A.M.

5. Now find out what time you were born and place the sun in the appropriate house.

6. Label the edge of that house with your Sun sign. You now have a description of your basic character and your fundamental drives. You can also see in what areas of life on Earth you will be most likely to focus your constant energy and center your activity.

7. If you are really feeling ambitious, label the rest of the houses with the signs, starting with your Sun sign, in order, still in a *counterclockwise direction.* When you get to Pisces, start over with Aries and keep going until you reach the house behind the Sun.

8. Look to house number 1. The sign that you have now labeled and attached to house number 1 is your Rising sign. It will color your self-image, outlook, physical constitution, early life and whole orientation to life. Of course this is a mere approximation, since there are many complicated calculations that must be made with respect to adjustments for birth time, but if you read descriptions of the sign preceding and the sign following the one you have calculated in the above manner, you may be able to identify yourself better. In any case, when you get through labeling all the houses, your drawing should look something like this:

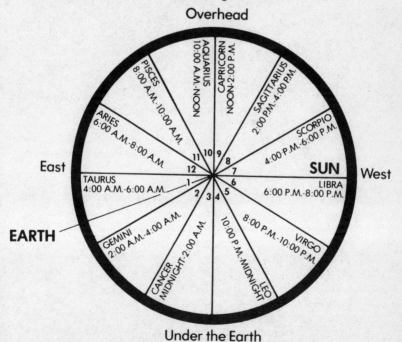

Basic chart illustrating the position of the Sun in Scorpio, with the Ascendant Taurus as the Rising Sign.

This individual was born at 5:15 P.M. on October 31 in New York City. The Sun is in Scorpio and is found in the 7th house. The Rising sign, or the sign governing house number 1, is Taurus, so this person is a blend of Scorpio and Taurus.

Any further calculation would necessitate that you look in an ephemeris, or table of planetary motion, for the positions of the rest of the planets for your particular birth year. But we will take the time to define briefly all the known planets of our Solar System and the Sun to acquaint you with some more of the astrological vocabulary that you will be meeting again and again. (See page 21 for a full explanation of the Moon in all the Signs.)

THE PLANETS AND SIGNS THEY RULE

The signs of the Zodiac are linked to the planets in the following way. Each sign is governed or ruled by one or more planets. No matter where the planets are located in the sky at any given moment, they still rule their respective signs, and when they travel through the signs they rule, they have special dignity and their effects are stronger.

Following is a list of the planets and the signs they rule. After looking at the list, go back over the definitions of the planets and see if you can determine how the planet ruling *your* Sun sign has affected your life.

SIGNS	RULING PLANETS
Aries	Mars, Pluto
Taurus	Venus
Gemini	Mercury
Cancer	Moon
Leo	Sun
Virgo	Mercury
Libra	Venus
Scorpio	Mars, Pluto
Sagittarius	Jupiter
Capricorn	Saturn
Aquarius	Saturn, Uranus
Pisces	Jupiter, Neptune

THE PLANETS
OF THE
SOLAR SYSTEM

Here are the planets of the Solar System. They all travel around the Sun at different speeds and different distances. Taken with the Sun, they all distribute individual intelligence and ability throughout the entire chart.

The planets modify the influence of the Sun in a chart according to their own particular natures, strengths and positions. Their positions must be calculated for each year and day, and their function and expression in a horoscope will change as they move from one area of the Zodiac to another.

Following, you will find brief statements of their pure meanings.

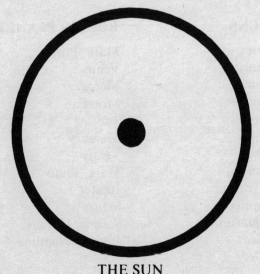

THE SUN

SUN

This is the center of existence. Around this flaming sphere all the planets revolve in endless orbits. Our star is constantly sending out its beams of light and energy without which no life on Earth would be possible. In astrology it symbolizes everything we are trying to become, the center around which all of our activity in life will always revolve. It is the symbol of our basic nature and describes the natural and constant thread that runs through everything that we do from birth to death on this planet.

To early astrologers, the sun seemed to be another planet because it crossed the heavens every day, just like the rest of the bodies in the sky.

It is the only star near enough to be seen well—it is, in fact, a dwarf star. Approximately 860,000 miles in diameter, it is about ten times as wide as the giant planet Jupiter. The next nearest star is nearly 300,000 times as far away, and if the Sun were located as far away as most of the bright stars, it would be too faint to be seen without a telescope.

Everything in the horoscope ultimately revolves around this singular body. Although other forces may be prominent in the charts of some individuals, still the Sun is the total nucleus of being and symbolizes the complete potential of every human being alive. It is vitality and the life force. Your whole essence comes from the position of the Sun.

You are always trying to express the Sun according to its position by house and sign. Possibility for all development is found in the Sun, and it marks the fundamental character of your personal radiations all around you.

It is the symbol of strength, vigor, wisdom, dignity, ardor and generosity, and the ability for a person to function as a mature individual. It is also a creative force in society. It is consciousness of the gift of life.

The underdeveloped solar nature is arrogant, pushy, undependable and proud, and is constantly using force.

MERCURY

Mercury is the planet closest to the Sun. It races around our star, gathering information and translating it to the rest of the system. Mercury represents your capacity to understand the desires of your own will and to translate those desires into action.

In other words it is the planet of Mind and the power of communication. Through Mercury we develop an ability to think, write, speak and observe—to become aware of the world around us. It colors our attitudes and vision of the world, as well as our capacity to communicate our inner responses to the outside world. Some people who have serious disabilities in their power of verbal communication have often wrongly been described as people lacking intelligence.

Although this planet (and its position in the horoscope) indicates your power to communicate your thoughts and perceptions to the world, intelligence is something deeper. Intelligence is distributed throughout all the planets. It is the relationship of the planets to each other that truly describes what we call intelligence. Mercury rules speaking, language, mathematics, draft and design, students, messengers, young people, offices, teachers and any pursuits where the mind of man has wings.

VENUS

Venus is beauty. It symbolizes the harmony and radiance of a rare and elusive quality: beauty itself. It is refinement and delicacy, softness and charm. In astrology it indicates grace, balance and the aesthetic sense. Where Venus is we see beauty, a gentle drawing in of energy and the need for satisfaction and completion. It is a special touch that finishes off rough edges. It is sensitivity, and affection, and it is always the place for that other elusive phenomenon: love. Venus describes our sense of what is beautiful and loving. Poorly developed, it is vulgar, tasteless and self-indulgent. But its ideal is the flame of spiritual love—Aphrodite, goddess of love, and the sweetness and power of personal beauty.

MARS

This is raw, crude energy. The planet next to Earth but outward from the Sun is a fiery red sphere that charges through the horoscope with force and fury. It represents the way you reach out for new adventure and new experience. It is energy and drive, initiative, courage and daring. The power to start something and see it through. It can be thoughtless, cruel and wild, angry and hostile, causing cuts, burns, scalds and wounds. It can stab its way through a chart, or it can be the symbol of healthy spirited adventure, well-channeled constructive power to begin and keep up the drive. If you have trouble starting things, if you lack the get-up-and-go to start the ball rolling, if you lack aggressiveness and self-confidence, chances are there's another planet influencing your Mars. Mars rules soldiers, butchers, surgeons, salesmen—any field that requires daring, bold skill, operational technique or self-promotion.

JUPITER

This is the largest planet of the Solar System. Scientists have recently learned that Jupiter reflects more light than it receives from the Sun. In a sense it is like a star itself. In astrology it rules good luck and good cheer, health, wealth, optimism, happiness, success and joy. It is the symbol of opportunity and always opens the way for new possibilities in your life. It rules exuberance, enthusiasm, wisdom, knowledge, generosity and all forms of expansion in general. It rules actors, statesmen, clerics, professional people, religion, publishing and the distribution of many people over large areas.

Sometimes Jupiter makes you think you deserve everything, and you become sloppy, wasteful, careless and rude, prodigal and lawless, in the illusion that nothing can ever go wrong. Then there is the danger of over-confidence, exaggeration, undependability and over-indulgence.

Jupiter is the minimization of limitation and the emphasis on spirituality and potential. It is the thirst for knowledge and higher learning.

SATURN

Saturn circles our system in dark splendor with its mysterious rings, forcing us to be awakened to whatever we have neglected in the past. It will present real puzzles and problems to be solved, causing delays, obstacles and hindrances. By doing so, Saturn stirs our own sensitivity to those areas where we are laziest.

Here we must patiently develop *method,* and only through painstaking effort can our ends be achieved. It brings order to a horoscope and imposes reason just where we are feeling least reasonable. By creating limitations and boundary, Saturn shows the consequences of being human and demands that we accept the changing cycles inevitable in human life. Saturn rules time, old age and sobriety. It can bring depression, gloom, jealousy and greed, or serious acceptance of responsibilities out of which success will develop. With Saturn there is nothing to do but face facts. It rules laborers, stones, granite, rocks and crystals of all kinds.

The Outer Planets

The following three are the outer planets. They liberate human beings from cultural conditioning, and in that sense are the law breakers. In early times it was thought that Saturn was the last planet of the system—the outer limit beyond which we could never go. The discovery of the next three planets ushered in new phases of human history, revolution and technology.

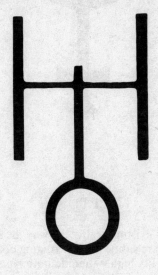

URANUS

Uranus rules unexpected change, upheaval, revolution. It is the symbol of total independence and asserts the freedom of an individual from all restriction and restraint. It is a breakthrough planet and indicates talent, originality and genius in a horoscope. It usually causes last-minute reversals and changes of plan, unwanted separations, accidents, catastrophes and eccentric behavior. It can add irrational rebelliousness and perverse bohemianism to a personality or a streak of unaffected brilliance in science and art. It rules technology, aviation and all forms of electrical and electronic advancement. It governs great leaps forward and topsy-turvy situations, and *always* turns things around at the last minute. Its effects are difficult to ever really predict, since it rules sudden last-minute decisions and events that come like lightning out of the blue.

NEPTUNE

Neptune dissolves existing reality the way the sea erodes the cliffs beside it. Its effects are subtle like the ringing of a buoy's bell in the fog. It suggests a reality higher than definition can usually describe. It awakens a sense of higher responsibility often causing guilt, worry, anxieties or delusions. Neptune is associated with all forms of escape and can make things seem a certain way so convincingly that you are absolutely sure of something that eventually turns out to be quite different.

It is the planet of illusion and therefore governs the invisible realms that lie beyond our ordinary minds, beyond our simple factual ability to prove what is "real." Treachery, deceit, disillusionment and disappointment are linked to Neptune. It describes a vague reality that promises eternity and the divine, yet in a manner so complex that we cannot really fathom it at all. At its worst Neptune is a cheap intoxicant; at its best it is the poetry, music and inspiration of the higher planes of spiritual love. It has dominion over movies, photographs and much of the arts.

PLUTO

Pluto lies at the outpost of our system and therefore rules finality in a horoscope—the final closing of chapters in your life, the passing of major milestones and points of development from which there is no return. It is a final wipeout, a closeout, an evacuation. It is a distant, subtle but powerful catalyst in all transformations that occur. It creates, destroys, then recreates. Sometimes Pluto starts its influence with a minor event or insignificant incident that might even go unnoticed. Slowly but surely, little by little, everything changes, until at last there has been a total transformation in the area of your life where Pluto has been operating. It rules mass thinking and the trends that society first rejects, then adopts and finally outgrows.

Pluto rules the dead and the underworld—all the powerful forces of creation and destruction that go on all the time beneath, around and above us. It can bring a lust for power with strong obsessions.

It is the planet that rules the metamorphoses of the caterpillar into a butterfly, for it symbolizes the capacity to change totally and forever a person's life style, way of thought and behavior.

FAMOUS PERSONALITIES

ARIES: Hans Christian Andersen, Pearl Bailey, Marlon Brando, Wernher Von Braun, Charlie Chaplin, Joan Crawford, Da Vinci, Bette Davis, Doris Day, W. C. Fields, Alec Guinness, Adolf Hitler, William Holden, Thomas Jefferson, Nikita Khrushchev, Elton John, Arturo Toscanini, J. P. Morgan, Paul Robeson, Gloria Steinem, Lowell Thomas, Vincent van Gogh, Tennessee Williams

TAURUS: Fred Astaire, Charlote Brontë, Carol Burnett, Irving Berlin, Bing Crosby, Salvador Dali, Tchaikovsky, Queen Elizabeth II, Duke Ellington, Ella Fitzgerald, Henry Fonda, Sigmund Freud, Orson Welles, Joe Louis, Lenin, Karl Marx, Golda Meir, Eva Peron, Bertrand Russell, Shakespeare, Kate Smith, Benjamin Spock, Barbra Streisand, Shirley Temple, Harry Truman

GEMINI: Mikhail Baryshnikov, Boy George, Igor Stravinsky, Carlos Chavez, Walt Whitman, Bob Dylan, Ralph Waldo Emerson, Judy Garland, Paul Gauguin, Allen Ginsberg, Benny Goodman, Bob Hope, Burl Ives, John F. Kennedy, Peggy Lee, Marilyn Monroe, Joe Namath, Cole Porter, Laurence Olivier, Harriet Beecher Stowe, Queen Victoria, John Wayne, Frank Lloyd Wright

CANCER: "Dear Abby," David Brinkley, Yul Brynner, Pearl Buck, Marc Chagall, Jack Dempsey, Mildred (Babe) Zaharias, Mary Baker Eddy, Henry VIII, John Glenn, Ernest Hemingway, Lena Horne, Oscar Hammerstein, Helen Keller, Ann Landers, George Orwell, Nancy Reagan, Rembrandt, Richard Rodgers, Ginger Rogers, Rubens, Jean-Paul Sartre, O. J. Simpson

LEO: Neil Armstrong, Russell Baker, James Baldwin, Emily Brontë, Wilt Chamberlain, Julia Child, Cecil B. De Mille, Ogden Nash, Amelia Earhart, Edna Ferber, Arthur Goldberg, Dag Hammarskjöld, Alfred Hitchcock, Mick Jagger, George Meany, George Bernard Shaw, Napoleon, Jacqueline Onassis, Henry Ford, Francis Scott Key, Andy Warhol, Mae West, Orville Wright

VIRGO: Ingrid Bergman, Warren Burger, Maurice Chevalier, Agatha Christie, Sean Connery, Lafayette, Peter Falk, Greta Garbo, Althea Gibson, Arthur Godfrey, Goethe, Buddy Hackett, Michael Jackson, Lyndon Johnson, D. H. Lawrence, Sophia Loren, Grandma Moses, Arnold Palmer, Queen Elizabeth I, Walter Reuther, Peter Sellers, Lily Tomlin, George Wallace

LIBRA: Brigitte Bardot, Art Buchwald, Truman Capote, Dwight D. Eisenhower, William Faulkner, F. Scott Fitzgerald, Gandhi, George Gershwin, Micky Mantle, Helen Hayes, Vladimir Horowitz, Doris Lessing, Martina Navratalova, Eugene O'Neill, Luciano Pavarotti, Emily Post, Eleanor Roosevelt, Bruce Springsteen, Margaret Thatcher, Gore Vidal, Barbara Walters, Oscar Wilde

SCORPIO: Vivien Leigh, Richard Burton, Art Carney, Johnny Carson, Billy Graham, Grace Kelly, Walter Cronkite, Marie Curie, Charles de Gaulle, Linda Evans, Indira Gandhi, Theodore Roosevelt, Rock Hudson, Katherine Hepburn, Robert F. Kennedy, Billie Jean King, Martin Luther, Georgia O'Keeffe, Pablo Picasso, Jonas Salk, Alan Shepard, Robert Louis Stevenson

SAGITTARIUS: Jane Austen, Louisa May Alcott, Woody Allen, Beethoven, Willy Brandt, Mary Martin, William F. Buckley, Maria Callas, Winston Churchill, Noel Coward, Emily Dickinson, Walt Disney, Benjamin Disraeli, James Doolittle, Kirk Douglas, Chet Huntley, Jane Fonda, Chris Evert Lloyd, Margaret Mead, Charles Schulz, John Milton, Frank Sinatra, Steven Spielberg

CAPRICORN: Muhammad Ali, Isaac Asimov, Pablo Casals, Dizzy Dean, Marlene Dietrich, James Farmer, Ava Gardner, Barry Goldwater, Cary Grant, J. Edgar Hoover, Howard Hughes, Joan of Arc, Gypsy Rose Lee, Martin Luther King, Jr., Rudyard Kipling, Mao Tse-tung, Richard Nixon, Gamal Nasser, Louis Pasteur, Albert Schweitzer, Stalin, Benjamin Franklin, Elvis Presley

AQUARIUS: Marian Anderson, Susan B. Anthony, Jack Benny, Charles Darwin, Charles Dickens, Thomas Edison, John Barrymore, Clark Gable, Jascha Heifetz, Abraham Lincoln, John McEnroe, Yehudi Menuhin, Mozart, Jack Nicklaus, Ronald Reagan, Jackie Robinson, Norman Rockwell, Franklin D. Roosevelt, Gertrude Stein, Charles Lindbergh, Margaret Truman

PISCES: Edward Albee, Harry Belafonte, Alexander Graham Bell, Frank Borman, Chopin, Adelle Davis, Albert Einstein, Jackie Gleason, Winslow Homer, Edward M. Kennedy, Victor Hugo, Mike Mansfield, Michelangelo, Edna St. Vincent Millay, Liza Minelli, John Steinbeck, Linus Pauling, Ravel, Diana Ross, William Shirer, Elizabeth Taylor, George Washington

SAGITTARIUS

CHARACTER ANALYSIS

People born under this ninth sign of the Zodiac are quite often self-reliant and intelligent. Generally, they are quite philosophical in their outlook on life. They know how to make practical use of their imagination.

There is seldom anything narrow about a Sagittarian. He is generally very tolerant and considerate. He would never consciously do anything that would hurt another's feelings. He is gifted with a good sense of humor and believes in being honest in his relationships with others. At times he is a little short of tact. He is so intent on telling the truth that sometimes he is a bit blunt. At any rate, he means well, and people who enjoy their relationship with him are often willing to overlook this flaw. He may even tell people true things about themselves that they do not wish to hear. At times this can cause a strain in the relationship. The Sagittarian often wishes that others were as forthright and honest as he is—no matter what the consequences.

The person born under this sign is often positive and optimistic. He likes life. He often helps others to snap out of an ill mood. His joie de vivre is often infectious. People enjoy being around the Sagittarian because he is almost always in a good mood. Quite often people born under the sign of Sagittarius are fond of the outdoors. They enjoy sporting events and often excel in them. Many of them are fond of animals—especially horses. Generally speaking they are healthy—in mind and limb. They have pluck; they enjoy the simple things of life. Fresh air and good comradeship are important to them. On the other hand, they are fond of developing their minds. Many Sagittarians cannot read or study enough. They like to keep abreast of things. They are interested in theater and the arts in general. Some of them are rather religious. Some choose a religious life.

Because they are outgoing for the most part, they sometimes come in touch with situations that others are never confronted with. In the long run this tends to make their life experiences quite rich and varied. They are well-balanced. They like to be active; they enjoy using their intellects.

It is important to the person born under this sign that justice prevails. They dislike seeing anyone treated unfairly. If the Sagittarian feels that the old laws are out-of-date or unrealistic he will fight to have them changed. At times he can be quite a rebel. It is important to him that law is carried out impartially. In matters of law, he often excels.

Sagittarians are almost always fond of travel. It seems to be imbedded in their natures. At times, they feel impelled to get away from familiar surroundings and people. Far away places have a magical attraction for someone born under this sign. They enjoy reading about foreign lands and strange customs. Many people who are Sagittarians are not terribly fond of living in big cities; they prefer the quiet and greenery of the countryside. Of all the signs of the Zodiac the Sign of Sagittarius is closest to mother nature. They can usually build a trusting relationship with animals.

The Sagittarian is quite clever in conversation. He has a definite way with words. He is fond of a good argument. He knows how to phrase things exactly; his sense of humor often has a cheerful effect on his manner of speech. He is seldom without a joke of some sort. At times he is apt to hurt others with his wit, but this is never done intentionally. A slip of the tongue sometimes gets him into social difficulties. The person born under this sign often angers quite easily; however, they cool down quickly and are not given to holding grudges. They are willing to forgive and forget.

On the whole, the Sagittarian is good-natured and fun-loving. He finds it easy to take up with people of all sorts. In most cases, his social circle is rather large. People enjoy his company. Many of his friends share his interest in outdoor life and intellectual pursuits.

At times, he can be rather impulsive. He is not afraid of risk; on the contrary, at times he can be rather foolhardy in the way he courts danger. However, he is very sporting in all that he does, and if he should wind up the loser, he is not apt to waste much time grieving about it. He can be fairly optimistic—he believes in good luck.

Health

Often people born under the sign of Sagittarius are quite athletic. They are healthy-looking—quite striking in a robust way. Often they are rather tall and well-built. They are enthusiastic people and like being active or involved. Exercise may interest them a great deal. The Sagittarian cannot stand not being active. He has to be on the go. As he grows older, he seems to increase his strength and physical ability. At times he may have worries, but he never allows them to affect his humor or health.

It is important to the Sagittarian to remain physically sound. He is usually very physically fit, but his nervous system may be somewhat sensitive. Too much activity—even while he finds action attractive—may put a severe strain upon him after a time. The Sagittarian should try to concentrate his energies on as few objects as possible. However, usually he has his projects scattered here and there, and as a result he is easily exhausted. At times illnesses fall upon him rather suddenly. Some Sagittarians are accident-prone. They are not afraid of taking risks and as a result are sometimes careless in the way they do things. Injuries often come to them by way of sports or other vigorous activities.

At times, people of this sign try to ignore signs of illness —especially if they are engaged in some activity that has captured their interest. This results in a severe setback at times.

In later life, the Sagittarian sometimes suffers from stomach disorders. High blood pressure is another ailment that might affect him; he should also be on guard for signs of arthritis and sciatica. In spite of these possible dangers, the average Sagittarian manages to stay quite youthful and alert through his interest in life.

Occupation

The Sagittarian is someone who can be relied upon in a work situation. He is loyal and dependable. He is an energetic worker, anxious to please his superiors. He is forward-looking by nature and enjoys working in modern surroundings and toward progressive goals. Challenges do not frighten him. He is rather flexible and can work in confining situations even though he may not enjoy it. Work which gives him a chance to move about and meet new people is well suited to his character. If he has to stay in one locale he is apt to become sad and ill-humored. He can take orders but he would rather be in a situation where he does not have to. He is difficult to please at times, and may hop from job to job before feeling that it is really time to settle down. He does his best work when he is allowed to work on his own.

The Sagittarian is interested in expressing himself in the work he does. If he occupies a position which does not allow him to do this, he will seek outside activities that give him a chance to develop in a direction which interests him.

Some Sagittarians do well in the field of journalism; others make good teachers and public speakers. They are generally quite flexible and would do well in many different positions. Some excel as foreign ministers or in music; others do well in government work or in publishing.

The person born under this sign is often more intelligent than the average man. The cultivated Sagittarian knows how to employ his intellectual gifts to their best advantage. In politics and religion, the Sagittarian often displays considerable brilliance.

He is generally pleasant to work with; he is considerate of his colleagues and would do nothing that might upset their working relationship. Because he is so self-reliant he often inspires others. He likes to work with detail. His ideas are often quite practical and intelligent. The Sagittarian is curious by nature and is always looking for ways of increasing his knowledge.

The people born under this sign are almost always generous. They rarely refuse someone in need, but are always willing to share what they have. Whether he is up or down, the Sagittarian can always be relied upon to help someone in dire straits. His attitude toward life may be happy-go-lucky in general. He is difficult to depress no matter what his situation. He is optimistic and forward-looking. Money always seems to fall into his hands; it's seldom a problem for him.

The average Sagittarian is interested in expansion and promotion. Sometimes these concerns weaken his projects rather than strengthen them.

He is interested in large profit and is sometimes willing to take risks to secure it. In the long run he is successful. He has a flair for carrying off business deals well. It is the cultivated Sagittarian who prepares himself well in business matters so that he is well-supported in his interests by knowledge, as well as by experience.

The average person born under this sign is more interested in contentment and joy than in material gain. However he will do his best to make the most of profit when it comes his way.

Home and Family

Not all Sagittarians are very interested in home life. Many of them set great store in being mobile. Their activities outside the home may attract them more than those inside the home. Not exactly homebodies, Sagittarians, however, can adjust themselves to a stable domestic life if they put their minds to it.

People born under this sign are not keen on luxuries and other displays of wealth. They prefer the simple things. Anyone entering their home should be able to discern this. They are generally neat; they like a place that has plenty of space—not too cluttered with imposing furniture.

Even when he settles down, the Sagittarian likes to keep a small corner of his life just for himself; independence is important to him. If necessary, he'll insist upon it, no matter what the situation. He likes a certain amount of beauty in his home, but he may not be too interested in keeping things looking nice—his interests lead him elsewhere. Housekeeping may bore him to distraction. If he is forced to stick to a domestic routine he is liable to become somewhat disagreeable.

Children bring him a great deal of happiness. He is fond of family life. Friends generally drop in any old time to visit a Sagittarian for they know they will always be welcomed and properly entertained. The Sagittarian's love of his fellow man is well known.

When children are small, he may not understand them too well, even though he tries. He may feel he is a bit too clumsy to handle them properly—although this may be far from the case. As they begin to grow up and develop definite personalities, the Sagittarian's interest grows. There is always a strong tie between children and the Sagittarian parent.

Children are especially drawn to Sagittarians because they seem to understand them better than other adults.

One is apt to find children born under this sign a little restless and disorganized at times. They are usually quite independent in their ways and may ask for quite a bit of freedom while still young. They don't like being fussed over by adults. They like to feel that their parents believe in them and trust them on their own.

Social Relationships

The Sagittarian enjoys having people around. It is not difficult for him to make friends. He is very sociable by nature. Most of the friends he makes, he keeps for life. As a rule, the person born under this sign is rather broadminded; he is apt to have all sorts of friends. He appreciates people for their good qualities, however few they may have. He is not quick to judge and is often very forgiving. He is not impressed by what a friend has in the way of material goods.

The Sagittarian is generally quite popular. He is much in demand socially; people like him for his easy disposition and his good humor. His friendship is valued by others. Quite often in spite of his chumminess, the Sagittarian is rather serious; light conversation may be somewhat difficult for him.

He believes in speaking his mind—in saying what he feels—yet at times, he can appear rather quiet and retiring. It all depends on his mood. Others may feel that there are two sides to his personality because of this quirk in his nature; for this reason it may be difficult for some people to get to know him. In some instances, he employs his silence as a sort of protection. When people pierce through however and don't leave him in peace, he can become rather angry.

On the whole, he is a kind and considerate person. His nature is gentle and unassuming. With the wrong people though, he can become somewhat disagreeable. He can become angry quite easily at times; however, he cools down quickly and is willing to let bygones be bygones. He never holds a grudge against anyone. Companionship and harmony in all social relationships is quite necessary for the Sagittarian; he is willing to make some sacrifices for it. The partner for someone born under this sign must be a good listener. There are times when the Sagittarian feels it is necessary to pour his heart out. He is willing to listen to another's problems, too. His mate or loved one should be able to take an interest in his hobbies and such. If not, the Sagittarian may be tempted to go his own way even more.

The Sagittarian says what he means; he doesn't beat around the bush. Being direct is one of his strongest qualities. Sometimes it pays off; sometimes it doesn't. He is often forgetful that the one he loves may be more sensitive than she allows herself to appear—even to him. He has a tendency to put his foot in his mouth at times. However, his mate should be able to overlook this flaw in his character or else try to correct it in some subtle way. At times, when joking broadly he has the ability to strike a sensitive chord in his loved one and this may result in a serious misunderstanding. The cultivated Sagittarian learns his boundaries; he knows when not to go too far. Understanding his partner's viewpoint is also an important thing for someone born under this sign to learn.

LOVE AND MARRIAGE

Sagittarians are faithful to their loved ones. They are affectionate in nature and not at all possessive. Love is important for them spiritually as well as physically. For some people born under this sign, romance is a chance to escape reality—it is a chance for adventure. Quite often, the Sagittarian's mate finds it difficult to keep up with him—he is so active and energetic. When Sagittarians fall in love, however, they are quite easy to handle.

Sagittarians do like having freedom. They will make concessions in a steady relationship; still there will be a part of themselves that they keep from others. He or she is very keen on preserving his individual rights, no matter what sort of relationship he is engaged in. The Sagittarian's ideals are generally high and they are important to him. He is looking for someone with similar standards, not someone too lax or conventional.

In love, the Sagittarian may be a bit childlike at times. As a result of this he is apt to encounter various disappointments before he has found the one meant for him. At times he or she says things he really shouldn't and this causes the end of a romantic relationship. The person born under this sign may have many love affairs before he feels he is ready to settle down with just one person. If the person he loves does not exactly measure up to his standards, the Sagittarian is apt to overlook this—depending on how strong his love is—and accept the person for what that person is.

On the whole, the Sagittarian is not an envious person. He is willing to allow his or her partner needed freedoms—within reason. The Sagittarian does this so that he will not have to jeopardize his own liberties. Live and let live could easily be his motto. If his ideals and freedom are threatened, the Sagittarian fights hard to protect what he believes is just and fair.

He does not want to make any mistakes in love, so he takes his time when choosing someone to settle down with. He is direct and positive when he meets the right one; he does not waste time.

The average Sagittarian may be a bit altar-shy. It may take a bit of convincing before Sagittarians agree that married life is right for them. This is generally because they do not want to lose their freedom. The Sagittarian is an active person who enjoys being around a lot of other people. Sitting quietly at home does not interest him at all. At times it may seem that he or she wants to have things his own way, even in marriage. It may take some doing to get him to realize that in marriage, as in other things, give and take plays a great role.

Romance and the Sagittarius Woman

The Sagittarian woman is often kind and gentle. Most of the time she is very considerate of others and enjoys being of help in some way to her friends. She can be quite active and, as a result, be rather difficult to catch. On the whole, she is optimistic and friendly. She believes in looking on the bright side of things. She knows how to make the best of situations that others feel are not worth salvaging. She has plenty of pluck.

Men generally like her because of her easy-going manner. Quite often she becomes friends with a man before venturing on to romance. There is something about her that makes her more of a companion than a lover. She can best be described as sporting and broad-minded.

She is almost never possessive; she enjoys her own freedom too much to want to make demands on that of another person.

She is always youthful in her disposition. She may seem rather guileless at times. Generally it takes her longer really to mature than it does others. She tends to be impulsive and may easily jump from one thing to another. If she has an unfortunate experience in love early in life, she may shy away from fast or intimate contacts for a while. She is usually very popular. Not all the men who are attracted to her see her as a possible lover, but more as a friend or companion.

The woman born under this sign generally believes in true love. She may have several romances before she decides to settle down. For her there is no particular rush. She is willing to have a long romantic relationship with the man she loves before making marriage plans.

The Sagittarius woman is often the outdoors type and has a strong liking for animals—especially dogs and horses. Quite often she excels in sports. She is not generally someone who is content to stay at home and cook and take care of the house. She would rather be out attending to her other interests. When she does household work, however, she does it well.

She makes a good companion as well as a wife. She usually enjoys participating with her husband in his various interests and affairs. Her sunny disposition often brightens up the dull moments of a love affair.

At times her temper may flare, but she is herself again after a few moments. She would never butt into her husband's business affairs, but she does enjoy being asked for her opinion from time to time. Generally she is up to date on all that her husband is doing and can offer him some pretty sound advice.

The Sagittarius woman is seldom jealous of her husband's interest in other people—even if some of them are of the opposite sex. If she has no reason to doubt his love, she never questions it.

She makes a loving and sympathetic mother. Quite often she will play with her children. Her cheerful manner makes her an invaluable playmate.

Romance and the Sagittarius Man

The Sagittarius man is often an adventurer. He likes taking chances in love as well as in life. He may hop around quite a bit—from one romance to another—before really thinking about settling down. Many men born under this sign feel that marriage would mean the end of their freedom—so they avoid it as much as possible. Whenever a romance becomes too serious, they move on. Many Sagittarians are rather impulsive in love. Early marriages for some often end unpleasantly. The Sagittarian is not a very mature person—even at an age when most others are. He takes a bit more time. He may not always make a wise choice in a love partner.

He is affectionate and loving but not at all possessive. Because he is rather lighthearted in love, he sometimes gets into trouble.

Most Sagittarius men find romance an exciting adventure. They make attentive lovers and are never cool or indifferent. Love should also have a bit of fun in it for him too. He likes to keep things light and gay. Romance without humor—at times—is difficult for him to accept. The woman he loves should also be a good sport. She should have as open and fun-loving a disposition as he has—if she is to understand him properly.

He wants his mate to share his interest in the outdoor life and animals. If she is good at sports, she is likely to win his heart, for the average Sagittarian generally has an interest in athletics of various sorts—from bicycling to baseball.

His mate must also be a good intellectual companion; someone who can easily discuss those matters which interest her Sagittarian. Physical love is important to him—but so is spiritual love. A good romance will contain these in balance.

His sense of humor may sometimes seem a little unkind to someone who is not used to being laughed at. He enjoys playing jokes now and again; it is the child in his nature that remains a part of his character even when he grows old and gray.

He is not a homebody. He is responsible, however, and will do what is necessary to keep a home together. Still and all, the best wife for him is one who can manage household matters single-handedly if need be.

He loves children—especially as they grow older and begin to take on definite personalities.

Woman—Man

SAGITTARIUS WOMAN
ARIES MAN

In some ways, the Aries man resembles an intellectual mountain goat leaping from crag to crag. He has an insatiable thirst for knowledge. He's ambitious and is apt to have his finger in many pies. He can do with a woman like you—someone attractive, quick-witted, and smart.

He is not interested in a clinging vine kind of wife, but someone who is there when he needs her; someone who listens and understands what he says; someone who can give advice if he should ever need it . . . which is not likely to be often. The Aries man wants a woman who will look good on his arm without hanging on it too heavily. He is looking for a woman who has both feet on the ground and yet is mysterious and enticing . . . a kind of domestic Helen of Troy whose face or fine dinner can launch a thousand business deals if need be. That woman he's in search of sounds a little like you, doesn't she? If the shoe fits, put it on. You won't regret it.

The Aries man makes a good husband. He is faithful and attentive. He is an affectionate kind of man. He'll make you feel needed and loved. Love is a serious matter for the Aries man. He does not believe in flirting or playing the field—especially after he's found the woman of his dreams. He'll expect you to be as constant in your affection as he is in his. He'll expect you to be one hundred percent his; he won't put up with any nonsense while romancing you.

The Aries man may be pretty progressive and modern about many things; however, when it comes to pants wearing, he's downright conventional: it's strictly male attire. The best position you can take in the relationship is a supporting one. He's the boss and that's that. Once you have learned to accept that, you'll find the going easy.

The Aries man, with his endless energy and drive, likes to relax in the comfort of his home at the end of the day. The good homemaker can be sure of holding his love. He's keen on slippers and pipe and a comfortable armchair. If you see to it that everything in the house is where he expects to find it, you'll have no difficulty keeping the relationship on an even keel.

Life and love with an Aries man may be just the medicine you need. He'll be a good provider. He'll spoil you if he's financially able.

He's young at heart and can get along with children easily. He'll spoil them every chance he gets.

SAGITTARIUS WOMAN
TAURUS MAN

If you've got your heart set on a man born under the sign of Taurus, you'll have to learn the art of being patient. Taureans take their time about everything—even love.

The steady and deliberate Taurus man is a little slow on the draw; it may take him quite a while before he gets around to popping that question. For the woman who doesn't mind twiddling her thumbs, the waiting and anticipating almost always pays off in the end. Taurus men want to make sure that every step they take is a good one—particularly, if they feel that the path they're on is one that leads to the altar.

If you are in the mood for a whirlwind romance, you had better cast your net in shallower waters. Moreover, most Taureans prefer to do the angling themselves. They are not keen on a woman taking the lead; once she does, they are liable to drop her like a dead fish. If you let yourself get caught on a Taurean's terms, you'll find that he's fallen for you—hook, line, and sinker.

The Taurus man is fond of a comfortable homelife. It is very important to him. If you keep those home fires burning you will have no trouble keeping that flame in your Taurean's heart aglow. You have a talent for homemaking; use it. Your taste in furnishings is excellent. You know how to make a house come to life with colors and decorations.

Taurus, the strong, steady, and protective Bull may not be your idea of a man on the move, still he's reliable. Perhaps he could be the anchor for your dreams and plans. He could help you to acquire a more balanced outlook and approach to your life. If you're given to impulsiveness, he could help you to curb it. He's the man who is always there when you need him.

When you tie the knot with a man born under Taurus, you can put away fears about creditors pounding on the front door. Taureans are practical about everything including bill-paying. When he carries you over that threshold, you can be certain that the entire house is paid for, not only the doorsill.

As a housewife, you won't have to worry about putting aside your many interests for the sake of back-breaking house chores. Your Taurus husband will see to it that you have all the latest time-saving appliances and comforts.

Your children will be obedient and orderly. Your Taurus husband will see to that.

SAGITTARIUS WOMAN
GEMINI MAN

The Gemini man is quite a catch. Many a woman has set her cap for him and failed to bag him. Generally, Gemini men are intelligent, witty, and outgoing. Many of them tend to be versatile.

On the other hand, some of them seem to lack that sort of common sense that you set so much store in. Their tendency to start a half-dozen projects, then toss them up in the air out of boredom may do nothing more than exasperate you.

One thing that causes a Twin's mind and affection to wander is a bore, but it is unlikely that an active woman like you would ever allow herself to be accused of dullness. The Gemini man that has caught your heart will admire you for your ideas and intellect—perhaps even more than for your homemaking talents and good looks.

A strong willed woman could easily fill the role of rudder for her Gemini's ship-without-a-sail. The intelligent Gemini is often aware of his shortcomings and doesn't mind if someone with better bearings gives him a shove in the right direction—when it's needed. The average Gemini doesn't have serious ego-hangups and will even accept a well-deserved chewing out from his mate or girlfriend gracefully.

A successful and serious-minded Gemini could make you a very happy woman, perhaps, if you gave him half the chance. Although he may give you the impression that he has a hole in his head, the Gemini man generally has a good head on his shoulders and can make efficient use of it when he wants. Some of them, who have learned the art of being steadfast, have risen to great heights in their professions. President Kennedy was a Gemini as was Thomas Mann and William Butler Yeats.

Once you convince yourself that not all people born under the sign of the Twins are witless grasshoppers, you won't mind dating a few—to test your newborn conviction. If you do wind up walking down the aisle with one, accept the fact that married life with him will mean your taking the bitter with the sweet.

Life with a Gemini man can be more fun than a barrel of clowns. You'll never be allowed to experience a dull moment. But don't leave money matters to him or you'll both wind up behind the eight ball.

Gemini men are always attractive to the opposite sex. You'll perhaps have to allow him an occasional harmless flirt—it will seldom amount to more than that if you're his proper mate.

The Gemini father is a pushover for children. See to it that you keep them in line; otherwise they'll be running the house.

SAGITTARIUS WOMAN
CANCER MAN

Chances are you won't hit it off too well with the man born under Cancer if your plans concern love, but then, Cupid has been known to do some pretty unlikely things. The Cancerian is a very sensitive man—thin-skinned and occasionally moody. You've got to keep on your toes—and not step on his—if you're determined to make a go of the relationship.

The Cancer man may be lacking in some of the qualities you seek in a man, but when it comes to being faithful and being a good provider, he's hard to beat.

The perceptive woman will not mistake the Crab's quietness for sullenness or his thriftiness for penny-pinching. In some respects, he is like that wise old owl out on a limb; he may look like he's dozing but actually he hasn't missed a thing. Cancerians often possess a well of knowledge about human behavior; they can come across with some pretty helpful advice to those in trouble or in need. He can certainly guide you in making investments both in time and money. He may not say much, but he's always got his wits about him.

The Crab may not be the match or catch for a woman like you; at times, you are likely to find him downright dull. True to his sign, he can be fairly cranky and crabby when handled the wrong way. He is perhaps more sensitive than he should be.

If you're smarter than your Cancer friend, be smart enough

not to let him know. Never give him the idea that you think he's a little short on brain power. It would send him scurrying back into his shell—and all that ground lost in the relationship will perhaps never be recovered.

The Crab is most content at home. Once settled down for the night or the weekend, wild horses couldn't drag him any farther than the gatepost—that is, unless those wild horses were dispatched by his mother. The Crab is sometimes a Momma's boy. If his mate does not put her foot down, he will see to it that his mother always comes first. No self-respecting wife would ever allow herself to play second fiddle—even if it's to her old gray-haired mother-in-law. With a little bit of tact, however, she'll find that slipping into that number-one position is as easy as pie (that legendary one his mother used to bake).

If you pamper your Cancer man, you'll find that "Mother" turns up increasingly less—at the front door as well as in conversations.

Cancerians make protective, proud, and patient fathers.

SAGITTARIUS WOMAN
LEO MAN

For the woman who enjoys being swept off her feet in a romantic whirlwind fashion, Leo is the sign of such love. When the Lion puts his mind to romancing, he doesn't stint. It's all wining and dining and dancing till the wee hours of the morning.

Leo is all heart and knows how to make his woman feel like a woman. The girl in constant search of a man she can look up to need go no farther: Leo is ten-feet tall—in spirit if not in stature. He's a man not only in full control of his faculties but in full control of just about any situation he finds himself in. He's a winner.

The Leo man may not look like Tarzan, but he knows how to roar and beat his chest if he has to. The woman who has had her fill of weak-kneed men finds in a Leo someone she can at last lean upon. He can support you not only physically but spiritually as well. He's good at giving advice that pays off.

Leos are direct people. They don't believe in wasting time or effort. They almost never make unwise investments.

Many Leos rise to the top of their professions; through example, they often prove to be a source of great inspiration to others.

Although he's a ladies' man, the Leo man is very particular about his ladies. His standards are high when it comes to love interests. The idealistic and cultivated woman should have no trouble keeping her balance on the pedestal the Lion sets her on. Leo believes that romance should be played on a fair give-and-take basis. He won't stand for any monkey business in a love relationship. It's all or nothing.

You'll find him a frank, off-the-shoulder person; he generally says what is on his mind.

If you decide upon a Leo man for a mate, you must be prepared to stand behind him full-force. He expects it—and usually deserves it. He's the head of the house and can handle that position without a hitch. He knows how to go about breadwinning and, if he has his way (and most Leos do have their own way), he'll see to it that you'll have all the luxuries you crave and the comforts you need.

It's unlikely that the romance in your marriage will ever die out. Lions need love like flowers need sunshine. They're ever amorous and generally expect similar attention and affection from their mates. Leos are fond of going out on the town; they love to give parties, as well as to go to them.

Leos make strict fathers, generally. They love their children but won't spoil them.

SAGITTARIUS WOMAN
VIRGO MAN

Although the Virgo man may be a bit of a fussbudget at times, his seriousness and dedication to common sense may help you to overlook his tendency to sometimes be overcritical about minor things.

Virgo men are often quiet, respectable types who set great store in conservative behavior and levelheadedness. He'll admire you for your practicality and tenacity . . . perhaps even more than for your good looks. He's seldom bowled over by a glamour-puss. When he gets his courage up, he turns to a serious and reliable girl for romance. He'll be far from a Valentino while dating. In fact, you may wind up making all the passes. Once he does get his motor running, however, he can be a warm and wonderful fellow—to the right girl.

He's gradual about love. Chances are your romance with him will start out looking like an ordinary friendship. Once he's sure you're no fly-by-night flirt and have no plans of taking him for a ride, he'll open up and rain sunshine all over your heart.

Virgo men tend to marry late in life. The Virgo believes in holding out until he's met the right girl. He may not have many names in his little black book; in fact, he may not even have a black book. He's not interested in playing the field; leave that to men of the more flamboyant signs. The Virgo man is so particular that he may remain romantically inactive for a long period. His girl has to be perfect or it's no go. If you find yourself feeling weak-kneed for a Virgo, do your best to convince him that perfect is not so important when it comes to love; help him to realize that he's missing out on a great deal by not considering the near perfect or whatever it is you consider yourself to be. With your surefire perseverance, you will most likely be able to make him listen to reason and he'll wind up reciprocating your romantic interests.

The Virgo man is no block of ice. He'll respond to what he feels to be the right feminine flame. Once your love-life with a Virgo man starts to bubble, don't give it a chance to fall flat. You may never have a second chance at winning his heart.

If you should ever have a falling out with him, forget about patching it up. He'd prefer to let the pieces lie scattered. Once married, though, he'll stay that way—even if it hurts. He's too conscientious to try to back out of a legal deal of any sort.

The Virgo man is as neat as a pin. He's thumbs down on sloppy housekeeping. Keep everything bright, neat, and shiny . . . and that goes for the children, too, at least by the time he gets home from work. Chocolate-coated kisses from Daddy's little girl go over like a lead balloon with him.

SAGITTARIUS WOMAN
LIBRA MAN

If there's a Libran in your life, you are most likely a very happy woman. Men born under this sign have a way with women. You'll always feel at ease in a Libran's company; you can be yourself when you're with him.

The Libra man can be moody at times. His moodiness is often puzzling. One moment he comes on hard and strong with declarations of his love, the next moment you find that he's left you like yesterday's mashed potatoes. He'll come back, though; don't worry. Librans are like that. Deep down inside he really knows what he wants even though he may not appear to.

You'll appreciate his admiration of beauty and harmony. If you're dressed to the teeth and never looked lovelier, you'll get a ready compliment—and one that's really deserved. Librans don't indulge in idle flattery. If they don't like something, they are tactful enough to remain silent.

Librans will go to great lengths to preserve peace and harmony—they will even tell a fat lie if necessary. They don't like showdowns or disagreeable confrontations. The frank woman is all for getting whatever is bothering her off her chest and out into the open, even if it comes out all wrong. To the Libran, making a clean breast of everything seems like sheer folly sometimes.

You may lose your patience while waiting for your Libra friend to make up his mind. It takes him ages sometimes to make a decision. He weighs both sides carefully before comitting himself to anything. You seldom dillydally—at least about small things—and so it's likely that you will find it difficult to see eye to eye with a hesitating Libran when it comes to decision-making methods.

All in all, though, he is kind, considerate, and fair. He is interested in the "real" truth; he'll try to balance everything out until he has all the correct answers. It's not difficult for him to see both sides of a story.

He's a peace-loving man. The sight of blood is apt to turn his stomach.

Librans are not show-offs. Generally, they are well-balanced, modest people. Honest, wholesome, and affectionate, they are serious about every love encounter they have. If one should find that the girl he's dating is not really suited to him, he will end the relationship in such a tactful manner that no hard feelings will come about.

The Libra father is firm, gentle, and patient.

SAGITTARIUS WOMAN
SCORPIO MAN

Many find the Scorpio's sting a fate worse than death. When his anger breaks loose, you had better clear out of the vicinity.

The average Scorpio may strike you as a brute. He'll stick pins into the balloons of your plans and dreams if they don't line up with what he thinks is right. If you do anything to irritate him—just anything—you'll wish you hadn't. He'll give you a sounding out that would make you pack your bags and go back to Mother—if you were that kind of a girl.

The Scorpio man hates being tied down to homelife—he would rather be out on the battlefield of life, belting away at whatever he feels is a just and worthy cause, instead of staying home nestled in a comfortable armchair with the evening paper. If you are a girl who has a homemaking streak—don't keep those home fires burning too brightly too long; you may just run out of firewood.

As passionate as he is in business affairs and politics, the Scorpio man still has plenty of pep and ginger stored away for lovemaking.

Most women are easily attracted to him—perhaps you are no exception. Those who allow a man born under this sign to sweep them off their feet, shortly find that they're dealing with a pepper pot of seething excitement. The Scorpio man is passionate with a capital P, you can be sure of that. But he's capable of dishing out as much pain as pleasure. Damsels with fluttering hearts who, when in the embrace of a Scorpio, think "This is it," had better be in a position moments later to realize that "Perhaps this isn't it."

Scorpios are blunt. An insult is likely to whiz out of their mouths quicker than a compliment.

If you're the kind of woman who can keep a stiff upper lip, take it on the chin, turn a deaf ear, and all of that, because you feel you are still under his love spell in spite of everything: lots of luck.

If you have decided to take the bitter with the sweet, prepare yourself for a lot of ups and downs. Chances are you won't have as much time for your own affairs and interests as you'd like. The Scorpio's love of power may cause you to be at his constant beck and call.

Scorpios like fathering large families. They love children but quite often they fail to live up to their responsibilities as a parent.

SAGITTARIUS WOMAN
SAGITTARIUS MAN

The woman who has set her cap for a man born under the sign of Sagittarius may have to apply an awful amount of strategy before she can get him to drop down on bended knee. Although some Sagittarians may be marriage-shy, they're not ones to skitter away from romance. A high-spirited woman may find a relationship with a Sagittarian—whether a fling or "the real thing"—a very enjoyable experience.

As a rule, Sagittarians are bright, happy, and healthy people. They have a strong sense of fair play. Often they're a source of inspiration to others. They're full of ideas and drive.

You'll be taken by the Sagittarian's infectious grin and his lighthearted friendly nature. If you do wind up being the woman in his life, you'll find that he's apt to treat you more like a buddy than the love of his life. It's just his way. Sagittarians are often chummy instead of romantic.

You'll admire his broadmindedness in most matters—including those of the heart. If, while dating you, he claims that he still wants to play the field, he'll expect you to enjoy the same liberty. Once he's promised to love, honor, and obey, however, he does just that. Marriage for him, once he's taken that big step, is very serious business.

A woman who has a keen imagination and a great love of freedom will not be disappointed if she does tie up with a Sagittarian. The Sagittarius man is often quick-witted. Men of this sign have a genuine interest in equality. They hate prejudice and injustice.

If he does insist on a night out with the boys once a week, he won't scowl if you decide to let him shift for himself in the kitchen once a week while you pursue some of your own interests. He believes in fairness.

He's not much of a homebody. Quite often he's occupied with faraway places either in his dreams or in reality. He enjoys—just as you do—being on the go or on the move. He's got ants in his pants and refuses to sit still for long stretches at a time. Humdrum routine—especially at home—bores him. At the drop of a hat, he may ask you to whip off your apron and dine out for a change. He likes surprising people. He'll take great pride in showing you off to his friends. He'll always be a considerate mate; he will never embarrass or disappoint you intentionally.

He's very tolerant when it comes to friends and you'll most likely spend a lot of time entertaining people.

Sagittarians become interested in their children when the children are out of the baby stage.

SAGITTARIUS WOMAN
CAPRICORN MAN

A with-it girl like you is likely to find the average Capricorn man a bit of a drag. The man born under this sign is often a closed up person and difficult to get to know. Even if you do get to know him, you may not find him very interesting.

In romance, Capricorn men are a little on the rusty side. You'll probably have to make all the passes.

You may find his plodding manner irritating and his conservative, traditional ways downright maddening. He's not one to take a chance on anything. "If it was good enough for my father, it's good enough for me" may be his motto. He follows a way that is tried and true.

Whenever adventure rears its tantalizing head, the Goat will turn the other way; he's just not interested.

He may be just as ambitious as you are—perhaps even more so—but his ways of accomplishing his aims are more subterranean or, at least, seem so. He operates from the background a good deal of the time. At a gathering you may never even notice him, but he's there, taking everything in, sizing everyone up, planning his next careful move.

Although Capricorns may be intellectual to a degree, it is not generally the kind of intelligence you appreciate. He may not be as quick or as bright as you; it may take him ages to understand a simple joke.

If you do decide to take up with a man born under this sign of the Goat, you ought to be pretty good in the "Cheering Up" department. The Capricorn man often acts as though he's constantly being followed by a cloud of gloom.

The Capricorn man is most himself when in the comfort and privacy of his own home. The security possible within four walls can make him a happy man. He'll spend as much time as he can at home. If he is loaded down with extra work, he'll bring it home instead of finishing it up at the office.

You'll most likely find yourself frequently confronted by his relatives. Family is very important to the Capricorn—*his* family that is. They had better take an important place in your life, too, if you want to keep your home a happy one.

Although his caution in most matters may all but drive you up the wall, you'll find that his concerned way with money is justified most of the time. He'll plan everything right down to the last penny.

He can be quite a scolder with children. You'll have to step in and smooth things out.

SAGITTARIUS WOMAN
AQUARIUS MAN

Aquarians love everybody—even their worst enemies sometimes. Through your love relationship with an Aquarian you'll find yourself running into all sorts of people, ranging from near-genius to downright insane . . . and they're all friends of his.

As a rule, Aquarians are extremely friendly and open. Of all the signs, they are perhaps the most tolerant. In the thinking department, they are often miles ahead of others.

You'll most likely find your relationship with this man a challenging one. Your high respect for intelligence and imagination may be reason enough for you to set your heart on a Water Bearer. You'll find that you can learn a lot from him.

In the holding-hands phase of your romance, you may find that your Water Bearing friend has cold feet. Aquarians take quite a bit of warming up before they are ready to come across with that first goodnight kiss. More than likely, he'll just want to be your pal in the beginning. For him, that's an important first step in any relationship—love, included. The "poetry and flowers" stage—if it ever comes—will come later. The Aquarian is all heart; still, when it comes to tying himself down to one person and for keeps, he is almost always sure to hesitate. He may even try to get out of it if you breathe down his neck too heavily.

The Aquarius man is no Valentino and wouldn't want to be. The kind of love-life he's looking for is one that's made up mainly of companionship. Although he may not be very romantic, the memory of his first romance will always hold an important position in his heart. Some Aquarians wind up marrying their childhood sweethearts.

You won't find it difficult to look up to a man born under the sign of the Water Bearer, but you may find the challenge of trying to keep up with him dizzying. He can pierce through the most complicated problem as if it were a matter of $2 + 2$. You may find him a little too lofty and high-minded—but don't judge him too harshly if that's the case; he's way ahead of his time—your time, too, most likely.

If you marry this man, he'll stay true to you. Don't think that once the honeymoon is over, you'll be chained to the kitchen sink forever. Your Aquarius husband will encourage you to keep active in your own interests and affairs. You'll most likely have a minor tiff now and again but never anything serious.

Kids love him and vice-versa. He'll be as tolerant with them as he is with adults.

SAGITTARIUS WOMAN
PISCES MAN

The man born under Pisces is quite a dreamer. Sometimes he's so wrapped up in his dreams that he's difficult to reach. To the average, active woman, he may seem a little sluggish.

He's easygoing most of the time. He seems to take things in his stride. He'll entertain all kinds of views and opinions from just about everyone, nodding or smiling vaguely, giving the impression that he's with them one hundred percent while that may not be the case at all. His attitude may be "why bother" when he's confronted with someone wrong who thinks he's right. The Pisces man will seldom speak his mind if he thinks he'll be rigidly opposed.

The Pisces man is oversensitive at times—he's afraid of getting his feelings hurt. He'll sometimes imagine a personal affront when none's been made. Chances are you'll find this complex of his maddening; at times you may feel like giving him a swift kick where it hurts the most. It wouldn't do any good, though. It would just add fuel to the fire of his complex.

One thing you'll admire about this man is his concern for people who are sickly or troubled. He'll make his shoulder available to anyone in the mood for a good cry. He can listen to one hard-luck story after another without seeming to tire. When his advice is asked, he is capable of coming across with some words of wisdom. He often knows what is bugging someone before that person is aware of it himself. It's almost intuitive with Pisceans, it seems.

Still, at the end of the day, this man will want some peace and quiet. If you've got a problem when he comes home, don't unload it in his lap. If you do, you are liable to find him short-tempered. He's a good listener but he can only take so much.

Pisceans are not aimless although they may seem so at times. The positive sort of Pisces man is quite often successful in his profession and is likely to wind up rich and influential. Material gain, however, is never a direct goal for a man born under this sign.

The weaker Pisces are usually content to stay on the level where they find themselves. They won't complain too much if the roof leaks or if the fence is in need of repair.

Because of their seemingly laissez-faire manner, people under this sign—needless to say—are immensely popular with children. For tots they play the double role of confidant and playmate. It will never enter the mind of a Pisces to discipline a child, no matter how spoiled or incorrigible that child becomes.

Man—Woman

SAGITTARIUS MAN
ARIES WOMAN

The Aries woman is quite a charmer. When she tugs at the strings of your heart, you'll know it. She's a woman who's in search of a knight in shining armor. She is a very particular person with very high ideals. She won't accept anyone but the man of her dreams.

The Aries woman never plays around with passion; she means business when it comes to love.

Don't get the idea that she's a dewy-eyed Miss. She isn't. In fact, she can be pretty practical and to-the-point when she wants. She's a girl with plenty of drive and ambition. With an Aries woman behind you, you are liable to go far in life. She knows how to help her man get ahead. She's full of wise advice; you only have to ask. In some cases, the Aries woman has a keen business sense; many of them become successful career women. There is nothing backward or retiring about her. She is equipped with a good brain and she knows how to use it.

Your union with her could be something strong, secure, and romantic. If both of you have your sights fixed in the same direction, there is almost nothing that you could not accomplish.

The Aries woman is proud and capable of being quite jealous. While you're with her, never cast your eye in another woman's direction. It could spell disaster for your relationship. The Aries woman won't put up with romantic nonsense when her heart is at stake.

If the Aries woman backs you up in your business affairs, you can be sure of succeeding. However, if she only is interested in advancing her own career and puts her interests before yours, she can be sure to rock the boat. It will put a strain on the relationship. The over-ambitious Aries woman can be a pain in the neck and make you forget that you were in love with her once.

The cultivated Aries woman makes a wonderful wife and mother. She has a natural talent for homemaking. With a pot of paint and some wallpaper, she can transform the dreariest domicile into an abode of beauty and snug comfort. The perfect hostess—even when friends just happen by—she knows how to make guests feel at home.

You'll also admire your Arien because she knows how to stand on her own two feet. Hers is an independent nature. She won't break down and cry when things go wrong, but will pick herself up and try to patch up matters.

The Aries woman makes a fine, affectionate mother.

SAGITTARIUS MAN
TAURUS WOMAN

The woman born under the sign of Taurus may lack a little of the sparkle and bubble you often like to find in a woman. The Taurus woman is generally down-to-earth and never flighty. It's important to her that she keep both feet flat on the ground. She is not fond of bounding all over the place, especially if she's under the impression that there's no profit in it.

On the other hand, if you hit it off with a Taurus woman, you won't be disappointed in the romance area. The Taurus woman is all woman and proud of it, too. She can be very devoted and loving once she decides that her relationship with you is no fly-by-night romance. Basically, she's a passionate person. In sex, she's direct and to-the-point. If she really loves you, she'll let you know she's yours—and without reservations.

Better not flirt with other women once you've committed yourself to her. She's capable of being very jealous and possessive.

She'll stick by you through thick and thin. It's almost certain that if the going ever gets rough, she won't go running home to her mother. She can adjust to the hard times just as graciously as she can to the good times.

Taureans are, on the whole, pretty even-tempered. They like to be treated with kindness. Pretty things and soft objects make them purr like kittens.

You may find her a little slow and deliberate. She likes to be safe and sure about everything. Let her plod along if she likes;

don't coax her, but just let her take her own sweet time. Everything she does is done thoroughly and, generally, without mistakes.

Don't deride her for being a slow-poke. It could lead to flying pots and pans and a fireworks display that could put Bastille Day to shame. The Taurus woman doesn't anger readily but when prodded often enough, she's capable of letting loose with a cyclone of ill-will. If you treat her with kindness and consideration, you'll have no cause for complaint.

The Taurean loves doing things for her man. She's a whiz in the kitchen and can whip up feasts fit for a king if she thinks they'll be royally appreciated. She may not fully understand you, but she'll adore you and be faithful to you if she feels you're worthy of it.

The Taurus woman makes a wonderful mother. She knows how to keep her children well-loved, cuddled, and warm. She may have some difficult times with them when they reach adolescence, though.

SAGITTARIUS MAN
GEMINI WOMAN

You may find a romance with a woman born under the sign of the Twins a many splendoured thing. In her you can find the intellectual companionship you often look for in a friend or mate. A Gemini girl friend can appreciate your aims and desires because she travels pretty much the same road as you do intellectually . . . that is, at least part of the way. She may share your interests but she will lack your tenacity.

She suffers from itchy feet. She can be here, there . . . all over the place and at the same time, or so it would seem. Her eagerness to move about may make you dizzy, still you'll enjoy and appreciate her liveliness and mental agility.

Geminians often have sparkling personalities; you'll be attracted by her warmth and grace. While she's on your arm you'll probably notice that many male eyes are drawn to her—she may even return a gaze or two, but don't let that worry you. All women born under this sign have nothing against a harmless flirt once in a while. They enjoy this sort of attention; if the Gemini feels she is already spoken for, however, she will never let such attention get out of hand.

Although she may not be as handy as you'd like in the kitchen, you'll never go hungry for a filling and tasty meal. The Gemini girl is always in a rush; she won't feel like she's cheating by breaking out the instant mashed potatoes or the frozen peas. She may not be much of a good cook but she is clever; with a dash of this and a suggestion of that, she can make an uninteresting TV dinner taste like something out of a Jim Beard cookbook. Then, again, maybe you've struck it rich and have a Gemini girl friend who finds complicated recipes a challenge to her intellect. If so, you'll find every meal a tantalizing and mouth-watering surprise.

When you're beating your brains out over the Sunday crossword puzzle and find yourself stuck, just ask your Gemini girl; she'll give you all the right answers without batting an eyelash.

Like you, she loves all kinds of people. You may even find that you're a bit more particular than she. Often all that a Geminian requires is that her friends be interesting . . . and stay interesting. One thing she's not able to abide is a dullard.

Leave the party-organizing to your Gemini sweetheart or mate and you'll never have a chance to know a dull moment. She'll bring out the swinger in you if you give her half the chance.

A Gemini mother enjoys her children. Like them, she's often restless, adventurous, and easily bored.

SAGITTARIUS MAN
CANCER WOMAN

If you fall in love with a Cancer woman, be prepared for anything. The Cancerian is sometimes difficult to understand when it comes to love. In one hour, she can unravel a whole gamut of emotions that will leave you in a tizzy. She'll undoubtedly keep you guessing.

You may find her a little too uncertain and sensitive for your liking. You'll most likely spend a good deal of time encouraging her—helping her to erase her foolish fears. Tell her she's a living doll a dozen times a day and you'll be well loved in return.

Be careful of the jokes you make when in her company—don't let any of them revolve around her, her personal interests, or her family. If you do, you'll most likely reduce her to tears. She can't stand being made fun of. It will take bushels of roses and tons of chocolates—not to mention the apologies—to get her to come back out of her shell.

In matters of money-managing, she may not easily come around to your way of thinking. Money will never burn a hole in her pocket. You may get the notion that your Cancerian sweetheart or mate is a direct descendent of Scrooge. If she has her way, she'll hang onto that first dollar you earned. She's not only that way with money, but with everything right on up from bakery string to jelly jars. She's a saver; she never throws anything away, no matter how trivial.

Once she returns your "I love you," you'll find you have an affectionate, self-sacrificing, and devoted woman on your hands. Her love for you will never alter unless you want it to. She'll put you high upon a pedestal and will do everything—even if it's against your will—to keep you up there.

Cancer women love homelife. For them, marriage is an easy step. They're domestic with a capital D. The Cancerian will do her best to make your home comfortable and cozy. She, herself, is more at ease at home than anywhere else. She makes an excellent hostess. The best in her comes out when she is in her own environment.

Cancer women make the best mothers. Each will consider every complaint of her child a major catastrophe. With her, children always come first. If you're lucky, you'll run a close second. You'll perhaps see her as too devoted to the children. You may have a hard time convincing her that her apron strings are a little too tight.

SAGITTARIUS MAN
LEO WOMAN

If you can manage a girl who likes to kick up her heels every now and again, then the Leo woman was made for you. You'll have to learn to put away jealous fears when you take up with a woman born under this sign, as she's often the kind that makes heads turn and tongues wag. You don't necessarily have to believe any of what you hear—it's most likely just jealous gossip or wishful thinking.

The Leo girl has more than a fair share of grace and glamour. She knows it, generally, and knows how to put it to good use. Needless to say, other women in her vicinity turn green with envy and will try anything short of shoving her into the nearest lake in order to put her out of the running.

If she's captured your heart and fancy, woo her full-force—if your intention is eventually to win her. Shower her with expensive gifts and promise her the moon—if you're in a position to go that far—then you'll find her resistance beginning to weaken. It's not that she's such a difficult cookie—she'll probably make a lot over you once she's decided you're the man for her—but she does enjoy a lot of attention. What's more, she feels she's entitled to it. Her mild arrogance, however, is becoming. The Leo woman knows how to transform the crime of excessive pride into a very charming misdemeanor. It sweeps most men—or rather, all men—right off their feet. Those who do not succumb to her leonine charm are few and far between.

If you've got an important business deal to clinch and you have doubts as to whether you can bring it off as you should, take your Leo wife along to the business luncheon and it'll be a cinch that you'll have that contract—lock, stock, and barrel—in your pocket before the meeting is over. She won't have to say or do anything . . . just be there at your side. The grouchiest oil magnate can be transformed into a gushing, obedient schoolboy if there's a Leo woman in the room.

If you're rich and want to see to it that you stay that way, don't give your Leo spouse a free hand with the charge accounts and credit cards. When it comes to spending, Leo tend to overdo. If you're poor, you have no worries because the luxury-loving Leo will most likely never recognize your existence—let alone, consent to marry you.

As a mother, she's both strict and easy. She can pal around with her children and still see to it that they know their places. She won't spoil them but she'll be a loving and devoted parent.

SAGITTARIUS MAN
VIRGO WOMAN

The Virgo woman may be a little too difficult for you to understand at first. Her waters run deep. Even when you think you know her, don't take any bets on it. She's capable of keeping things hidden in the deep recesses of her womanly soul—things she'll only release when she's sure that you're the man she's been looking for. It may take her some time to come around to this decision. Virgo girls are finnicky about almost everything; everything has to be letter-perfect before they're satisfied. Many of them have the idea that the only people who can do things right are Virgos.

Nothing offends a Virgo woman more than slovenly dress, sloppy character, or a careless display of affection. Make sure your tie is not crooked and that your shoes sport a bright shine before you go calling on this lady. Keep your off-color jokes for the locker room; she'll have none of that. Take her arm when crossing the street. Don't rush the romance. Trying to corner her in the back of a cab may be one way of striking out. Never criticize the way she looks—in fact, the best policy would be to agree with her as much as possible. Still, there's just so much a man can take; all those dos and don'ts you'll have to observe if you want to get to first base with a Virgo may be just a little too much to ask of you. After a few dates, you may come to the conclusion that she just isn't worth all that trouble. However, the Virgo woman is mysterious enough, generally speaking, to keep her men running back for more. Chances are you'll be intrigued by her airs and graces.

If lovemaking means a lot to you, you'll be disappointed at first in the cool ways of your Virgo girl. However, under her glacial facade there lies a hot cauldron of seething excitement. If you're patient and artful in your romantic approach, you'll find that all that caution was well worth the trouble. When Virgos love, they don't stint. It's all or nothing as far as they're concerned. Once they're convinced that they love you, they go all the way right off the bat—tossing all cares to the wind.

One thing a Virgo woman can't stand in love is hypocrisy. They don't give a hoot about what the neighbors say if their hearts tell them "Go ahead!" They're very concerned with human truths—so much so that if their hearts stumble upon another fancy, they're liable to be true to that new heartthrob and leave you standing in the rain. She's honest to her heart and will be as true to you as you are with her, generally. Do her wrong once, however, and it's farewell.

Both strict and tender, she tries to bring out the best in her children.

SAGITTARIUS MAN
LIBRA WOMAN

You'll probably find that the girl born under the sign of Libra is worth more than her weight in gold. She's a woman after your own heart.

With her, you'll always come first—make no mistake about that. She'll always be behind you 100 percent, no matter what you do. When you ask her advice about almost anything, you are likely to get a very balanced and realistic opinion. She is good at thinking things out and never lets her emotions run away with her when clear logic is called for.

As a homemaker she is hard to beat. She is very concerned with harmony and balance. You can be sure she'll make your house a joy to live in; she'll see to it that the home is tastefully furnished and decorated. A Libran cannot stand filth or disarray—it gives her goose-bumps. Anything that does not radiate harmony, in fact, runs against her orderly grain.

She is chock-full of charm and womanly ways. She can sweep just about any man off his feet with one winning smile. When it comes to using her brains, she can out-think almost anyone and, sometimes, with half the effort. She is diplomatic enough, though, never to let this become glaringly apparent. She may even turn the conversation around so that you think you were the one who did all the brain-work. She couldn't care less, really, just as long as you wind up doing what is right.

The Libra woman will put you up on a pretty high pedestal. You are her man and her idol. She'll leave all the decision-making—large or small—up to you. She's not interested in running things and will only offer her assistance if she feels you really need it.

Some find her approach to reason masculine; however, in the areas of love and affection the Libra woman is *all* woman. She'll literally shower you with love and kisses during your romance with her. She doesn't believe in holding out. You shouldn't, either, if you want to hang onto her.

She is the kind of girl who likes to snuggle up to you in front of the fire on chilly autumn nights . . . the kind of girl who will bring you breakfast in bed on Sunday. She'll be very thoughtful about anything that concerns you. If anyone dares suggest you're not the grandest guy in the world, she'll give that person what-for. She'll defend you till her dying breath. The Libra woman will be everything you want her to be.

She'll be a sensitive and loving mother. Still, you'll always come before the children.

SAGITTARIUS MAN
SCORPIO WOMAN

The Scorpio woman can be a whirlwind of passion—perhaps too much passion to really suit you. When her temper flies, you'd better lock up the family heirlooms and take cover. When she chooses to be sweet, you're apt to think that butter wouldn't melt in her mouth . . . but, of course, it would.

The Scorpio woman can be as hot as a *tamale* or as cool as a cucumber, but whatever mood she's in, she's in it for real. She does not believe in posing or putting on airs.

The Scorpio woman is often sultry and seductive—her femme fatale charme can pierce through the hardest of hearts like a laser ray. She may not look like Mata Hari (quite often Scorpios resemble the tomboy next door) but once she's fixed you with her tantalizing eyes, you're a goner.

Life with the Scorpio woman will not be all smiles and smooth-sailing; when prompted, she can unleash a gale of venom. Generally, she'll have the good grace to keep family battles within the walls of your home. When company visits, she's apt to give the impression that married life with you is one great big joy-ride. It's just one of her ways of expressing her loyalty to you—at least in front of others. She may fight you tooth and nail in the confines of your living room, but at a ball or during an evening out, she'll hang onto your arm and have stars in her eyes.

Scorpio women are good at keeping secrets. She may even keep a few buried from you if she feels like it.

Never cross her up on even the smallest thing. When it comes to revenge, she's an eye-for-an-eye woman. She's not too keen on forgiveness—especially if she feels she's been wronged unfairly. You'd be well-advised not to give her any cause to be jealous, either. When the Scorpio woman sees green, your life will be made far from rosy. Once she's put you in the doghouse, you can be sure that you're going to stay there a while.

You may find life with a Scorpio woman too draining. Although she may be full of the old paprika, it's quite likely that she's not the kind of girl you'd like to spend the rest of your natural life with. You'd prefer someone gentler and not so hot-tempered . . . someone who can take the highs with the lows and not complain . . . someone who is flexible and understanding. A woman born under Scorpio can be heavenly, but she can also be the very devil when she chooses.

As a mother, a Scorpio is protective and encouraging.

SAGITTARIUS MAN
SAGITTARIUS WOMAN

You'll most likely never come across a more good-natured girl than the one born under the sign of Sagittarius. Generally, they're full of bounce and good cheer. Their sunny dispositions seem almost permanent and can be relied upon even on the rainiest of days.

Women born under this sign are almost never malicious. If ever they seem to be, it is only seeming. Sagittarians are often a little short on tact and say literally anything that comes into their pretty little heads—no matter what the occasion. Sometimes the words that tumble out of their mouths seem downright cutting and cruel. Still, no matter what the Sagittarian says, she means well. The Sagittarius woman is quite capable of losing some of her friends—and perhaps even some of yours—through a careless slip of the lip.

On the other hand, you are liable to appreciate her honesty and good intentions. To you, qualities of this sort play an important part in life. With a little patience and practice, you can probably help cure your Sagittarian of her loose tongue; in most cases, she'll give in to your better judgement and try to follow your advice to the letter.

Chances are, she'll be the outdoors type of girlfriend. Long hikes, fishing trips, and white-water canoeing will most likely appeal to her. She's a busy person; no one could ever call her a slouch. She sets great store in mobility. She won't sit still for one minute if she doesn't have to.

She is great company most of the time and, generally, lots of fun. Even if your buddies drop by for poker and beer, she won't have any trouble fitting in.

On the whole, she is a very kind and sympathetic woman. If she feels she's made a mistake, she'll be the first to call your attention to it. She's not afraid to own up to her own faults and short-comings.

You might lose your patience with her once or twice. After she's seen how upset her shortsightedness or tendency to blabber-mouth has made you, she'll do her best to straighten up.

The Sagittarius woman is not the kind who will pry into your business affairs. But she'll always be there, ready to offer advice if you need it.

The Sagittarius woman is seldom suspicious. Your word will almost always be good enough for her.

She is a wonderful and loving friend to her children.

SAGITTARIUS MAN
CAPRICORN WOMAN

If you are not a successful businessman or, at least, on your way to success, it's quite possible that a Capricorn woman will have no interest in entering your life. Generally speaking, she is a very se-curity-minded female; she'll see to it that she invests her time only in sure things. Men who whittle away their time with one unsuc-cessful scheme or another, seldom attract a Capricorn. Men who are interested in getting somewhere in life and keep their noses close to the grindstone quite often have a Capricorn woman behind them, helping them to get ahead.

Although she is a kind of "climber," she is not what you could call cruel or hard-hearted. Beneath that cool, seemingly calculating, exterior, there's a warm and desirable woman. She just happens to think that it is just as easy to fall in love with a rich or ambitious man as it is with a poor or lazy one. She's prac-tical.

The Capricorn woman may be keenly interested in rising to the top, but she'll never be aggressive about it. She'll seldom step on someone's feet or nudge competitors away with her elbows. She's quiet about her desires. She sits, waits, and watches. When an opening or opportunity does appear, she'll latch onto it lickety-split. For an on-the-move man, an ambitious Capricorn wife or girlfriend can be quite an asset. She can probably give you some very good advice about business matters. When you invite the boss and his wife for dinner, she'll charm them both right off the ground.

The Capricorn woman is thorough in whatever she does: cooking, cleaning, making a success out of life . . . Capricorns make excellent hostesses as well as guests. Generally, they are very well-mannered and gracious, no matter what their backgrounds are. They seem to have a built-in sense of what is right. Crude behavior or a careless faux-pas can offend them no end.

If you should marry a woman born under Capricorn, you need never worry about her going on a wild shopping spree. Capricorns are careful with every cent that comes into their hands. They understand the value of money better than most women and have no room in their lives for careless spending.

The Capricorn girl is usually very fond of family—her own, that is. With her, family ties run very deep. Don't make jokes about her relatives; she won't stand for it. You'd better check her family out before you get down on bended knee; after your marriage you'll undoubtedly be seeing a lot of them.

Capricorn mothers train their children to be polite and kind.

SAGITTARIUS MAN
AQUARIUS WOMAN

If you find that you've fallen head over heels for a woman born under the sign of the Water Bearer, you'd better fasten your safety belt. It may take you quite a while actually to discover what this girl is like—and even then, you may have nothing to go on but a string of vague hunches. The Aquarian is like a rainbow, full of bright and shining hues; she's like no other girl you've ever known. There is something elusive about her—something delightfully mysterious. You'll most likely never be able to put your finger on it. It's nothing calculated, either; Aquarians don't believe in phony charm.

There will never be a dull moment in your life with this Water Bearing woman; she seems to radiate adventure and magic. She'll most likely be the most open-minded and tolerant woman you've ever met. She has a strong dislike for injustice and prejudice. Narrow-mindedness runs against her grain.

She is very independent by nature and quite capable of shifting for herself if necessary. She may receive many proposals of marriage from all sorts of people without ever really taking them seriously. Marriage is a very big step for her; she wants to be sure she knows what she's getting into. If she thinks that it will seriously curb her independence and love of freedom, she's liable to shake her head and give the man his engagement ring back—if indeed she's let the romance get that far.

The line between friendship and romance is a pretty fuzzy one for an Aquarius. It's not difficult for her to remain buddy-buddy with an ex-lover. She's tolerant, remember? So if you should see her in close conversation with an old love, don't jump to any hasty conclusions.

She's not a jealous person herself and doesn't expect you to be, either. You'll find her pretty much of a free spirit most of the time. Just when you think you know her inside-out, you'll discover that you don't really know her at all, though.

She's a very sympathetic and warm person; she can be helpful to people in need of assistance and advice.

She'll seldom be suspicious even if she has every right to be. If she loves a man, she'll forgive him just about anything. If he allows himself a little fling, chances are she'll just turn her head the other way. Her tolerance does have its limits, however, and her man should never press his luck at hanky-panky.

She makes a bighearted mother; her good qualities rub off on her children.

SAGITTARIUS MAN
PISCES WOMAN

Many a man dreams of a sensitive Pisces woman. You're perhaps no exception. She's ladylike and proper. Your business associates and friends will be dazzled by her warmth and femininity. Although she's a charmer, there is a lot more to her than just a pretty exterior. There is a brain ticking away behind that soft, womanly facade. You may never become aware of it—that is, until you're married to her. It's no cause for alarm, however; she'll most likely never use it against you.

If she feels you're botching up your married life through careless behavior or if she feels you could be earning more money than you do, she'll tell you about it. But any wife would, really. She will never try to usurp your position as head and breadwinner of the family.

No one had better dare say an uncomplimentary word about you in her presence. It's likely to cause her to break into tears. Pisces women are usually very sensitive beings. Their reaction to adversity, frustration, or anger is just a plain, good, old-fashioned cry. They can weep buckets when so inclined.

Treat her with tenderness and generosity and your relationship will be an enjoyable one. She's most likely fond of chocolates. A bunch of beautiful flowers will never fail to make her eyes light up. See to it that you never forget her birthday or your anniversary. These things are very important to her.

She makes a strong, self-sacrificing mother.

SAGITTARIUS

LUCKY NUMBERS: 1997

Lucky numbers and astrology can be linked through the movements of the Moon. Each phase of the thirteen Moon cycles vibrates with a sequence of numbers for your Sign of the Zodiac over the course of the year. Using your lucky numbers is a fun system that connects you with tradition.

New Moon	First Quarter	Full Moon	Last Quarter
Dec. 10 ('96)	Dec. 17 ('96)	Dec. 24 ('96)	Jan. 1
3 6 3 7	1 8 4 1	2 3 5 7	9 4 0 2
Jan. 8	Jan. 15	Jan. 23	Jan. 31
2 8 6 6	4 0 6 7	6 3 5 9	9 4 7 4
Feb. 7	Feb. 14	Feb. 22	March 2
4 8 2 9	6 7 1 4	8 8 3 7	0 1 7 2
March 8	March 15	March 23	March 31
2 5 3 9	9 1 6 8	1 5 0 3	3 9 4 7
April 7	April 14	April 22	April 29
7 5 2 3	6 8 1 7	5 6 9 6	6 0 4 2
May 6	May 14	May 22	May 29
2 8 9 3	3 5 7 1	0 8 5 9	9 3 0 7
June 5	June 12	June 20	June 27
7 8 2 4	4 6 0 5	8 5 2 6	9 7 4 5
July 4	July 12	July 19	July 26
5 8 0 3	3 7 0 5	3 2 5 8	6 3 4 7
August 3	August 11	August 18	August 24
7 9 2 6	6 1 4 0	9 5 8 1	7 8 2 4
Sept. 1	Sept. 9	Sept. 16	Sept. 23
4 6 0 5	5 8 5 9	4 3 0 8	9 3 5 7
Oct. 1	Oct. 9	Oct. 15	Oct. 22
7 2 0 9	9 6 0 3	7 2 8 9	3 6 8 1
Oct. 31	Nov. 7	Nov. 14	Nov. 21
5 0 3 9	9 4 7 5	5 2 3 6	8 2 4 8
Nov. 29	Dec. 7	Dec. 13	Dec. 21
0 6 3 7	7 0 8 5	2 6 9 2	4 9 4 0
Dec. 29	Jan. 5 ('98)	Jan. 12 ('98)	Jan. 20 ('98)
2 8 3 6	6 4 1 2	3 5 7 5	9 0 4 7

SAGITTARIUS

YEARLY FORECAST: 1997

*Forecast for 1997 Concerning Business
and Financial Matters, Job Prospects,
Travel, Health, Romance and Marriage
for Those Born with the Sun
in the Zodiacal Sign of Sagittarius.
November 23–December 20*

For those born under the influence of the sun in the zodiacal sign
of Sagittarius, which is ruled by Jupiter, the planet of wisdom,
expansiveness, and freedom, 1997 promises to be a year when
lasting achievements are possible. Sagittarius people are the
astrological Archers, always fixing your sights on the next goal.
Now it will be more important than ever to keep your long-term
aspirations in mind and remain single-minded in your efforts to
reach them. You will have added determination, and an extra
capacity for perseverance, to aid you in your quest. In all aspects
of your life, both personal and professional, the main risk is taking the easy option and settling for second best. This will not satisfy you in the long run and will be a crime against your basic
nature.

Professionally, you will tend to be more outspoken and even
aggressive in your approach to business affairs and ventures. This
can lead to quick results, especially when you are confronted with
obstacles or stiff opposition. However, it will be more difficult to
maintain an even keel in partnership and cooperative ventures
because of your impatience. Financially, there are greater possibilities of receiving some money from an unexpected or even
unknown source. At the same time, there continues to be a
greater risk of deception, or self-deception, where money matters
are concerned. You will find the best job opportunities in lines of
work where you are given scope to express your creative urges
and individuality. Routine, humdrum work will tend to leave you

more restless than ever. Long-distance travel can be satisfying, especially in connection with business or for educational purposes. Such journeys will be more subject than usual to last-minute changes in schedule. You are likely to suffer fewer health problems this year. The main threat to Sagittarius health will be tension and a nervous disposition. This can be an important year for romance. Even the most freedom-loving Sagittarius single may decide to settle down and tie the matrimonial knot. Above all, it is a year when you are likely to experience greater emotional maturity and discover a new stability where matters of the heart are concerned.

For Sagittarius career and business people, 1997 is a year to translate your personal vision and long-term goals into definitive action. Your sense of purpose has both advantages and disadvantages. From the positive side, it gives you the staying power to keep plugging away at projects which a less disciplined person would almost certainly give up on. This is especially important if the project in question has your personal stamp upon it, and you identify closely with what you are doing. From the negative side, however, there is a greater risk of intimidating associates and allies, not to mention competitors. Try not to be too obsessive in the pursuit of your goals; otherwise you can become almost intolerable to work with. The best professional opportunities this year are those that involve you in a fair degree of travel, particularly over short distances. Alternatively, activities that involve an original and intuitive type of mental quickness which you have not activated before should be a most enjoyable challenge. There will also be more opportunities this year to convert a serious hobby or spare-time interest into a viable commercial and business proposition. This process can sometimes be lonely and very challenging, but there is nothing quite so fulfilling as putting your creative stamp on what you are doing and bringing something new into the world. Use the first week of the year, and the period between March 8 and June 19, for breaking through logjams and removing obstacles that others have placed in your path. These periods strike the keynote for your achievements during the remainder of the year. Between August 14 and September 27 is favorable for operating behind the scenes, acting by stealth rather than out in the open. During this period you need to be extra cautious about whom you decide to trust with your most confidential plans and strategies. From November 9 to December 17 there are more opportunities for boosting personal earnings through routine career and business endeavors. Extra income at this time can be particularly useful in helping to bring holiday cheer and comfort to those who are less fortunate than you.

Where money matters are concerned, this year represents a break with the past. Either suddenly or subtly, your main source of income is likely to change. Even more importantly, your personal attitude to money is also likely to flip-flop. You will find it easier to trust in life to provide you with the money you want and need. This is especially important if you decide to take the brave but difficult step of striking out on your own to earn an income from your creative or artistic endeavors. When money is needed, it is likely to appear. Financial good fortune may come your way purely by chance, or by what appears to be chance. At the same time, there is a greater risk of being misled where money matters are concerned. Someone you trust may not be as reliable as you had hoped or assumed. It is important to be more careful with money and valuable possessions; the risk of theft of embezzlement is also greater. The first three weeks of the year are excellent for capitalizing on recent breakthroughs or generous offers that you received during the Christmas period. This is also a time when you should find it easier to earn more for the work you do. Throughout the year, be prepared for some additional expenditure in connection with children.

This promises to be an interesting year for work and occupational affairs. A guiding hand seems to be helping you make the right decisions, or even making the right decisions without your conscious cooperation. Very few people born under the sign of Sagittarius are cut out to follow in other people's footsteps and do the same simple jobs day in and day out. The unusual is what appeals to you most. This can prompt you to sacrifice job security and a dependable source of income. Unusual job opportunities may come your way this year. If you aim to become a well-paid athlete or sports commentator, or you would like to get into the entertainment industry, you may get the breakthrough for which you have been hoping. Attend trials and auditions even if you think that your chances are slim; talent spotters are likely to have a higher estimate of your abilities than you do. If you feel trapped in a repetitious, boring job, structure your escape with care, and be patient. Rash decisions only lead to regrets. It would be foolish to burn your bridges by leaving your job with nothing else to go to. Guard against a certain restlessness which prevents you from keeping your mind on the task at hand. Do not spend too much time chatting with co-workers or gossiping on the telephone behind your employer's back. Think carefully about what you most want to do. Talk things over with people older and more experienced than yourself. They may be able to steer you away from a mistake you are about to make.

The Sagittarius longing for distant horizons and the unknown is especially strong this year. Strangely, however, it may not translate into an urge for distant travel. Instead, you will prefer traveling closer to home and even in your own home itself, through reading, study, and creative endeavors. Travel to distant places or foreign countries may be required by your business and work, or in connection with romance and other matters of the heart. Getting away from your usual locale can also help broaden your mind and educate you about past cultures and civilizations. After mid-May you are not likely to feel at ease too far from home. Between July 23 and August 22 is good for making a business trip or for visiting present or future in-laws. That is also the best period for entertaining guests in your home.

This year should present you with fewer setbacks or problems relating to health. More than ever, it is a positive attitude to life that helps to ensure your well-being. There is no better medicine than doing what you enjoy. Being forced to do what you hate can almost literally poison your whole system. Try to lead a more orderly life. Too much rushing around, meals eaten at irregular hours, and lack of sleep are the kind of lifestyle which is not conducive to your good health. Between August 14 and September 28 be extra careful about what you eat and drink, especially if traveling in foreign countries; there is a greater risk of infections or food poisoning. During this same period also be more careful when operating machinery or driving a car that you are unfamiliar with; accidents could occur then. From April 20 until May 20 is good for scheduling routine health checkups and also for giving up a habit you know is unhealthy for you.

Do not deceive yourself where love and romance are concerned. If you do, you could miss a great opportunity. As a Sagittarius you tend to idealize love to the extent that you sometimes turn your back on real opportunity for a fulfilling romance. Settling down is not quite the boring experience which you may imagine. Chance encounters, in the most unlikely of situations or circumstances, can bring you together with the person with whom you may decide to spend the rest of your life. Already married Sagittarius couples, or those involved in long-term relationships, may want to plan a second honeymoon. Love grows through careful nurturing and must not be allowed to fade through habit and overfamiliarity. Go out of your way to let that special person in your life know how much you care and appreciate all that is done for you.

DAILY FORECAST

January–December 1997

JANUARY

1. WEDNESDAY. Fair. This first day of the new year is likely to bring out the best in you. There is nothing that thrills or excites you more than battling against the odds and plunging into the unknown. Pursue the fulfillment of secret hopes and dreams regardless of the opinions voiced by the people around you. Individuals in positions of authority and power are easier to win over to your way of thinking. Be impersonal with them, and impartial; attempts on your part at becoming too friendly could be misinterpreted. You can become the guiding force in group and club activities, but do not expect to rise unopposed. Ignore idle gossipers; as a Sagittarius you have an innate sense of what is true and what is false.

2. THURSDAY. Variable. Be yourself, and above all trust yourself. Money and prosperity are not as important as you may think, or as crucial as someone may wish you to believe. Personal charm can work wonders. Disarm people with your straightforwardness, your honesty, and your refreshing love of beauty and nature. This day brings you a step closer to the fulfillment of a romantic hope or dream. It is the goodness in your partner's heart that matters, not how much they own or how attractive they are. Accept an invitation to a party or other social function. Try not to be offended if someone appears to be letting you down or breaking a promise; they are probably not doing so intentionally.

3. FRIDAY. Disconcerting. This can be an uneven, upsetting day. Attempting to keep up with events is likely to prove difficult, if not impossible. People tend to keep changing their minds, not too worried if that means changing your schedule in the process. Unexpected information may take you by surprise and cause you to rethink your plans for the future. This information could relate to politics and the business world, or could be of a much more personal and intimate nature. An unpleasant episode in your life which you thought was behind you for good may be resurrected. Although new neighbors can be less considerate and quiet than their predecessors, get to know them before forming a firm opinion.

4. SATURDAY. Good. You can afford to sit back and watch how things develop. Today you can achieve more by doing nothing than by taking an active role. This is especially true with sensitive situations involving diplomacy and secrecy. Influential people with whom you rub shoulders can prove unexpectedly helpful. If they offer to further your personal or financial affairs by working on your behalf behind the scenes, accept the offer. Nonetheless, beware of becoming implicated in anything that is definitely illegal or underhanded. Someone you knew, or met, a long time ago could reappear in your life and offer to assist you in a money-making venture.

5. SUNDAY. Easygoing. Life has mysterious ways which are often impossible to understand. Do not even try; just acknowledge them and take advantage of them. Someone may give you money, or something precious, with purely altruistic motives. This is definitely not the day for staring the proverbial gift horse in the mouth. All money-making enterprises relating to the oceans, to fishing, and to oil are favored. Do not doubt yourself. Above all, do not become discouraged if a problem is not responding to your attempts to find a remedy. Be thankful for the insight you have been given so far; it will help you to do a better job in the future.

6. MONDAY. Quiet. This promises to be a fairly uneventful beginning to the week. Be especially gentle with those around you. They will appreciate small but meaningful gestures. Give thanks where thanks are due. This is a good day for putting together personal plans which will allow you to further your own interests during the next month or two. By all means ask others for their financial or moral support, but avoid shouting your cause too loudly; a good scheme is its own best advocate. The same applies to trying to get co-workers or your spouse to see your point of view. Modesty and humility are your best allies. A secret project that you have been involved in for a while may start to pay financial dividends.

7. TUESDAY. Demanding. Sagittarius men and women are likely to be more appreciated and admired than ever. Smile, and the world will smile with you. A new romantic liaison may be in the offing, perhaps with someone you have fancied for a long time but who seemed not to reciprocate your feelings. You will be glad this time that your assumption was probably wrong. This is an auspicious day for all creative and artistic ventures. Your flair for self-expression should stand you in good stead. You cannot afford today to take risks with money. Acquaintances may try to persuade you that they are indeed your true friends; the harder they try to persuade you, the less genuine they probably are.

8. WEDNESDAY. Promising. This day favors all new enterprises and fresh beginnings. For Sagittarius men and women, conditions are especially good where new financial projects or ventures are concerned. Influential people are more helpful than usual. If you work as an employee, a pay raise is likely. You can also earn a substantial bonus in return for particularly outstanding work or as a reward for putting in some additional overtime if requested to do so. Sagittarius who employ others may want to consider extra incentives to keep workers happy and productive. Make it clear to them individually and collectively how much you value their contributions.

9. THURSDAY. Deceptive. Not everything is exactly as it seems. Beware of people bearing gifts; their motives are unlikely to be what they appear. Someone who makes a particularly generous offer is almost certainly either a trickster or a fool, possibly both. Think at least twice before committing yourself by making promises or by giving assurances. Someone may be trying to trick you by keeping certain facts concealed from you. Attempting to keep children on the straight and narrow can be an almost impossible task. Disciplining them is necessary; avoiding making yourself seem to be their enemy will not be so easy.

10. FRIDAY. Calm. Keep to yourself throughout the day. Catch up on telephone calls you have been intending to make but have not found the time to do. You may also want to visit friends or relatives. However, there are certain ideas and plans that you should keep mum about for the moment. Think your ideas through carefully and patiently before spilling the beans to anyone else. Do not allow yourself to be rushed into arrangements with which you are not entirely happy. Neighbors can be surprisingly helpful, but try to avoid getting in their debt; kindness sometimes has a price tag attached to it. Writing a letter to a former colleague is probably better than talking to them in person.

11. SATURDAY. Slow. This is a helpful day for finishing off tasks and finalizing plans. There are certain things in your life that you really need dispense with or dispose of. A family reunion is starred. It can be a happy occasion emotionally, and may also leave you better off financially. Friends can prove to be a real liability today. Plans for a pleasant evening at home may be interrupted by bad timing or lack of tact on the part of one of your friends. If you do not want to be disturbed, refuse to answer the phone or the doorbell. Think twice before lending money to a close acquaintance, let alone someone who is not so close. If you do lend it, you are unlikely ever to see it again.

12. SUNDAY. Fair. Morning hours can be particularly favorable for Sagittarius professionals and business people. The early bird catches the worm, and this weekend confirms that rule. Influential people who are willing to listen to you can prove more of a help than you suspected or even hoped. This morning is also good for shopping of any kind, especially for antiques, furniture, or other bric-a-brac; you may pick up a real bargain. Financial advice offered by a relative can prove very sound. However, this is another sensitive day for all matters relating to friendship. It seems that friendship and love cannot be mixed or melded now.

13. MONDAY. Variable. You can afford to take a well-calculated risk. Your Sagittarius intuition and hunches are more likely to prove accurate and correct, particularly where finances and investments are concerned. However, guard against jeopardizing business profits and your hard-earned savings. In making an investment, experiment with small sums at first; if you are comfortable and successful you can be more adventurous later. Youngsters may land in trouble, not only causing you extra worry but also somewhat tarnishing your own good name. Minor arguments or disputes can easily escalate into major shouting matches. Try not to let old grudges, resentments, or prejudices undermine your naturally good judgment.

14. TUESDAY. Easygoing. All artistic and creative enterprises are favored. Taking up a new hobby may be exactly what you need to balance your energies and bring a fresh outlook and perspective into your life. Try to appreciate that money-making is not the guiding principle or main objective. There are other things that matter more, such as the enjoyment and satisfaction that come from self-expression. This is a good day for an outing to the theater, especially with loved ones. Reading is also favored; sometimes there is nothing better than curling up with a good novel or detective story. Try to put romance before business, even if you have to pencil it in on your calendar.

15. WEDNESDAY. Tricky. This is not a good day for taking risks of any kind. People can be surprisingly two-faced where money is concerned. Even those who you assume have your best interests at heart may be quite prepared to back out of a deal at the crucial moment. You are probably partly to blame unless you keep a grip on reality. If you imagine that life is one long vacation, you are in for a big surprise. Sagittarius in the acting or entertainment fields must distinguish more sharply between the fantasy world of work and the greater world of reality in which you live. A youngster, perhaps your own child, may not be telling the whole truth.

16. THURSDAY. Changeable. Stick to your guns. Do not keep changing your mind, especially where work plans and schedules are concerned. It is important that other people know exactly where you stand. Carefully weigh the options available to you before making a decision. Words spoken in haste are almost certain to be misinterpreted or misunderstood. If you are expecting a visitor, try to be at home when they drop by even if they are late. It is probably worth waiting in case they turn up in an hour or two. Charm can work wonders, especially for Sagittarius employees. Look for ways to enjoy your work more and to give good service to others in the process. Get to bed early tonight.

17. FRIDAY. Misleading. Once again it seems that you may be anticipating too much or allowing your optimism to blind you to reality. Do not expect people occupying positions of power to help you just because it is in their power to do so. It is possible that a superior is nursing a secret grudge against you precisely because you are talented and your prospects are promising. Not everything that goes on behind closed doors is aboveboard or impartial. Check the credentials of unexpected visitors to make sure they are who they claim to be. Take care of your health a little more vigorously than you have been doing. This is a time when you can trust your own diagnosis of aches or pains rather than rushing to consult a professional.

18. SATURDAY. Pleasant. This is likely to be a pleasant day providing that you avoid the temptation to go too far too fast.

Sagittarius are notorious for an ability to say the right words but at the wrong moment. Try harder not to create friction and not to hurt people's feelings. What you intend as plain honesty may be interpreted as rudeness by others. Allow those with whom you associate on a daily basis to plan the schedule and take the initiative. Bearing a grudge against a former lover or employer could lead to losing a unique opportunity to bring more emotional security into your life. Being willing and able to forgive and forget helps all of your relationships but helps you most of all.

19. SUNDAY. Positive. This is another day when you are wise to take a backseat and allow loved ones to be in charge. Compromise is almost certainly the best policy; there is no dishonor in backing down in regards to a contentious issue. A legal problem may solve itself without any active intervention on your part, which can save you a considerable amount of money as well as aggravation. Officials or other people in authority are more likely to take your side in matters of a financial nature. Someone you meet today for the first time may open lucrative new doors for you. Grab at a money-making opportunity before it passes you by.

20. MONDAY. Unsettling. The worst thing you can do is walk around with a chip on your shoulder. Let bygones be bygones. It is foolish to continue nursing a resentment against someone who carelessly or accidentally offended you in the past. Joint funds need protecting; this is true with regard to both business and personal finances. Look for ways to save on taxes; consulting an accountant or other financial adviser could save you a lot. Consider becoming more involved in neighborhood or community activities; they could lead to all sorts of new opportunities and adventures. A friend who has a certain idea in mind should be given a fair hearing; you are bound to benefit.

21. TUESDAY. Disquieting. Do not be soft-hearted or soft-headed, especially where money matters are concerned. Strive to be factual and impartial. Above all, do not allow good looks or charm to turn your head or sway your opinion. An attractive-sounding investment is probably not as foolproof as it looks. Be sure to read the small print; if still in doubt, obtain expert advice before acting. Sagittarius involved in research or investigative work of any kind stand a greater risk of being lured off the track and up some blind alley. Try not to confuse romantic and financial issues. Beware of emotional blackmail on the part of a loved one or a friend.

22. WEDNESDAY. Fair. An older family member may offer you just the help and encouragement that you need. If you are trying to turn a creative or artistic endeavor into a viable money-making venture, you may be discovered by a talent scout, making this your lucky day. Give youngsters in your care, and especially your own children, all the support they need. Try to treat them all equally. Allow them to benefit from your experience and, above all, from your mistakes. Do not risk your savings in a new investment scheme or through any type of gambling. Guard against taking on a new financial partner without first thoroughly investigating their past performance.

23. THURSDAY. Unsettling. People who have known you a long time can prove a positive influence. You are likely to find that your recent suspicions about them are unfounded. The morning favors study and self-improvement endeavors. Preparing for an examination or oral presentation can be difficult, especially if you are just starting out in a new locale. However, the discipline involved is just what you need at present. Try to get your priorities right where long-term plans and interests are concerned. Unfortunately, certain people you respect and on whom you depend may have a rather shortsighted view of your potential. Be prepared to part ways with someone who has been deliberately holding you back or bad-mouthing you behind your back.

24. FRIDAY. Good. This is a favorable day for planning a vacation. Take your time going through travel brochures. Find out who offers the best rates and the best package deals. As a Sagittarius you are happiest when left free to do your own thing. This is particularly true when on vacation in a distant place; renting a car is a better idea than being one of the herd on a tour bus. There is probably no need to book anything yet; give yourself and the family a few more days to decide. Today also favors launching a new publicity or advertising campaign. You are an excellent proponent of worthy causes and an asset to any humanitarian group or society. Give your time as well as your money.

25. SATURDAY. Rewarding. Sagittarius business people seldom pay attention to weekends or holidays where work priorities are concerned. Today you have good reason for pushing ahead with career interests and professional ventures, provided that loved ones have no objection. Do what you can to streamline business finances; also look for ways to cut down on unnecessary expenses and overhead without making any real sacrifices. In all matters, both professional and personal, be prepared to take the bull by the horns. It is better to bring old resentments or grudges out into the open rather than allowing them to fester. In this way they can be talked out and resolved once and for all.

26. SUNDAY. Successful. This is another good day for keeping ahead and placing yourself in the strongest possible position for the week ahead. A few telephone calls to colleagues will allow you to test the probable response to a new venture you would like to launch during the next few days. This is also a favorable time for catching up with correspondence relating to career matters. If you are temporarily unemployed, one or two letters of application to the right person may be all that is needed to put you back on the employment track. Make good use of the contacts you have. Spend time preparing a new, more upbeat cover letter to present yourself in the best possible light.

27. MONDAY. Satisfactory. Loved ones can be exceptionally supportive and reassuring. Their practical advice on matters relating to money or to your career may prove invaluable; after all, they have your best interests at heart. This is a favorable day for Sagittarius employees or business owners involved in fashion design or in the sale of clothing. Be prepared to spend a little extra in order to appeal both to the general public and to a more limited clientele; first impressions are very important. It will be easier for Sagittarius employees to gain favors from a boss who has tended to be rather strict and tough in the past.

28. TUESDAY. Fortunate. A friend could be a rather disruptive influence, particularly during the morning. However, the disruption may turn out to be to your advantage after all. Be prepared to do someone a good turn, even if you feel that they will be ungrateful and unappreciative. Do not allow the negativity of other people to deter you from an act of personal generosity. This is a favorable day for taking a more active role in organizing neighborhood activities, especially of a humanitarian nature. You are likely to be surprised at the number of people who agree with your ideals and aspirations and are willing to pitch in to help. The evening is favorable for socializing.

29. WEDNESDAY. Frustrating. People may be late for appointments, leaving your schedule for the day in shambles. Business colleagues are either unwilling or unable to see your point where the financial side of the business is concerned. Their reluctance to give you the go-ahead for a new venture may temporarily paralyze your initiative. Do not listen to gossip, especially concerning a close friend. Keep a sharp eye and a close grip on children if you are out at a shopping center; there is a greater risk of becoming separated from them in a crowd. It is a good time to examine your motives in trying to help make the world a better place; you do not have to go far from home to have an impact.

30. THURSDAY. Disconcerting.   You need to keep a cool head and remain both patient and philosophical. A financial disappointment is not as serious as you might first have feared. However, it is still cause for concern and may prompt you to examine what you have been doing with your own and other people's funds. Beware of someone who claims to be a friend; this person may be only using you to get ahead. Do not push self-sacrifice too far. A little common sense should show you that you also need to take good care of yourself and take into account your personal priorities and interests.

31. FRIDAY. Difficult.   Once again you could be your own worst enemy. Guard against being caught up in your own idealism and tendency to view people through rose-colored glasses. Even people occupying positions of authority and power are not above suspicion of corruption or shady dealing. Be very careful to whom you reveal a secret; this is especially important when it comes to secret new business ventures. Drive with extra care and thought. A car swerving out of hidden side roads can be a real menace. Also stay very alert in parking lots, protecting yourself against a fender-bender by looking both ways twice.

FEBRUARY

1. SATURDAY. Deceptive.   The new month starts on a contemplative note. Events in January have shown you that not everything is what it seems, and that you need to dig beneath the surface in order to more fully understand what is really going on. The key to future success in the world lies, surprisingly, in greater self-knowledge. A more introspective and inward-looking attitude should help you understand not only yourself but also the motivation of other people. Money remains a delicate issue. It is a subject on which you cannot afford to be ruled by your heart or by emotional considerations alone. Be more careful about the feelings you are willing to reveal to others.

2. SUNDAY. Fair. The day starts on a nervous note. The problem involves investing too much physical and emotional energy in minor matters which are not that important. Try to be more detached, and do not allow small setbacks to ruffle you. Later on you are likely to feel increasingly sure of yourself and of your capabilities. Some energetic sports may be just what you need to bring you to life. Sagittarius patients who are recovering from an operation, accident, or serious illness should continue to follow doctor's orders to the letter. You are likely to realize the benefits of having a hobby that truly fulfills and satisfies you, taking your mind off worries at least for a while.

3. MONDAY. Quiet. Avoid creating too many waves in your lunge for achievement and self-promotion. The gentle approach remains the best. Be frank and open in expressing your wishes or needs, but do not be surprised if others have a rather different point of view. Your personal integrity is your largest asset and will win others around to your side in the long run. This is not a day when you can afford to sit on the fence where partnership issues are concerned. If you do not speak up for yourself you cannot expect others to consider your plans. Meeting the brother or sister of a close acquaintance for the first time can lead to a pleasant new relationship.

4. TUESDAY. Difficult. Financial problems may be right around the corner if you insist on buying on credit. Try in all matters today to follow the path of least resistance. Avoid confrontation at all costs, especially when there is money at stake; let other people fight it out among themselves. Do not allow yourself to be bullied into taking a certain course of action when your Sagittarius instincts say no. Listen to your own inner voice rather than to others, even if they happen to be good friends. Your attitude when it comes to creative or artistic endeavors may be a little too serious. Avoid letting what starts off as a means of self-fulfillment become a matter of mere duty or drudgery.

5. WEDNESDAY. Starred. Some quick thinking can save you a dollar or two. Be prepared to try hard bargaining; you may be surprised by the results. Writing a letter can be just what is required to spur someone into action on your behalf. If you need to make any financial decisions, be sure to read up on the latest business and economic trends. And do not hesitate to ask for expert advice, even if you have to pay for it. A chance encounter, in the street or in another public place, could literally transform your life. This is particularly true where romance is concerned. Be more open with loved ones; honesty is the best policy. Trust yourself and others will trust you.

6. THURSDAY. Excellent. Today, like yesterday, is full of surprises and unique opportunities. Be prepared for the best; take full advantage of people's generosity and kindness. All affairs of the heart continue to be especially favored. A new romantic attraction is likely to develop, possibly with a partner considerably older than you or from a totally different background. Alternatively, renewing contact with an old flame may lead to your attraction sparking back to life. A second honeymoon could be just the thing to renew and refresh a long-term relationship. Buy something special for someone who is very special to you; do not wait for a birthday or anniversary to present your gift.

7. FRIDAY. Tricky. This is a good day for new beginnings and fresh starts. Do not look for immediate results; the seed first has to be dug into the earth before it will bear fruit. Your loved ones are likely to be especially encouraging; there is nothing better than having someone at your side who really believes in you. Extend a helping hand to a person in need and you will end up with a friend for life who will never forget your kindness. Attempts at breaking a deadlock situation affecting your business or personal finances are likely to be successful. However, do not believe everything that you hear or are told. Someone is stirring up gossip and deliberately trying to confuse you.

8. SATURDAY. Disquieting. You may be uncomfortable in a number of different ways. Breaking old patterns and habits can be difficult. Ironically, the more you want to break them, the harder it can be to be free of them. Persevere, even in the face of discouragement; there are some goals that can only be achieved with continual determination. A certain family member may be a nuisance, especially if they are attempting to make you feel guilty. Do not give in to any form of emotional blackmail. Try not to allow an interest in antiques or a similar hobby to become an obsession. Having guests in your home may make you feel uncomfortable and cramped.

9. SUNDAY. Fortunate. A problem is likely to resolve itself unexpectedly, with no real effort on your part. A family or domestic reconciliation may be imminent. There is greater readiness on all sides to forgive and forget. A hunch is likely to pay off. If you are looking for a new home or property, trust your instincts and follow your feelings. You may spot hidden potential that has gone unnoticed by everyone else. Redecorating your home can be a special pleasure, particularly if you are able to add some unique artistic touches of your own. There are worthwhile opportunities for converting a hobby into a major source of income and enjoying every minute of it.

10. MONDAY. Fair. Try to gather momentum in whatever you are doing. Keep up your concentration and new horizons are bound to open up for you, especially in work of a creative or artistic nature. Allow projects to flow without too many preconceived ideas. Trust yourself and your capacities. Do not be afraid to express new ideas or thoughts that come to you, even if they seem rather daring. Work in a protected, quiet area. Interruptions, especially from friends, can prove annoying and may fatally disturb your stream of concentration. Children can become quite a handful. For Sagittarius parents and teachers, knowing where to draw the line in controlling youngsters is something that never comes easily.

11. TUESDAY. Exciting. Someone you hardly know may do you a great service. This is a fine day for all attempts at mediation. You should be able to reach a compromise agreement either in a domestic or professional context. You are likely to shine in a conference or other smaller meeting. People wielding influence and power can be especially impressed by your creative abilities, offering just the opening you have been hoping to get. Now is the time to take a more active or even aggressive stand in efforts to make the world a better place in which to live. This evening favors socializing and meeting new people.

12. WEDNESDAY. Variable. You may become a victim of jealousy at work. Fellow employees may resent your lucky streak or your knack of always ending up on your feet. Do not be surprised if they find fault with you over the smallest matters and even report you to the boss. Try not to allow yourself to be provoked; keep calm, and the storm will pass. Sagittarius supervisors or business owners need to be stricter in enforcing discipline and in drawing up guidelines for employees. Guard against making optimistic promises or giving assurances you may never be able to fulfill. One short letter written and sent off today could have favorable repercussions for you before the end of the month.

13. THURSDAY. Lucky. Enjoy all that is going on today. Even routine duties can be a pleasure. Life is too short for long faces and frowns. Seek out cheerful company; spend more time with those you love. Your ability to spot opportunities has never been as useful as today. You have a special talent for anticipating future trends and can easily capitalize on this ability. This is also a fine day for speech making: you are sure to impress your audience not just with your eloquence but also with the importance and relevance of your message. Encourage a friend to go all out to achieve a secret hope; your sustained belief in his or her ability can make a significant impact on the outcome.

14. FRIDAY. Stressful. Choose the issues most important to you, and be prepared to fight. Now is your chance to show certain people just how much they have been underestimating you and undervaluing your abilities. Anyone who crosses swords with you will soon discover just what they are up against. Do not take no for an answer. If you need the support of a friend, you should have no trouble finding at least one shoulder to lean on. In all of your endeavors, concentrate on achieving results that will benefit not just you but others as well. Work done in solitude can bear surprisingly fruitful results. Treasure someone's secret and keep it locked in your heart.

15. SATURDAY. Sensitive. This is an important day for romance and for relationships in general. Try to smooth some ruffled feathers, especially if you have been a little tactless or negligent lately. A chance encounter could develop into a romantic attraction. The afternoon or evening is favorable for going out on a first date. Try to develop a greater sense of emotional calm. As a Sagittarius you have a strong tendency to overreach, perhaps even to the extent of making a spectacle of yourself in public. It can be useful to be a little less flamboyant. The people most important to you appreciate you for what you are, not for how you present yourself outwardly.

16. SUNDAY. Cautious. Take things one step at a time. You may be expecting far too much of a youngster, perhaps a child of your own. Children can buckle under the weight of emotional investment that you place in them. People born under the sign of Sagittarius consider nothing more important than personal freedom. However, you can sometimes be very careless in imposing restrictions on the freedom of those around you. Try not to dominate situations. In competitive games and sports, remember that a good loser can be a much better friend or associate than an arrogant winner. Romantic partners need to be treated with extra sensitivity; otherwise a minor disagreement could turn into a serious quarrel.

17. MONDAY. Difficult. This start to the new workweek finds you in a vulnerable position. Events may place you in a predicament which you feel unable to handle. This is a good time to confess to certain shortcomings or lack of in-depth knowledge. If you are involved in research or investigations of any kind, you are likely to encounter obstacles. People may not just be unwilling to divulge information but could actively obstruct your inquiries. Avoid arguing about joint funds; you are almost bound to end up the loser. A delay in paying bills could cost you plenty. An old friend may display a cool attitude which hurts you more than you are willing to admit.

18. TUESDAY. Quiet. External pressures of work or other routine commitments are considerably reduced. Use the extra time to delve a little deeper into issues that concern you deeply. The illness of someone close to you may be stirring up emotions which you need to face rather than run away from. If you are involved in counseling or treatment of any kind, take stock of your situation and assess just how much you are benefiting from the therapeutic process. Do not be tempted to take promises at face value. There are depths of meaning and significance to even the most insignificant comments. A large business corporation may prove willing to donate to a cause that is important to you; do not hesitate to ask.

19. WEDNESDAY. Fortunate. A goal that you have been striving to reach, perhaps for years, is at last within your grasp. You need to be more single-minded. As a Sagittarius Archer you almost always have one goal in life which is more dominant than any other. Be honest with yourself; do not fritter away your time and energy on distractions or issues of secondary importance. Self-discipline and patience are almost certain to get you where you want to go. This is an auspicious time for making new commitments and setting long-term goals. Be specific about just what you want out of life. An older relative may fail to appreciate your sense of humor but still is behind you all the way.

20. THURSDAY. Unsettling. Misunderstandings are likely. Double-check the exact place and time of any meeting before setting out. If mailing off an important letter, be sure you have the address and the zip code exactly right. Mail addressed to you could be held up en route; try to get people to send you faxes or e-mail instead. This can be a frustrating day for Sagittarius students. Concentration will be difficult to maintain for any length of time. Also, check with your teacher to make sure you are studying the right chapter. Trying to communicate with foreigners can be frustrating due to the language barrier.

21. FRIDAY. Frustrating. There are times when switching on the Sagittarius charm simply does not work; this is one of them. Flamboyant behavior on your part is almost sure to be inappropriate; be more restrained in how you dress and what you say. Think twice before making a romantic approach; you could find yourself regretting it and feeling foolish. Someone from a distance knows how to manipulate your emotions; beware. If you judge a person merely by outward appearance you will miss the essential. Guard against spoiling youngsters; you may think you are being kind but you could really be doing them a disservice. Do not waste valuable time on the telephone or toying with computer games.

22. SATURDAY. Disquieting. A conflict between career and domestic interests may seem difficult to resolve. Be sure that you are not inventing reasons for keeping your family at arm's length. Be honest with yourself about your feelings, even if you are not prepared to be completely honest with them. Getting an important career project finished by the deadline may be more difficult than you anticipate; do not exhaust yourself in the process. If you are continuing to bear a grudge against someone, try to appreciate that your negative feelings will hurt you more than them. This is not the best of days for entertaining influential people or trying to change their views.

23. SUNDAY. Disconcerting. Your thoughts are likely to focus on career and professional issues. It is important that you become more modest in your aspirations. Aim too high and you are almost sure to be disappointed, too low and you do a disservice to yourself. Trying to impress influential people is not the best way of ensuring success. Instead, boost your reputation by doing what you are best at rather than by trying to sell yourself as a jack-of-all-trades. There are too many glory-seekers in the world already; do not add another one to their number. Routine business matters can be furthered by focusing on more monotonous and less interesting chores. Be prepared to listen to a friend who wants to confide in you.

24. MONDAY. Fair. Sagittarius professionals may be able to sneak a victory when everyone's back is turned. Diplomacy is the best approach. Resist the temptation to shout your virtues from the rooftop. People who can benefit from what you have to offer will find their way to you in the most unlikely and unexpected of ways. What seems to you to be a gesture of self-sacrifice is well worth making; the benefits can far outweigh the efforts or apparent losses involved. This is not the best day for socializing; the company you choose is likely to be rather brash and loud. However, an unexpected visit from a neighbor could prove exciting and unusual.

25. TUESDAY. Calm. Focus on the financial side of routine business matters. Try to trim down unnecessary expenditures, especially on frivolous items. Wise investment of recent profits is important; guard against taking poorly calculated risks. Listen to the small voice of your intuition, but do not yet act on it. Group or club activities provide an ideal outlet for your energy; concentrate on relaxation and enjoyment rather than aiming for peaks of excitement. Let a friend who is in emotional difficulties know that you are willing to help when and if they ask. However, this is not to say you should shoulder all of their problems.

26. WEDNESDAY. Variable. Be honest and straightforward, even if you suspect that others are being dishonest in relation to you. Do not gamble money on risky ventures. Admire beauty by all means, but do not let yourself be seduced by it. A close acquaintance may be hiding something from you. Lend money to a person who claims to be your friend and you may never see the money, or the friend, again. Correspondence or a package received through the mail could cheer you up. It is not true that love is impossible to express in words. If you are separated by physical distance from a romantic partner, put your feelings in a letter. Family members know how to bring out the best in you.

27. THURSDAY. Misleading. The day gets off to an uneven and erratic start. Traveling may prove unusually difficult. Allow plenty of time to get to your destination, especially if you have an important appointment. You may receive disappointing news about someone you once knew. A change of neighbors can be disturbing for you. This is a good day for entertaining clients or influential people. Property or real estate transactions can be furthered, especially with the help of people who operate behind the scenes. Inside information can give you an important financial break. A longtime friend may offer some valuable advice.

28. FRIDAY. Easygoing. This last day of the month should be plain sailing for you. There is less pressure on you to perform or to conform. A more inward-looking attitude is likely to be helpful. Be true to yourself; there is no better way to make yourself happy. Privacy is probably more important to you than you realize. Be prepared to move things around at home, or at work if possible, to provide solitude for yourself. This is a day for planning rather than putting strategies into action. The time for taking the next important step is not too far in the future, but do not force the pace. Visiting someone who is sick or weak can do them a world of good.

MARCH

1. SATURDAY. Fair. Avoid the temptation to make mountains out of molehills. Try to realize that you may be hiding behind your high principles, cloaking your personal desires and self-interest with grand notions of right and justice. Be more lenient toward family members who fail to live up to your ideals. Pondering what happened in the past not only wastes your valuable time but also can make you moody and needlessly sad. Push ahead full steam with long-term creative endeavors; the results of your labor may surprise even you. Jump at an opportunity to take a vacation at short notice, even if it means putting your plans in limbo for a short while.

2. SUNDAY. Good. Sometimes you have to be shamelessly honest about your wishes and desires. However, do not risk hurting someone's feelings or giving the impression that you are purely selfish. A family reunion should be enjoyable, giving you a true taste of all the good aspects of belonging to a clan. Domestic matters are likely to be uppermost in your mind. This is a fine time for doing some redecorating at home. Even if you live in temporary or rented accommodations, it is always possible to add little touches that give the place your personal signature. Someone you love is likely to come around to your way of thinking at long last. Resist saying I told you so.

3. MONDAY. Difficult. There may be one particular issue relating to money which is bothering you. Unfortunately, this is not the time to confront free-spenders directly. If you attempt to do so, you could end up having to take a defensive position even though you are in the right. Do not indulge in gossip, although you should not be surprised if others do so. Parents or other older family members may believe or suspect something about you which is hardly flattering. Try to be more tactful yourself where other people's feelings are concerned. The fact that they are not diplomatic with regard to you is no excuse for reacting in the same way to them.

4. TUESDAY. Useful. Your superior, boss, or other influential people may grant an extension to an impossible deadline; at last you can take a deep breath and relax. Otherwise, this is a good day for bringing existing projects or activities to a successful close. Jobs finished today may win you a bonus or substantial commission. All real estate and property affairs are favored. Red tape and bureaucracy should be less of a problem, and you may actually find yourself very thankful that the authorities look into matters in such small detail. Entertaining someone important is a good idea. Even consider inviting the person to stay overnight in your home.

5. WEDNESDAY. Unpredictable. Trying to discover the whereabouts of some object or possession could take up a good part of the day. Making sense of figures for recent personal expenditure can prove difficult, perhaps impossible. Make an extra effort to be more careful in keeping track of your personal spending. Do not throw away receipts; store them, especially if the purchased article is under a manufacturer's guarantee. There are certain questions about sources of income or wealth which should never be asked of someone; be discreet and tactful even if you are longing to know. This evening is a good time for socializing at home and also for a night out on the town with friends.

6. THURSDAY. Buoyant. Broaden your horizons. Allow a little more optimism to intrude into your short-term plans and calculations. Smile and the world will smile with you. Now is a particularly favorable time for developing new skills. Consider taking a brush-up course in a former skill that has become rusty from disuse. Reading the local newspaper will not only provide you with valuable information about local activities and politics but also put you on the track of a real bargain through the classified advertisements. New plans launched today may be blessed with a greater share of success than even you anticipate.

7. FRIDAY. Slow. Some fear or anxiety could be holding you back from releasing your full potential. Just because you may have failed at something in the past does not mean that you will not succeed this time around. Be encouraged by those who seem to have more faith in you than you do yourself. Do not allow someone who knows you a bit too well from the past try to persuade that you cannot change. You can do so by becoming free of patterns which have tended to hold you back. A delay in processing real estate or property transactions may be causing you some anxiety but try not to worry too much.

8. SATURDAY. Positive. This is an ideal day for activities designed to bring you closer to your roots. Surround yourself with people and objects which protect and nourish your deeper self. Strive to draw closer to a state of simplicity and almost childlike innocence. You have nothing to prove to others, and nothing to prove to yourself; just be what you are. The bonds linking you with family members are drawing closer. Poking around in a secondhand or antique shop can lead to discovering some beautiful old clothes or other usable objects. If you are going out tonight, spend a little extra time choosing what to wear.

9. SUNDAY. Fair. Be prepared to forgive and forget. This is another of those days when disagreements or personality differences cannot be solved through confrontation, or even by trying to discuss the problem openly. There are times when it is better to pretend that you have not noticed; in this way problems will start to go away by themselves. Go out of your way not to start a fight with a friend or family member who seems to be valuing their career above their relationship with you. A heated discussion will only alienate them further. This is a favorable day for all kinds of recreation and entertainment. Sports, especially of a physical kind, can be a good way of burning off feelings of frustration.

10. MONDAY. Fortunate. This is an auspicious start to the workweek. A greater sense of optimism can help you rise above trivial problems and see how insignificant they really are. Your financial decisions are likely to be inspired and timely. Act on a hunch and you could achieve results that surprise others, not to mention yourself. Do not take no for an answer when confronted by a difficult person in the business world. If you cannot shout down the opposition, you may be able to find ways of bypassing them altogether. Your reputation can be boosted in unexpected and unforeseen ways. This is the time to assume a more prominent profile in the public eye.

11. TUESDAY. Tricky. Conditions do not favor taking chances, especially where money is concerned. There are too many hidden factors of which you are not yet aware. Guard against going behind people's backs; they will soon find out, and can be extremely offended. Sagittarius parents may be worrying about a youngster who you sense is not telling you the whole truth. There is no point attempting to force information out of them; distancing themselves from you is probably only a stage in the difficult process of growing up. Try to find out more hard facts by talking to their teacher or the parents of their friends.

12. WEDNESDAY. Mixed. The morning can be a rather frustrating time at work. A well-intentioned colleague may now unintentionally undo some of the hard work you have immersed yourself in over the past few days or even weeks. Do not expect teamwork or other cooperative ventures to proceed without at least one major misunderstanding. Achieving a balance of power in decision-making processes is likely to be especially difficult. Try not to be late for work; your employer may view tardiness more seriously than you anticipate. Later in the day is good for bringing to a close specific jobs or transactions which have been dragging on for some time. The evening favors being with your romantic partner at home.

13. THURSDAY. Starred. This day favors attempts to get ahead with routine assignments, run-of-the-mill jobs, and other humdrum chores. Not even the most boring task is without some sort of challenge. Listening to music is an ideal way of turning chores into a pleasurable event. View the need for greater discipline in routine work as a test rather than a source of discouragement. People who try to get you to work harder or faster are probably genuinely interested in bringing out the best in you and helping you to develop your talents. Some extra money may come your way quite unexpectedly.

14. FRIDAY. Variable. Teamwork and partnership ventures enter an exciting new phase today. Seize fresh opportunities before it is too late. New horizons can open up in teaching, writing, or lecturing. A legal dispute may be resolved in your favor. Loved ones can be surprisingly supportive and encouraging, even with regard to your creative endeavors in which they previously showed no interest. Children may make you feel justifiably proud. Do not be too quick to sign a contract; you are likely to regret it. Someone at home may forget to pass on an important message or tell you about new mail.

15. SATURDAY. Uncertain. A family member may be feeling more isolated and out on a limb than you realize. Try to give the same degree of support that was recently given to you, especially at an emotional level. Loved ones need to feel they are really important to you and appreciated. Parents may have a rather disruptive influence on marital and partnership affairs; try to ensure that they do not load the dice against you. Colleagues are unlikely to share your enthusiasm for a particular venture, which could cause some friction. If you want to move ahead with a particular project this weekend, you probably have to work on your own. An unexpected visitor may turn up at the door bearing a gift.

16. SUNDAY. Disquieting. Trying to discuss a delicate financial subject with loved ones may be greeted with a less than enthusiastic reception. Choose your words with care; there is a greater risk of misunderstandings. Youngsters may force you to make some unforeseen expenditure. The particular type of expense involved may be long term rather than a one-shot purchase, possibly requiring you to do some juggling with your finances. If you are involved in research or investigative work, be more sensitive to other people's privacy. Know when not to ask embarrassing questions. Do not continue to put off dealing with a taxation matter.

17. MONDAY. Difficult. Do what you can to improve future economic security both for yourself and for loved ones. New pension, insurance, and retirement plans are worth looking into more carefully; they could be worthwhile alternatives. Focus on pooling resources, both mental and financial. Influential people may bar the way to progress in a certain business venture, possibly out of a sense of jealousy. Do nothing that might antagonize officials or other individuals occupying positions of authority and power; they can become ruthless if they suspect you are trying to provoke them. This is not the best of days for trying to impress superiors or clients.

18. TUESDAY. Fair. You may not be the best person to manage your own money, even if you excel at handling other people's finances on their behalf. This is a favorable day for sorting out matters relating to a legacy or inheritance. Be realistic about your own financial needs; do not think primarily of other people's interests. A business merger which is in the works, or on the point of materializing, may be just what is needed to give your own ambitions and professional aspirations that crucial extra boost. Competition can bring out the best in you. Chess or other board games can be a perfect way of relaxing while also challenging and developing your mental powers.

19. WEDNESDAY. Changeable. Affairs relating to people or places at a distance are assuming extra significance in your life. It is important to develop a more philosophical, long-term approach with regard to them. Do not give up because of a few minor setbacks. View problems as a challenge to be overcome, not a cause for despair. Break down a major project into manageable components. Seriously think about ways to better yourself through study or other forms of self-improvement. Higher education can open new doors for you. Do not let irritations or anxieties at home spill over into your business life. In professional activities you need to keep cool, calm, and in control.

20. THURSDAY. Frustrating. You may be aiming at the stars, as your Sagittarius nature inspires you to do. But getting to the stars is not a simple matter. Learn to be more realistic. Put your ideas to the test before committing yourself to them. Without patience and self-discipline you will find it difficult to achieve any aspiration. Ask people who are older or more experienced than you for advice on a certain matter. A negative response to your idea or proposal may be a question of sour grapes more than anything else. Children are apt to be more sensitive than you think. Avoid saying or doing anything which might give them an inferiority complex.

21. FRIDAY. Disconcerting. Your main problem today stems from trying too hard. A display of intense ambition can frighten people or put them on guard. Attempt to be more diplomatic, and especially to be more modest. However single-minded and serious you are in your motivations and aspirations, aim to develop a calmer and more serene appearance when dealing with other people. Guard against associating with dubious people or organizations. Your natural tendency to see only the best in everyone can blind you to their less positive side. If you feel tired, the need to focus on matters outside the home can make you resentful, which in turn contributes to your need for more rest and release from stress.

22. SATURDAY. Lucky. Be more conscious of your reputation and of the need to preserve and protect your good name. This may seem like a frivolous, purely enjoyable day, but at the same time you are managing to make a good impression on people whose assessment of you really matters. Today is ideal for home entertaining; you are certain to make a very impressive host. Be quick to kiss and make up if you get into an argument with a loved one. You will find it easier to touch people's hearts and make them feel they are one of the family. This is a good day for planning a journey or actually taking one, especially for purposes of entertainment and enjoyment.

23. SUNDAY. Manageable. You may at last rediscover a valuable possession mislaid a while ago and given up as lost for good. This is a day when emotions run high. Make additional allowances for family members or other people who seem to be behaving rather irrationally. Your fondness for pursuing activities that take you away from the family can create a conflict, but the problem is not as serious as it might appear. In group or club activities, avoid involvement in any activity which is on the borderline between socially acceptable and illegal. A friend in trouble may ask you for help; do not turn your back.

24. MONDAY. Variable. It is important to make sure that the money aspect involved in any close association is clearly understood. Failure to do so can create long-term misunderstandings and eventual quarrels that are difficult to settle. Do not bury your head in the sand and try to pretend that a certain financial problem does not exist; that only aggravates the situation. An offer from a mutual friend of your partner or associate may not be quite as sound as it appears at first glance. Avoid rushing into any new venture without a great deal of careful thought. A considerate, generous action on the part of a neighbor could save you a great deal of trouble.

25. TUESDAY. Good.   You are at your best today in a group setting. You can shine among people who know and appreciate you. Meeting new people can be advantageous both socially and professionally. Take things slow and easy, though. Place more emphasis on just being with people rather than doing a lot of entertaining or questioning. This is a particularly good day for an audition or interview where your talents are on display for someone who is in a position to help you in the future. A well-calculated gamble may pay off. Take advantage of opportunities for combining business and pleasure, particularly at a distance from your home base.

26. WEDNESDAY. Difficult.   You may run headlong into trouble if you do not make ample allowance for the unexpected. Guard against planning your schedule too tightly; unforeseen delays are much more likely than normal. Someone from the past who suddenly shows up at your home or place of work could throw off your mental and emotional balance by confronting you with a situation you would prefer to avoid. And someone who presents you with a brilliant and unusual scheme may deliberately be concealing its risks and disadvantages from you. Plans for raising money for a charitable cause could suffer from an unpredicted setback. Do not put all of your eggs in one basket; keep your options open.

27. THURSDAY. Fair.   Take promises made to you with a grain of salt. A number of people are hardly likely to keep their word. You may find boastfulness upsetting because it shows you that the person's character is not quite what you had supposed. Dealing with a large business corporation can be successful. You can be especially fortunate if you have insider's knowledge on which to draw. New romance can flourish, enriching all aspects of your life with a light and warmth which may have been lacking recently. Sagittarius couples may want to consider taking a second honeymoon this spring and renewing the marriage vows in a formal ceremony.

28. FRIDAY. Exciting. Sagittarius people are ideally placed today to do a little behind-the-scenes wheeling and dealing; the financial benefits could be considerable. All endeavors aimed at raising funds for a charity or other worthwhile cause are likely to succeed beyond your expectations. Giving time, energy, or money to someone who is underprivileged or suffering from an illness makes you know you have done something worthwhile. Be good to yourself, too. You may have a tendency to take the blame for problems which are not your fault at all. Sagittarius teachers, social workers, and others involved in humanitarian ventures may win an important promotion or award.

29. SATURDAY. Starred. People tend to look to you for inspiration, strength, and advice. Be generous in giving to them. A hobby that you take seriously may give you more pleasure and a greater sense of fulfillment if you take a class to improve your skills, or teach one. This is the time to start thinking about realistic options for turning it into a source of income; the possibility is not as remote as you may think. This is another day when affairs of the heart are favored. Be prepared for the unexpected where romance is concerned. Opportunities that come along for Sagittarius singles are unlikely to be repeated for a long time to come.

30. SUNDAY. Mixed. Spend some time catching up with personal correspondence. Telephoning a distant family member can put your mind at ease. Where personal affairs and interests are concerned, this is a day for planning rather than for outright action. People in positions of authority may try to deny you an opportunity to enjoy yourself. Do not cross swords with in-laws or with the parents of your romantic partner; you are likely to regret it. Guard against involvement in speculative and other risky financial ventures, especially if there is any hint of becoming involved in something shady or illegal. Keep a closer watch on children, but do not interfere unless necessary.

31. MONDAY. Stressful. Your tendency to take unnecessary chances may work against you. Do not put your own money at stake merely for the sake of a whim or personal indulgence. Keep receipts for any purchases you make; you may need them. Do not be too trusting. Someone who tries to win your affection may not be what he or she appears to be. Romance may take you into rough emotional waters, triggering old fears and feelings of anger which you thought you had overcome. It is important to analyze these apparently negative feelings rather than try to ignore them. Your relationship depends on mutual understanding and trust.

APRIL

1. TUESDAY. Uncertain. Considerable uncertainty is hanging over financial affairs in general. Deciding how much to reveal about your personal finances is apt to be a sensitive issue. Guard against committing yourself to additional responsibility which could involve unforeseen expenses you have not been warned about in advance. This is especially important in regard to an application for a personal loan or mortgage. Business prospects are improving. A more dynamic and even aggressive outlook could help you make people realize that they have underestimated you and what you are capable of achieving. Looking for a lost document or other item may prove a time-consuming activity but worthwhile in the long run.

2. WEDNESDAY. Changeable. Unexpected news received this morning could throw you off balance for a while. However, what appears at first to be bad news is more likely than not to work out in your favor. Although you may be forced to change your normal route going to work, the change could actually be refreshing. It may even show you that the route you have become used to is not the best one after all. Conditions are especially good for getting correspondence backlogs out of the way. Try to tackle routine tasks in a more creative and adventurous spirit. Make business correspondence more personal and individualized; the recipient is likely to appreciate the human touch.

3. THURSDAY. Calm. There are fewer pressures and fewer demands on you. However, do not let the hours slip by without using them responsibly and creatively. The temptation to join in some gossip and even add to it could be strong, but try to resist. Talking about people behind their backs is disrespectful not only to them but also to yourself. This is a helpful day for Sagittarius people living by their wits. If you depend for your livelihood on your abilities in communicating or selling, expect some welcome news. Spend a little extra time focusing on your strategies; concentrate on the tactics that you recently proved to yourself are likely to be the most effective in the long run.

4. FRIDAY. Optimistic. You may be giving your parents or other older family members a harder time than you realize. It is fine to go your own way in true Sagittarius fashion and do only what you wish. However, a little more consideration for those who care deeply about you is sure to be appreciated. This can be an important day if you are involved in any type of creative endeavor. New contacts may introduce you to a whole new world of opportunity. Enlarging your circle of friends and acquaintances is almost certain to bring you into close touch with people who appreciate and value your abilities. This is an auspicious day for a marriage proposal or acceptance.

5. SATURDAY. Pleasant. Do not try to force the pace in business or professional ventures; by doing so you may only end up antagonizing your allies and colleagues as well as your competitors. Be more patient in attempting to resolve domestic disagreements or disputes. Try to appreciate that other people do not necessarily see matters in the same way that you do. Recreational outings or sporting activities involving your boss or other influential people are particularly favored. There is excellent opportunity for you to discuss a new plan that you are hatching in an offbeat setting. A gamble may pay off even better than you hope.

6. SUNDAY. Fair. Slow down a little. Unless you become more lighthearted in your attitude, there is a danger of turning even enjoyable activities into a duty and a chore. Do not doubt yourself or your own abilities. You are likely to become more aware than ever of an inner source of strength which can see you through difficult situations. Consider buying in bulk at a local discount store to stock up on supplies for the next few weeks or even months. Be sure to use any cents-off coupons that you have. It is also a good day for writing up a report or preparing an article for publication. Your new approach to an old subject is likely to prove highly challenging and thought-provoking.

7. MONDAY. Good. A softer approach to people is likely to prove especially effective. Sagittarius professionals will find there are definite advantages to being better prepared than the competition. Do not hesitate to switch on that Sagittarius charm, both in a professional setting and in a social context. Put your artistic flair to good use even in simple activities such as arranging books on a shelf. You may want to take up a new hobby. Follow your heart, and make some space and time for doing something you really enjoy and find fulfilling. Morning and evening hours are particularly starred for love and romance.

8. TUESDAY. Variable. Some quick thinking on your part may impress your boss more than you realize, or even more than they are willing to admit. Be clear in making a request for improved working conditions or a pay raise. Do not be surprised or discouraged if your employer cannot guarantee to meet your demands quite yet. This is a favorable day for writing and mailing off responses to job advertisements; be sure to present your credentials and experience in as impressive a way as possible. Guard against burning your bridges in routine occupational affairs. Do not leave one job without having a definite offer of another one.

9. WEDNESDAY. Disquieting. Stick to the work at hand. Do not take on more than you can handle comfortably and easily. Your reluctance to say no to people who try to take advantage of your generosity may be your undoing. Allow more time to get to your place of work and back home again. A particularly self-important colleague or co-worker may be a thorough nuisance, but try to keep out of the way to avoid any direct confrontation. Think twice before signing a contract or other important document. Crucial new information may come to light in the next few days which could radically change your mind about the issue in question. Drive with extra care; pedestrians as well as other drivers can be very unpredictable.

10. THURSDAY. Mixed. In partnership and cooperative ventures you may now be getting the wrong end of the stick. Do not assume too much about the motivation and intentions of your partners; you are almost sure to be wrong. And try not to think the worst of people; by doing so you can actually help bring out the worst in them. You are possibly being unfair to your mate, giving them a harder time than necessary. By all means be open and honest with loved ones, but do not expect them to share all of your woes and worries. There are some matters you simply must work out your own. Later in the day expect more opportunities, both professionally and personally.

11. FRIDAY. Changeable. There is a good chance for successful business growth and expansion through partnership and cooperative endeavors. Pooling different talents and abilities is just what is needed to present a stronger front, especially in advertising and public relations. This is a good day for entering a new phase in important negotiations. Keep a lower profile, and try to be more diplomatic in presenting your own interests and points of view. New creative endeavors can get off to a flying start, particularly if you are being helped along with any kind of sponsorship. Encourage children and youngsters to try something they have not done before.

12. SATURDAY. Quiet. Today is likely to be fairly uneventful and calm. Put any spare time to constructive use. Delve into certain matters in more depth, especially problems that have been troubling you. You may find that the solution has been lying there all the time, just below the surface. The public library is likely to provide all you could possibly need for furthering your research or investigation into a certain subject that fascinates or troubles you. If you are feeling out of your depth emotionally, do a little self-examination rather than simply expecting other people to provide you with all the answers. You have the willpower to make some important change.

13. SUNDAY. Cautious. You need to take more responsibility for your own actions while refusing to take the blame for the negative actions or decisions of other people. This may involve walking a rather thin line in order to avoid offending the people concerned. Sagittarius parents need to accept that child-rearing is a time-consuming and emotionally demanding commitment. If you try to offload this responsibility onto your partner, you may end up taking action for which you will find it difficult to forgive yourself at a later date. Persevere single-mindedly with career and professional interests but do not neglect loved ones or friends.

14. MONDAY. Deceptive. Deciding just how to invest joint funds or business profits can be especially difficult. Do not believe and take as gospel everything that financial experts or other influential people recommend. In today's complex world they may turn out to be no wiser about the best course of action than you are. What had seemed to be an attractive prospect for a merger may run up against opposition at an official level. There is no point refusing to fill out required forms or provide necessary information. If you are involved in any type of investigative work, double-check your most basic assumptions; you could be rushing up a blind alley.

15. TUESDAY. Sensitive. Some rather disconcerting or upsetting news received from someone at a distance may involve you in a change of plans. Be philosophical; try to adapt to the new situation rather than making a mountain out of a molehill by whining and complaining. This is especially true in case of last-minute alterations to vacation or travel plans. Sagittarius students may be disappointed to find that a particular course does not quite live up to expectations. Express your feelings openly and frankly to someone who is more experienced than yourself in such matters. Guard against putting all your eggs in one basket where new or potential employment opportunities are concerned. Do your best to keep your options open.

16. WEDNESDAY. Challenging.   Business plans and goals may require some revision, possibly on more than mere points of detail. Do not be too sure you are right about a particular issue. Your understanding of what justice is and is not may be slightly prejudiced and one-sided. This is a special day for romance. If it is true that love makes the world go around, events today could find you sharing this feeling of dynamism and dizziness. Try to be realistic in matters of the heart. Do not allow yourself to be taken in by mere appearances, or by glitz and glamour. Be careful to whom you lend money, and even to whom you reveal your personal income and finances.

17. THURSDAY. Variable.   Morning hours are best for pressing ahead with routine business activities. Sagittarius charm is likely to work wonders, especially in motivating people to do favors or provide that extra bit of help. Focus on presenting an attractive, confident public appearance. Even at the highest level of business or commerce, it is always the individual that counts. Also keep in mind the importance of first impressions. A new romantic attraction could develop at your place of work or through a colleague. Be more reasonable with people, especially later in the day. Guard against playing the martyr role and making a major issue out of what in fact is hardly that important.

18. FRIDAY. Contradictory.   Be extra patient this morning. Do not rush or you could end up exhausting yourself for nothing, and even making an enemy of someone who was once your ally. Try to control your Sagittarius temper, even if you happen to become aware of an outrageous injustice. Guard against interfering in the personal affairs of other people. Ambition is good, but too much can frighten people and make them avoid you. Later in the day favors dealing with staff and employment matters. A reassuring word in the ear of an especially promising employee will make him or her more aware of being appreciated. An end-of-week bonus will also be most welcome.

19. SATURDAY. Manageable.   You may be able to turn other people's confusion to your own advantage. Follow a hunch where financial matters are concerned rather than accepting the advice of experts as gospel. Sagittarius business people can leap ahead of competitors by pressing on with a new project while keeping it strictly under wraps. Communicating with people locally can prove a problem. Some correspondence you are expecting may have gone astray; try to check with the sender. Influential people are not altogether reliable and trustworthy. It is not that they necessarily want to mislead you, just that they may not be very good at their job.

20. SUNDAY. Good.   Strike out on your own. Do not shy away from acting as a beacon of inspiration to others. Friends, new or old, can be strongly attracted by the dynamism of your personality, and they are likely to become valuable associates. Press ahead with efforts to make the world a better place for everyone. Your enthusiasm for promoting a worthwhile cause can be highly contagious. Do not fear challenging existing institutions and established ways of thinking. Sagittarius people are always able to see farther ahead than others can see. You will be happiest doing something different; break away from the humdrum, the familiar, the ordinary and expected.

21. MONDAY. Positive.   This is an auspicious start to the new workweek. A breakthrough can bring you significantly closer to fulfilling a secret hope or dream. Your idealism continues to be infectious and inspiring to others. Let the sky be your limit, nothing lower, nothing less. New encounters are almost certain to lead to forming new friendships, which are apt to endure for a long time. Associating with current friends can be especially enjoyable and pleasant in a professional setting as well as a purely social context. Continue your efforts toward reform. Profit from a recent venture can be increased through wise reinvestment of surplus funds.

22. TUESDAY. Sensitive.   A discussion with someone at work can resolve a problem or misunderstanding. You are likely to find that the person becomes much warmer toward you than ever before. However, the uncertainties and doubts that remain in your mind are not so easily dismissed. The boss or another superior can be unhelpful when asked about your exact job prospects. Try not to read too much between the lines, but at the same be realistic. Do not set your sights too high. You need to keep a tight grip on your emotions; do not let them run away with you. Worries and fears tend to be contagious. A person who approaches you with a sob story is possibly not telling the whole truth.

23. WEDNESDAY. Difficult.   An apparently treacherous situation can be defused by confronting the problem head-on. Do not allow people in the business or professional world to become aware of your vulnerabilities; they could be only too happy to take advantage of them. Guard against being too casual in making or honoring promises. It is more important than you may now realize to honor your assurances down to the smallest detail. Try to keep everyone focused during discussions or a conference; minds tend to wander, confusing the main issues. Someone you have enjoyed working with may be transferred to a different department or move on to a new job altogether.

24. THURSDAY. Easygoing. Sagittarius people tend to have strong hunches but sometimes are reluctant to make use of them. Try your best to believe in yourself today. Your intuition is likely to be accurate. Guard against becoming involved in financial dealings of a shady nature, however strongly they are recommended. You can excel in all kinds of behind-the-scenes maneuvering. Sometimes it is just a little word or suggestion that tilts the balance in your favor. Take time away from pressure. Spend more time on your own, enjoying the luxuries of solitude and giving yourself a period of meditation.

25. FRIDAY. Rewarding. Try a new attack in your approach to creative or mental endeavors; you are likely to be successful if you start all over again. Purchasing or installing new equipment can help you further your personal aims. This could be a good time to think about upgrading your personal computers, or buying a computer if you had no need for one up until now. This is also a good day for pinning down individuals who should be able to help you with regard to employment in the near future. You should find it easier to contact such people and make a favorable impression on them. Sagittarius animal lovers may be asked to take in a stray; everyone knows you will not say no.

26. SATURDAY. Productive. Think big. Be more optimistic about what you are capable of achieving. Do not hesitate to ask for assistance in helping achieve your aims. What starts off as a casual conversation or bit of gossip could end up providing you with some extremely interesting inside information or a tangible offer. Some extra traveling, especially over a short distance, should help blow the cobwebs out of your mind and refresh your spirit. More involvement in community affairs and activities can give you a greater sense of belonging and sharing with the people who live close to you. Deal with a backlog of correspondence and feel the relief of getting it finally out of the way.

27. SUNDAY. Satisfactory. This is a good day for reflection. Make a commitment to yourself to develop a more understanding attitude toward the people you work with and for. New ideas are the most valuable of all. People dealing directly with the public know best of all what will be accepted by them and what is unlikely to succeed. You may have this firsthand knowledge, or you may have to rely on what you are told. Try to be more methodical in your thinking and planning, especially where personal finances are concerned. A meeting with an influential person, perhaps in a relaxed and casual setting, may have some useful spin-offs later in the year.

28. MONDAY. Unpredictable. Focus on equalizing income and expenditure so that you do not have to borrow, and you can soon get out of the red. Taking out a loan is always a somewhat frustrating experience, especially for Sagittarius people who so value freedom and independence. Do not believe what influential people promise unless they have actually signed on the dotted line; even then, be sure to read the small print as they may deliberately have inserted a bailout clause. Make sure there are no mix-ups about work arrangements, particularly if you are self-employed or are employed on a temporary basis. Evening plans are apt to fall through; find your own entertainment.

29. TUESDAY. Fair. There is a risk of getting out of bed on the wrong foot and feeling disoriented until you are brought down to earth with a bump. Do not hide your light under a bushel. If you can see the solution to someone else's problem, speak up. However, be extra sensitive to avoid raising delicate subjects such as problems involving health or work. People will be quick to take offense. A new romantic attraction could develop rapidly in a work or professional context. If you are already involved in a long-term relationship, you may find that your partner can be more actively helpful to your career than you had guessed.

30. WEDNESDAY. Mixed. By all means rejoice at today's good news, but do not overreact. Try not to hurt the feelings of someone less fortunate than you. A new opportunity that offers you a greater sense of freedom may seem threatening to your loved ones or romantic partner. Do not ignore the health complaint of someone you care for deeply. Even if the problem is entirely imaginary, it is still important because it happens to be real for them. Guard against attempts to mix business and pleasure, especially later in the day. Try not to become too attached to a certain piece of jewelry or other item; it may only cause you heartache if lost.

MAY

1. THURSDAY. Variable. Use this first day of the new month to finish off existing projects before embarking on new ones. Bringing to a close work that has been dragging on for some time not only gives you a sense of freedom and relief but also clears the decks for what you really want to do. Heart-to-heart discussions with family members or people who share your home can be particularly useful in helping to resolve minor domestic problems. You may be apprehensive about an upcoming test or test results, but try not to imagine the worst. There is no reason unfortunate events in the past should repeat themselves either now or in the near future.

2. FRIDAY. Disquieting. A certain amount of disruption at home is unavoidable. Try to keep calm in the face of physical or emotional disturbance. Do not allow anyone to provoke you into a rash action which sooner or later you will regret. Do something to brighten up your surroundings. A new framed poster or a plant can help to induce a more positive atmosphere. A feeling that your luck is running out where romance is concerned is at least partly your fault. Love is not a lottery. It takes a great deal of hard work and effort to build a truly enduring and worthwhile relationship. Keep trying even if you do not seem to be having an impact.

3. SATURDAY. Good. Try a more creative approach to your routine affairs and activities. Find a way to enjoy what you do, even the most trivial of tasks. Spending time with children is an ideal way of unwinding after the pressures of the past workweek. Bring out the child in yourself; let that inner youthfulness have free rein. If you have a special hobby, you should find your favored pastime particularly absorbing. It may provide the best outlet for the type of frustrations you have been encountering recently. Sagittarius men and women are likely to excel today in sports, games, and a display of skills and talents. A gamble may pay off, but do not push your luck.

4. SUNDAY. Mixed. A bad dream may make you reluctant to get out of bed this morning. A headache or other pain can make it difficult to face the world. You are almost sure to start feeling better by midday, if not earlier. A family member may make the kind of request or demand which you dread. Be firm with them, while also being fair. Expressing regret for something you recently did or said may be a useful, but painful, way to correct the more extravagant and less responsible side of your nature. Leave no doubt as to the love and appreciation you feel for your partner. Later in the day should be fine for socializing at home.

5. MONDAY. Deceptive. Think before you act, not the other way around. Rely on your brains, not your heart or your emotions. Try to be more detached and objective, especially where money matters are concerned. Keep important receipts for items you recently purchased. It is even worth holding on to the less important ones for the time being; you never know when you may need them. This is a good day for bulk buying and a shopping spree. Before leaving home, prepare a detailed list of what you need to purchase; it can be frustrating to get home and find you have forgotten the most important things. Do not base your actions on information that is probably out of date.

6. TUESDAY. Fair. This is a good day for pushing ahead in earnest with work and occupational affairs. Higher-ups are more likely to appreciate your commitment and seriousness. The quantity as well as quality of the work you produce now could qualify you for a significant promotion. Let your boss know that you have your sights set high. Try not to waste time in pointless gossip or chatting, especially with regard to your employer's time; they are likely to resent you wasting their money. Think twice before making a promise you may not be able to honor. This Sagittarius problem stems from your generous nature and could now become more acute.

7. WEDNESDAY. Manageable. Adopting a new, healthier diet may be just what you need to feel better. This is especially true if you have a demanding schedule every day and therefore have less time than usual to prepare or cook balanced meals. Healthy food can be surprisingly delicious and easy to make, and will leave you feeling much more satisfied than junk food. Conditions are excellent for approaching influential people in connection with work or business prospects. Your determination and ambition are likely to be valued and appreciated. Do not make life unnecessarily difficult for a family member by leaving a mess behind you; you do not have a personal maid following you around.

8. THURSDAY. Changeable. This is a good day for establishing new contacts which may lead to forming a cooperative or partnership venture. Be open to ideas and suggestions that challenge the norm and offer a viable alternative to traditional ways of doing things. Having access to a rapid, reliable communications system is especially important. For Sagittarius business people, looking at the latest developments in technology may be worth the time and effort. In all joint endeavors try not to shine too brightly; casting a shadow on your partners can make them resentful. Do not minimize the importance of attending at once to minor legal details.

9. FRIDAY. Manageable. Today is especially favorable for Sagittarius people having to go through any type of legal proceedings. It should be easier to arrive at an amicable agreement which is acceptable to all parties. A long-drawn-out court battle is the last thing you need at the moment. Make an effort to understand the feelings of the opposition by putting yourself in their shoes. Invite them to talk about their wishes, hopes, and fears; discuss feelings with them at greater length. A telephone call from someone you would like to get to know better is likely to brighten up the whole day. Carry extra cash if going out tonight.

10. SATURDAY. Pleasant. Delve into certain matters in greater depth. In the hustle and bustle of daily life it is sometimes difficult to give an issue that matters a lot to you the time and energy you would like to devote to it. Today you have the opportunity to correct this imbalance. Research a range of possibilities and investigate all alternatives. Be patient instead of making a rapid decision which is perhaps ill-informed and based on inadequate information. Be prepared to help someone out with a loan, or with managing their income. This can be a very productive day for working in a quiet office on your own. What you could not accomplish all week can be done in a matter of hours.

11. SUNDAY. Demanding. Even though this is the weekend, impose a little more discipline on yourself. Plant your goals firmly in your mind. Do not waste energy or time on secondary issues and distractions. Above all, do not take on more than you can safely manage. Any encounters with influential people can provide valuable opportunities for winning their support. However, there is nothing to be gained from making promises to anyone which you may be unable to honor when called upon to do so. Do not believe everything you read in the newspaper. Avoid acting on financial advice from people who probably know even less than you do.

12. MONDAY. Sensitive. Set your own psychological and emotional boundaries. Guard against infringing on other people's privacy; they are likely to resent it just as you would. In research work, be extra scrupulous about checking the credentials and reliability of your sources; otherwise you could be led astray. Try to keep up with bill payments, even if doing so means making a few personal expenditure sacrifices. Once you begin spending more than you earn, your debts could quickly accumulate and cause unnecessary worry in the weeks and months to come. This is a good day for attending to legal matters. Obtaining expert advice, if needed, is unlikely to prove a problem.

13. TUESDAY. Satisfactory. You may find that a certain fear, worry, or anxiety which you have been harboring is unfounded. Learn from this; try to realize how negative and also unnecessary worry can be. Be prepared to press ahead with long-term self-improvement plans. Do not expect to achieve results overnight; the most important aims and goals are only reached through perseverance. It may be possible to obtain financial backing, possibly from government sources or your employer, for a training course you would like to pursue. News received from someone at a distance is likely to confirm that you are indeed on the right track.

14. WEDNESDAY. Disconcerting. Avoid imposing extra physical and emotional strain on yourself. The boss may make additional demands which leave you feeling stressed and exhausted. Attempts by you to improve work efficiency may not be appreciated by higher-ups even though you are trying to do them a favor. This is a good day for drawing up the tentative outline of a new business proposal. However, do not yet submit them for official approval; the immediate response is unlikely to be favorable. Think twice before attempting to correct what you sense is a flagrant injustice; the official version of what is happening may be very different from your own perception.

15. THURSDAY. Frustrating. What you think is certain to please someone may, on the contrary, annoy them. Trying to placate loved ones can be difficult and thankless. A conflict between work and home responsibilities may be difficult to resolve at this moment. The tension may actually be made worse by attempts to smooth matters over. This is not a day when you can get away with playing the role of innocent victim; people will see through your strategy immediately. Being nice is not always the best solution when faced with a thorny problem. Sometimes a more direct, forthright approach is needed, especially if you must protect other people's interests as well as your own.

16. FRIDAY. Fair.   In career and professional ventures, do not try to run before you can walk. Take time to learn the ropes rather than overestimating your understanding of a situation. Influential people can be helpful. Having a sponsor or backer is especially reassuring and also financially advantageous. Being answerable to someone for your actions forces you to think out your strategy and tactics more carefully. Try not to be provoked by someone who challenges your credentials or disputes your abilities. In this case, as in all others, your actions speak louder than words. Spend tonight with a group, not as a twosome.

17. SATURDAY. Stimulating.   Give in to a feeling of wanting to withdraw from the hectic pace of daily existence and spend a little extra time alone. A few hours, even a few minutes, of privacy can be surprisingly therapeutic. Analyzing your actions and goals is sure to help you gain a deeper perspective regarding activities you are engaged in at the moment. People who operate behind the scenes can advise you on financial or business matters quite successfully. This is a particularly auspicious day for love and romance. A new romantic attraction could develop unexpectedly at a social function or gathering of acquaintances. A friendship may turn into a relationship that includes a hint of sensual love.

18. SUNDAY. Disquieting.   Children, especially your own, may be quite a handful. They are likely to make extra demands on your patience and understanding. Keep in mind that growing up can be rather painful. Try to remember how you felt and behaved when you were their age. Attempts at making the world a better place can encounter opposition from people whose self-interest lies in keeping things exactly as they are. In group or club activities, there is a greater risk of a leadership dispute arising between two people who are equally capable of doing the job. It would not be smart for you to try to play the role of mediator.

19. MONDAY. Tricky.   There is a greater risk of misunderstandings, especially where financial matters are concerned. It is more important than ever to ensure that the money aspect of any close associations is clearly understood by both parties concerned. Failure to do so could create problems and even give rise to accusations of deliberate dishonesty. Associating with friends and acquaintances should be pleasant but also a little stressful. Think twice before talking openly about your personal financial situation. And above all, do not reveal any secrets relating to somebody else. Keep a close watch on your wallet when you are in a crowd.

20. TUESDAY. Demanding. Sagittarius business people may be trailing behind current trendsetters and also not keeping up with technological change. Do not waste time pursuing what you hope will turn out to be a shortcut; it is almost certain to prove exactly the opposite. Unexpected surprises forced upon you by people you hardly know can be difficult to bear, but try not to overreact. Be a little more suspicious of salespeople trying to sell a special new product you have never heard about. Meeting with an influential person can be surprising and even mystifying; the eventual outcome is almost certain to be in your best long-term interests.

21. WEDNESDAY. Mixed. This is a good day for pushing ahead with private or secret ventures obscured from public scrutiny. Follow your hunches and intuitions, regardless of the current general wisdom on the subject. However, do not let the cat out of the bag by boasting prematurely of your achievements. Keep in mind the saying that a bird in the hand is worth two in the bush. There is a danger of allowing a venture that started out well to drift to a halt simply through laxness and overconfidence. Pursue any complaint you have against large business companies; the people involved may be willing to settle the matter discreetly to protect their public image.

22. THURSDAY. Stressful. Unlike yesterday, this is not a day when you can afford to go out to slay a corporate dragon. If you match yourself against people who are more powerful than you, it is likely that you will soon regret it. Look for a way to resolve problems without threats or court action, but do not expect to get any answers immediately. Time and a little more patience are needed. Emotions are running higher than usual, especially in cooperative and teamwork ventures. Be vocal in expressing your own preferences and points of view, but do not block other people's proposals as a matter of principle. Evening hours favor neighborhood activities rather than any traveling.

23. FRIDAY. Fair. You may be able to take a longer vacation this year than usual. Look for a way to combine your serious interests with pleasurable activities. Examining architecture or archaeological sites may appeal, giving you fresh insight into history. Allow youngsters, especially your own children, to make responsible decisions of their own; they are sure to appreciate being respected in this way. Being overly aggressive in business or professional ventures may unnecessarily make some enemies for you, which you can well do without. Go out tonight with friends who like you for exactly who you are.

24. SATURDAY. Useful. This is a good day for sorting out routine financial matters, especially relating to income and regular work. A little careful budgeting is certainly not out of place. Your greater degree of mental restlessness could make it difficult to concentrate for any prolonged period of time. Be careful to focus on one task or job at a time. If you jump from one to another, you are almost sure to make some unnecessary mistakes. Anxiety can deplete your physical and emotional resources and also upset your stomach. Try not to get deeply involved in other people's problems. Romantically, this may be a day you remember for the rest of your life.

25. SUNDAY. Variable. People are not so easily won over by smooth talk and persuasion. You are likely to encounter someone who has a closed mind. It is time to make an extra effort in breaking a habit which you know is unhealthy. Disobedient youngsters may be a problem because of the disruption they create. This is not the best day for any type of gambling. Even a risk which you think is well worth taking may prove to be rather foolish. The afternoon favors moving full speed ahead with business and career endeavors. By making the best use of the time available you should be in a strong position by the start of business tomorrow.

26. MONDAY. Deceptive. A feeling of frustration may be causing you to see a situation negatively. Instead, try to view it as a blessing, probably preventing you from getting entangled in something which would lead you far astray. Be careful with your money and personal possessions, especially if traveling in an area you are not familiar with. Someone who asks you to make an act of self-sacrifice may be exploiting you behind your back. Double-check the credentials of anyone who claims to be collecting money on behalf of a charitable or other worthwhile enterprise. The evening is auspicious for an outing with your partner or for attending an official business function.

27. TUESDAY. Manageable. The day starts off on an optimistic note. Your good cheer should prove contagious. A chance encounter, perhaps in a store or hallway, or on the street or a train, could develop into a meaningful friendship. Good news received from relatives or in-laws can remove a burden from your mind. This is a good day for Sagittarius teachers, politicians, and writers to express contrary views and gain acceptance for them. Take full advantage of an opportunity to address a gathering of people at a meeting or conference. This is another favorable day for romance. Make sure you do not leave work without having done all that is expected of you.

28. WEDNESDAY. Disquieting. This midweek day includes a domestic crisis, but only a minor one. Do not overreact to criticism, or take suggestions too personally. Above all, try not to let parents or other family members push your emotional buttons. This is a good day for sitting down with your partner or colleagues to discuss options in teamwork and cooperative ventures. Important new possibilities and ideas may emerge. Now is not the right time, however, to show your Sagittarius initiative and independence by acting as you think fit without obtaining prior approval from the other people involved. There should be an opportunity to demonstrate your ability to forgive and forget.

29. THURSDAY. Productive. It is worth contacting a few experts for advice regarding home improvements or necessary repairs in or around the home. This is also a good day for some do-it-yourself work, provided you have the required skills. Completing a particular job, or getting a heavy workload finally out of the way, is sure to give you a strong sense of relief and satisfaction. Influential people may be prepared to open doors for you, offering the kind of opportunity which you are unlikely to encounter often in a whole lifetime. Do not underestimate yourself or your abilities. This is an ideal time to enter into a partnership with a powerful, experienced individual.

30. FRIDAY. Fair. The domestic and romantic sides of your life may be difficult to reconcile. Older family members may interfere in your romantic affairs; when all is said and done, they probably mean well. This is a good day for browsing around in secondhand or antique stores. You may find an item that someone discarded as useless, but which you know how to put to good use. Later in the day favors a family get-together around the dinner table. Do not miss dinnertime unless you have a very important meeting. Even then, be sure to call. Try to make your home a more private and intimate place into which you and other loved ones can safely withdraw.

31. SATURDAY. Changeable. This is definitely not a time for doing anything just for old times' sake. Activities or interests which once absorbed you may now seem boring and pointless. Try not to be too serious in your search for pleasure and entertainment. A youngster may need disciplining; be firm but fair. Later in the day can be good for getting away from your usual surroundings. An unexpected visitor may be an ideal partner in a game or competitive activity, or simply ideal if you want to discuss recent developments. The evening tends to favor attending a formal or official function. Even a casual party may lead to a meaningful encounter.

JUNE

1. SUNDAY. Deceptive. A romance could be going smoothly in every way except financially. If one of you earns considerably more than the other, guard against creating a power imbalance. You may also have different priorities when it comes to spending money on entertainment and pleasure. These differences need to be resolved if the relationship is going to continue and develop. An honest conversation is needed; it may be up to you to get the ball rolling. An outing can be expensive but boring. If you are learning a new sport, you may have to spend more on equipment than you had bargained for; try to borrow or rent what you need.

2. MONDAY. Difficult. This is a difficult start to the working week for Sagittarius employees. You may have unwittingly made an enemy of someone who will not hesitate to make your life difficult. You could be getting more than your fair share of unpleasant or boring tasks. Address the problem before it escalates into unmanageable proportions. Written work of all kinds is apt to be time consuming. You may be asked to rewrite a report or a letter in order to change its tone. Stress can manifest in physical symptoms, such as a headache. Try not to push yourself beyond a sensible limit.

3. TUESDAY. Demanding. Current work projects continue to dominate your time. There is a danger that you may have bitten off more than you can chew. Guard against letting pride keep you from asking for assistance. A superior may be willing to reduce your responsibilities if you are genuinely struggling. This is not a time when you can afford to let work problems get you down. Discussing them with a sympathetic colleague can help keep things in perspective. Keep in mind that all anyone can ask you to give is your best shot. Catch up with routine domestic chores at home; pitch in and do a little more than your fair share.

4. WEDNESDAY. Variable.   If your week got off to a bad start, you should find that things improve today. Although you are still under some pressure in the workplace, there should be some lighthearted interludes which cheer you up. A telephone call from someone you recently met can do wonders for your morale. Make a point of arranging some social engagements. Having something to look forward to can make problems easier to handle. Getting caught up in your own life could mean that someone you love is feeling neglected. Get in touch with people who really matter to you. Avoid eating or drinking too much this evening; overindulging is not apt to agree with you.

5. THURSDAY. Starred.   Keep in mind that all successful relationships contain an element of hard work. This is a propitious time for fresh starts. If you are married, go out of your way to make your spouse feel special; the rewards should be more than satisfying. If you are single, guard against overdoing the Sagittarius aloofness. Someone is eager to get closer to you if you let them. This is a lucky day for a job interview or test taking. Do not be put off by someone's aggressive approach; it may be their way of sounding you out. If you are self-employed, this is a favorable time for taking on a new employee or a partner to share the pressure.

6. FRIDAY. Pleasant.   This should be an enjoyable end to the working week. Deadlines can be met with time to spare. Sagittarius business people may find that profits are up compared to this time last year. A business deal which is finalized today is likely to prove profitable. Your job satisfaction may be much higher than it was at the beginning of the week, especially if you work in the caring professions. Most of today's tasks should be rewarding. You can bring a special project to a satisfying conclusion. This is a time of increased closeness in your personal relationships. Let down your guard a little with someone new.

7. SATURDAY. Disquieting.   You may not be in the best of moods. Little things which you would normally not even notice are apt to irritate you. Guard against taking out a bad mood on those closest to you, especially children; they will only feel puzzled or hurt. This is a time when you are best left to your own devices. Refuse to be pressured into doing any favors or fulfilling social obligations if you feel that you are not up to making the necessary effort. A short-lived romance could be coming to an end. Even though you realize that it was not meant to be, it can still be hard to cope with feelings of rejection or inadequacy.

8. SUNDAY. Lucky. Sagittarius people who work weekends or shifts of antisocial hours at least should welcome the financial rewards. Even if you cannot imagine continuing this sort of time schedule indefinitely, you can at least salt away some extra money in the meantime. This is a good time for finding temporary work or an evening job if you need to boost your income. Devote some of your time to a hobby or outside interest. Academic or intellectual pursuits of all kinds are favored. Sagittarius students who are soon to take examinations may find it more effective to divide time between work and pleasure. You need a clear mind to absorb information.

9. MONDAY. Disconcerting. If you are trying to book a last-minute vacation you may find that what you want is in limited supply. It could be a case of having to take whatever there is; do not deliberate for too long or you could end up with nothing. Legal matters of all kinds can be tricky to handle. An official decision may not go in your favor; do not hesitate to appeal. Guard against signing any document you do not fully understand. It is essential to read the small print. Do not let others confuse or intimidate you with words you do not understand. Insist on a clear explanation.

10. TUESDAY. Difficult. Long-distance travel can be subject to delays. If you are traveling for business purposes it is wise to keep appointments as open-ended as possible. In this way it will not matter so much if you run behind schedule. Try to postpone important meetings until tomorrow or later in the week. Any formal applications, especially for a passport or visa, are unlikely to be straightforward. You may have to stand in a long line if you need something in a hurry. Avoid getting caught up in office politics or malicious gossip. Someone could be quick to repeat your words out of context. A loved one may refuse to discuss a sensitive issue.

11. WEDNESDAY. Mixed. You need to be extra well prepared for any business meeting. A certain individual could be in a faultfinding mood; you need to be word perfect. Double-check that you have all necessary paperwork and other materials before leaving for an appointment. It can be difficult to adjust to a new boss at first. You may feel that this person is making changes just for the sake of ensuring that their presence is felt. Try not to let your own routine suffer from too much disruption. This is a favorable time for making long-term financial plans. Invest in a private pension scheme if your employer does not provide one.

12. THURSDAY. Useful. This is a busy day for Sagittarius professionals, especially those who are self-employed. The key to success lies in being well organized so that minor matters do not get overlooked. Make a list of the day's tasks, then check them off as you go. In this way it should be easier to set priorities. You can be called upon to resolve a dispute. Your innate sense of fair play should come in handy. A new relationship may be slow getting off the ground because of work commitments on both sides. Try to agree on at least one evening you can spend together. Rely on past experience to help solve a personal dilemma.

13. FRIDAY. Fair. This morning is the most productive part of the day. You can bring new energy and dynamism to bear on a current project. This is not a time when you need to hesitate to take the lead or push forward your own proposals. A pay raise may be approved if you are prepared to push for it, but realize that it is not going to be handed to you on a silver platter. Going for a promotion can land you in a highly competitive situation. Later in the day can be a good time for socializing. You may feel the need to switch off completely from work matters. Choose the company of those people whose conversation is stimulating.

14. SATURDAY. Changeable. A personal item which you recently loaned out could be returned to you in a poor condition. Make a mental note not to lend your belongings to this person ever again. If you live with family members or roommates, this can be a good time for making new arrangements concerning joint bills. Make sure that you are neither paying more nor less than your fair share. House rules may need to be discussed and revised when everyone is present. Sagittarius singles should think carefully about letting a friendship develop into a romance. Keep in mind that many a love affair comes to an end, whereas a friendship can last for a lifetime.

15. SUNDAY. Good. This is a sociable day for most Sagittarius people. If you have recently ended a relationship, now is the time to pick up the thread of your social life again. Under current conditions you can learn who your true friends are. A display of loyalty and affection is sure be touching. A wish you have secretly been nurturing could be gratified today. Activities centering around a club or other organization can be fun. Raising money for a worthwhile cause should be easier than you expect, and more fun as well. Introduce a new partner to your closest friends; you should get a unanimous vote of approval.

16. MONDAY. Unsettling. A promised letter or check is unlikely to turn up in today's mail. You may be put in a position where you have no choice but to be angry. This is a time when others are quick to take advantage if you are too easygoing or forgiving. Guard against getting impatient if caught in heavy traffic; there is a greater risk of an accident, which could be your fault. There is also a possibility of running out of cash at an inconvenient time. Be sure to have a little extra money tucked away in your wallet. Appointments are likely to be postponed or canceled altogether. Put aside difficult work matters and make a fresh start on them tomorrow.

17. TUESDAY. Unpredictable. Your routine is likely to vary from the norm. You may be asked to take on certain tasks which are new to you. A superior may have more faith in your abilities than you have. Do not shy away from opportunities for advancement because of fear of failure. You never know what you can do until you try; you may discover hidden talents in yourself. In romance this is a time when it is probably best to keep a low profile; let the other person run after you. It is not usual in the Sagittarius nature to play hard to get, but subtle measures can be more effective than being too obvious or overly enthusiastic.

18. WEDNESDAY. Satisfactory. Self-motivation should come easily to you. In fact, you will prefer to be left to get on with a job by yourself. Anyone breathing down your neck is likely to cramp your style. You may be trusted with confidential information. Someone's faith in you can be flattering; give them your loyalty in return. In a personal relationship this is a good time to discuss a matter which has been bothering you for a while. One problem may have been magnified by keeping it to yourself for too long. Give a loved one the chance to dispel suspicions and so put your mind at rest. There is probably a simple explanation to what seems confusing.

19. THURSDAY. Variable. Working with children can be challenging, but you will have some especially rewarding moments. A project which requires creative input may take longer than you anticipated. Not every idea turns out to be a good one, but perseverance can pay off. Inspiration is likely to win through at the end of the day. This is a favorable time for buying or making new clothes for yourself. Feeling good about the way you look can do wonders for your self-confidence. If you decide to try a new hairstyle or color, make sure that you ask for advice in advance. There may be some hidden extra expenses. A night out can be fun but costly. Check the newspaper for free or low-cost alternatives.

20. FRIDAY. Difficult.   Friction within a close relationship may come to a head. Although your heart may sink at the thought of a showdown, keep in mind that this is probably the only way to clear the air. Try not to get too upset so that you avoid saying things you later regret. A casual romance needs to be either ended or put on a firmer footing. This is not a time when you should leave someone dangling. Try to be honest when it comes to talking about what you expect from a partner. Financially you could have to cut back in a number of areas. A friend who is well off is unlikely to understand your anxieties.

21. SATURDAY. Slow.   If you need to economize, make a point of staying away from a shopping mall. You can save money simply by not putting yourself in temptation's way. Buy only essentials at the supermarket. Young children may need more of your time and energy. If you do not feel equal to the task, rope in some helping hands or ask your partner to take over for a few hours. You could benefit from some time to yourself. This is not a favorable time for any type of gambling, even on what is touted as a sure thing; you could suffer heavy losses. Keep your aspirations within reason if you want to achieve financial stability as well as personal satisfaction.

22. SUNDAY. Sensitive.   There is no accounting for other people's moods. A friend may pull out of a long-standing arrangement with no satisfactory explanation or apology. Someone close to you can be hard to comprehend. You have to accept that you are being kept at arm's length at the moment for reasons best known to others. This is not a good time for being too demanding in any of your personal relationships. The more you want, the less someone is prepared to give. The best approach is to make your own plans for the day. The best company is a friend who always accepts you just as you are, or a pet if your friend is unavailable.

23. MONDAY. Uncertain. Sagittarius commuters can expect to have a difficult start to the day. Travel may be disrupted, making you late for work or for an appointment. Changes to your usual routine are unavoidable. In your business dealings this is a time when you should avoid trying to complete certain matters by telephone. A certain client is sure to respond better in a face-to-face meeting. Agreements of all kinds need to be confirmed in writing as soon as possible; otherwise someone may change their mind. Do not confide personal details to someone who is no more than an acquaintance. You could learn the hard way that they are indiscreet or unsympathetic.

24. TUESDAY. Demanding. Administrative matters are likely to take up a good deal of time. You may resent the amount of paperwork you are expected to shuffle. As a Sagittarius you are usually impatient with anything which smacks of red tape or bureaucracy. However, keep in mind that you probably cannot change the rules. It is in your own best interests to keep records and correspondence up to date. Meetings may run late because of petty disagreements or disputes. It can be tricky dealing with someone who seems unable to get to the point. This is a time to be guided by solid facts, not by hearsay. Rumors are almost certain to be untrue or, at best, half-truths.

25. WEDNESDAY. Fair. You may receive a surprising offer. It can be flattering to be sought after, but look carefully at what is being offered; it might not be as good as it sounds. Your long-term prospects must also be a consideration in any career decision. Guard against being swayed by financial benefits alone. If you are house hunting, confirm a mortgage rate before making an offer. Insurance is important, both on possessions and your life. If you are seeking a loan of any kind, shop around; interest rates may vary considerably. Spend time this evening with loved ones rather than going out with friends.

26. THURSDAY. Exciting. Recent efforts to advance your career are likely to bear fruit today. You may receive notification of a promotion or a substantial pay raise. This is a fortunate day for buying or selling property. All transactions are likely to go through without a hitch. If you are in the process of setting up your own business or applying for a personal loan, this can be a good time for securing financial backing. Find out if you qualify for a government grant. You may be able to go ahead with your plans sooner than you anticipate. This evening favors celebrating a special occasion such as an anniversary or a friend's birthday. Plan on being up later than usual.

27. FRIDAY. Confusing. Do not rely too much on other people's promises or assurances. Although their intentions may be sincere at the time, they could quickly forget what they say. It may be hard to forgive someone who lets you down without any warning, but at least you know where you stand on their list of priorities. In the workplace you may be called upon to sort out other people's problems or mistakes. One-to-one dealings need to be handled with extreme tact and diplomacy. A loved one can make a fuss about a matter which you regard as unimportant. Do not dismiss their concerns; try to understand as best you can and help arrive at a solution.

28. SATURDAY. Deceptive. If you are embarking upon a new romance, guard against raising your hopes too high or too quickly. You may still be seeing your new partner through rose-colored glasses. Ignore their obvious faults only at your own peril. A friend's well-meaning warning about someone who seems wrong for you should be heeded. If you are shopping for special items today, compare prices. There is a greater risk that you will end up paying too much. Make sure that you keep receipts and guarantees. A restaurant meal may prove unsatisfactory; ask for a reduction to your bill, or refuse to leave a tip.

29. SUNDAY. Variable. Part of the day has to be devoted to routine domestic tasks. Do not let others off the hook when it comes to household chores. Insist on a fair distribution of labor. This should be a quiet day on the whole. You will enjoy just watching television or puttering around at home. A friend or neighbor may drop by unannounced later in the day. They are unlikely to outstay their welcome if they sense that you are not in a very hospitable mood. Duty to family members should not be shirked; someone is hoping to hear from you more than you realize. Encourage youngsters to stand on their own two feet.

30. MONDAY. Unsettling. You might not be feeling at your physical best. A minor ailment can make you uncomfortable but not ill enough to justify taking time off. Getting through the day's tasks can be difficult. You may have a tendency to be absent-minded, or your concentration may wander at a critical moment. Extra rest could prove helpful. Do not rely too much on your memory. Make a note of important information while it is fresh in your mind. Also jot down appointments and social engagements on your calendar. Keep a copy of important correspondence that you send. Anticipate delays in travel after dark. You will be happiest at home tonight.

JULY

1. TUESDAY. Manageable. Someone who has been difficult to deal with lately may test your patience again today. Try to rise above the temptation to ignore them. This is a good time for tackling problems head-on; there is a greater chance of being able to resolve differences stemming from a personality clash. The day favors dealings with foreign contacts and with people from your past. Matters finalized today should prove lucrative. You may be able to combine a business trip with a pleasurable vacation. This evening lends itself to intellectual activities such as a trip to the theater or viewing an exhibition of an artistic nature.

2. WEDNESDAY. Slow. In the office you may have to cover for an absent colleague, which can make your workload greater than usual. A personal project may have to be put on the back burner for now. If you are taking messages for someone, be sure to immediately write them down word for word; this way you can be sure of passing on the correct information. You may have a tendency to be absentminded or forgetful about small details, so do not rely on your memory. Put this evening aside for relaxation. A loved one is looking forward to your company at home, especially if you have not spent much time together recently.

3. THURSDAY. Mixed. This morning is the best part of the day for work which involves close liaison with a colleague. Seek assistance or advice about a work matter which has you stumped; new input can get the ball rolling again. Avoid taking on too much all at the same time; you could end up putting yourself under unnecessary pressure. Now is the time to practice the art of delegating. Later in the day favors working alone, especially on projects which require close attention to detail and focused concentration. Intimate conversation with a loved one this evening could reveal the source of recent problems; do not shy away from doing all that you can to resolve them.

4. FRIDAY. Variable. Joint finances require some attention. Either you or your partner may have been overspending recently; now is the time to rework your budget for the remainder of the month. Careful planning now means that you can avoid having to dip into your savings or adding to your credit card debt. This is a day when you should avoid discussing your personal life with anyone other than a very close friend. Do not risk becoming the object of gossip; exercise some extra caution. Social invitations for this evening and the weekend are likely to be numerous. Sagittarius people usually love to party, but make sure that you also set aside some time for yourself on this spirited holiday.

5. SATURDAY. Useful. If you go out shopping you may be tempted to spend more than you can afford. Sagittarius people are known for a tendency toward extravagance, but this is a time to be sensible if not stingy. You will be glad that you did not spend when you have to meet other bills later in the month. Make a point of paying for purchases with cash rather than credit cards. In this way you are more likely to be realistic about how much things cost and how fast the cost adds up. Later in the day is a good time to get together with your closest friends. Accept a party invitation; it could be the perfect place for meeting new people of the opposite sex.

6. SUNDAY. Fair. Even if you have definite views concerning religion or spirituality, this is a time when you may find yourself changing some long-held opinions. Plans for the day can go awry when someone opts out of an arrangement. Aim to keep flexible. Do not put too much faith in someone who has often been unreliable in the past. Spend less time with a certain individual who is a drain on your mental or emotional energy. You will get most satisfaction from being with those who share your interests and outlook. If you want a favor, first try diplomatically asking for it outright. If that does not work, a heavy dose of flattery could be effective.

7. MONDAY. Misleading. If you are starting a new job or project you could find yourself thrown in at the deep end. People may take for granted that you know more than you do. You might not get an opportunity to ask all of the necessary questions. Your best approach is to proceed slowly, learning as much as you can until others are ready to help out. Business meetings of all kinds can be tricky and are almost sure to run over schedule. Some agenda items may have to be postponed until another time if it proves impossible to reach unanimous agreement. A proposal of your own may be voted down. Legal matters can be confusing; make sure that you understand all the clauses in the small print before signing any contract.

8. TUESDAY. Demanding. On this demanding day you have to be well organized in order to get through even half of your workload. Make an extra effort to prioritize. You may resent the amount of time you have to devote to work at the moment, especially if you cannot see a light at the end of the tunnel. If your personal life is suffering as a result of your professional commitments, look for ways to reorganize your working time so that you are more efficient. You might decide to postpone a social arrangement with friends this evening in favor of staying home with a good book and going to bed earlier than usual.

9. WEDNESDAY. Good. If you have not yet taken your summer vacation this is a good day for finalizing your plans. If you are able to go away on short notice there is a greater chance of finding a real travel bargain. If your business involves traveling abroad, do not put off applying for a visa or to renew your passport. If you are on the road today you could strike up an interesting conversation with a fellow passenger; this may lead to a new friendship or business relationship. This is an especially fortunate day for the Sagittarius who is self-employed. Outstanding invoices can be settled, which should ease the cash flow situation, and new orders can be finalized.

10. THURSDAY. Easygoing. This is a lucky day if you are interviewing for a new job or for a promotion. Hold out for the salary you know you deserve; there is a lot to be said for recognizing your own worth. A reward for your recent efforts or achievements at work may come your way. Praise from a superior can boost your morale or revive your flagging motivation. Financial backing for a new business venture should be easier to secure than you expect. If you work on commission you may be able to finalize a major deal. Later in the day favors an official or formal function of any kind, especially a dance or dinner party. Be sure to look your best tonight.

11. FRIDAY. Challenging. This is a busy end to the working week. Hopes of getting away early for the weekend may be squashed. Your workmates are under as much pressure as you are. This may help to stir up arguments or disputes as tension mounts, but try to take them in stride. Do not attach too much importance to criticisms blurted out in the heat of the moment. Someone is probably just letting off steam and may apologize voluntarily later on. Written work of all kinds can be more time consuming than you bargain for. Sagittarius students who are nearing exam time should now buckle down to reviewing for the big test.

12. SATURDAY. Stressful. A new romance which got off to a promising start may come to an end as quickly as it began. You may now realize that your expectations were too high to begin with. If you are left feeling rejected, it is important to seek the support and affirmation of close friends and family members. With their help you should find it easier to put the affair behind you. This is not a time for keeping personal anxieties to yourself. The Sagittarius tendency to put on a brave face is not always appropriate or helpful. You may not be at your competitive best if participating in a sports contest. The important thing is to be a graceful winner or loser; play for fun.

13. SUNDAY. Confusing. Although you may feel that a friend is not being entirely honest with you, this is not a good time for a confrontation. Even after a long talk with this person you will probably come out none the wiser. Others are keeping their own counsel at the moment; it is up to you to respect their right to do so. They will confide in you when they are ready. A social event today may cost far more than you had bargained for; be sure to allow for hidden extras. Avoid lending money to a friend unless you can afford to wait a long time to be repaid. The same can be said about personal belongings; something you loan out may be returned to you in poor condition or possibly not at all.

14. MONDAY. Lucky. The working week gets off to a promising start. You may finally be able to bring a long-standing project to a satisfying conclusion, although some small details may need to be finalized at at a later. Do not bank on any new contract or deal until you have the necessary signatures. For Sagittarius singles, this is a lucky day for romance. Someone who has been a secret admirer may now find a way of letting you know how much they like you. You have nothing to lose and everything to gain by agreeing to a date. Give a child in your family the help and encouragement they need to overcome shyness or to improve in a sport.

15. TUESDAY. Starred. This promises to be an enjoyable day at work. A new challenge could be just what you need, especially if work has seemed boring or repetitive lately. If you work as part of a large department, this is a good time to meet with colleagues. Clear communication contributes to a cheerful working atmosphere. Colleagues who are on vacation or are out sick will appreciate your efforts to keep them up to date. If you are going out today, allow extra time for your journeys; transportation may prove unreliable, particularly if you have a tight schedule. If eating out this evening, choose a restaurant which is cheap, cheerful, and noted for its salads or other light menu choices.

16. WEDNESDAY. Exciting. Sagittarius people are usually not shy and retiring. Today, though, you should allow yourself to blow your own trumpet long and loud. In this way you will get the recognition you richly deserve. Push your own ideas in the workplace, even if they seem farfetched or unconventional to your associates. You could make someone sit up and think. Others seem willing to follow your lead at the moment. Enjoy being a trendsetter. This is a good time for buying new clothes or accessories. Bring your wardrobe up to date; choose something in the latest fashion or color. A new look can do wonders for your self-confidence as well as attracting favorable attention.

17. THURSDAY. Rewarding. The day gets off to a cheerful start. A letter or card in the mail may have news of a loved one who lives abroad or is away on vacation. For Sagittarius business people this is a good day for doing a lot of work over the telephone. You should be able to tie up loose ends which do not require a face-to-face meeting. If you are interviewing for a job or taking an examination today you should find that your advance preparation pays off; the questions are likely to be straightforward. Any sort of academic work can be satisfying, whether it is for the purpose of getting a specific job or just to satisfy your own intellectual interests.

18. FRIDAY. Calm. You can work at your own pace. Someone who recently has been breathing down your neck should now back off and give you more autonomy, which is sure to suit the freedom-loving side of your Sagittarius nature. You should be on an even keel financially at the moment. If extra cash comes in, resist the temptation to spend it all at once; put some aside for that proverbial rainy day. If you find it hard to save on a regular basis, this is a favorable time for increasing your tax withholding as a means of forced savings. Plan a relaxing end to the week. Arrange to have dinner at home with someone you would not want to live without. Schedule a get-together with friends for the weekend.

19. SATURDAY. Stressful. If you have a family to look after you may feel overworked and underappreciated. It may seem that you never really get time off. It is up to you not to let loved ones take your services for granted. If help is not forthcoming, it is probably better to come right out and ask for it rather than silently play the role of martyr. An argument with a brother or sister could be in the cards. Resist the temptation to exaggerate in order to prove a point; understatement may be more convincing.

Young children can wear you out. Use all of your creative skills to keep them occupied and out from under your feet.

20. SUNDAY. Variable. This morning is an ideal time to sleep late, especially if you have been burning the candle at both ends recently. You probably need to recharge your batteries. A particularly vivid dream is worth writing down; the symbolism could be revealing once you ponder it or discuss it with someone close to you. Keep household chores to a minimum. Plans for a lazy afternoon may be ditched when you get a better offer. An unexpected telephone call can spur you into action on the tennis court or poolside. A friend with mechanical knowledge may be able to fix a problem you are having with your car; this could save you the hassle and expense of a garage bill.

21. MONDAY. Deceptive. The working week is apt to start off with a stack of administrative work. Most of this is tedious but necessary. Make a mental note to keep your filing and correspondence more up to date once you have cleared the backlog. For Sagittarius employers, this is a good time to hire temporary staff to get you through a busy period. If you are taking a temporary job, ask for a written contract stating the terms and salary. Money which is owed to you can be slow coming in. Now is the time to chase it up. If you are unemployed, make sure that you claim all the government benefits to which you are entitled.

22. TUESDAY. Disquieting. This can be a frustrating time if you are in the process of trying to sell property. The contract may be subject to delays. A prospective purchaser may pull out at the last moment, putting you back to square one. If you have found a property to buy, it may be worth paying for an independent survey. The faults which come to light could make you think twice about going ahead. All is probably not calm on the home front. Friction between you and a family member can cast a cloud over the evening. Brace yourself for an emotional scene with someone who is angry at themselves but taking out their anger on you.

23. WEDNESDAY. Tranquil. Being at home can be relaxing. Do your chores at a comfortable pace, maybe listening to some music or a talk show as you work. Time to yourself gives you a chance to think through an issue which is close to your heart but tugging at your emotions. If you have the option to work from home rather than going to the office, this is a good day for doing so. You will get more done if you minimize the chance of interruptions. This is a lucky time for finding rental accommodations. This may come through word of mouth, perhaps from a colleague. A lazy evening at home will probably appeal more than going out on the town.

24. THURSDAY. Good.   This is an especially productive day for Sagittarius people who depend on creative skills at work. Focus on new ideas as soon as possible; they are almost sure to bear fruit. If your work involves communicating with the public in any way, you should be able to make a definite impact on those you need to impress. You could get a lucky break just by being in the right place at the right time. This is also a good time for catching up with personal correspondence. Getting back into the habit of writing letters can save on your telephone bill. A night out can be fun this evening providing you do not overindulge in food or drink.

25. FRIDAY. Mixed.   You are apt to start off the day feeling sluggish or in low spirits. For Sagittarius singles, a recent disappointment in love may still be weighing heavily. Your best approach now is to get back into the social swing with renewed determination. Someone who always sparks your sense of humor is worth seeking out; laughter is the tonic you need right now. If life seems to be all work and no play, make a point of arranging some social activity for the weekend, especially if you live alone. The movies or the theater can be a good starting point for a night out; try to get your tickets in advance.

26. SATURDAY. Challenging.   You can expect a busy schedule today. Fortunately you thrive on this; it suits you better than having too little to do. You should be able to race through your usual chores at home and then participate without a guilty conscience in activities with your friends. If you are married you may want to socialize independently. A certain friend might be glad for the opportunity to see you alone for a change. Exercise caution if you become involved in a discussion about religion or politics. There is a greater risk of unintentionally offending someone you do not know well but hope to get to know better.

27. SUNDAY. Changeable.   A minor health problem may be starting to worry you. Do not try to ignore it; make a promise to yourself to call the doctor for an appointment tomorrow. This is a good time to consider alternative health treatments, such as acupuncture or homeopathy, for conditions which have failed to respond to conventional medicine. Whatever medical help you seek, choose a practitioner who comes recommended rather than picking one at random. Get some physical exercise, especially if you are sedentary during the week. If the weather is fine, outdoor sports should appeal to you. Avoid rich foods this evening, and try to keep alcohol to a minimum.

28. MONDAY. Disconcerting. This is unlikely to be an easy start to the working week. The first priority for Sagittarius employees is to arrive at work on time if not a little early. Someone in authority may choose to take you to task regarding punctuality if you are late. A superior may prove impossible to please today. Keep in mind that this probably says more about their character than it does about your professional abilities; try not to become discouraged or downhearted. Higher-ups may be under pressures that you know nothing about. If a friend comes to you with their problems, be willing to listen even if you cannot come up with the solutions that they want to hear.

29. TUESDAY. Difficult. Today is likely to be no easier than yesterday. Your best approach is to stay cool rather than letting pressure get the better of you. If you stay calm in a crisis you will impress the people who matter and at the same time get the results that you are aiming to achieve. This is a time when others respond warmly to your Sagittarius charm and optimism. A job interview can be taxing, but this does not necessarily mean that you will not be offered the job. Being able to think on your feet could win the day. Try to put this evening aside for your partner or other loved ones; someone may be feeling neglected and underappreciated.

30. WEDNESDAY. Easygoing. Pressure at work is likely to ease off. You should be able to meet a deadline with time to spare. If you are self-employed this is a good day for going over your accounts. A meeting with your accountant or bank manager may also be helpful. A tax-saving idea is worth investigating further. This is also a good time for bringing your insurance needs up to date. Consider extending the coverage on your home contents to include recent purchases of technology equipment or jewelry. Also make sure that you have sufficient life insurance, especially if you are currently the main breadwinner in your family. Tuck away a little extra money in your wallet or safe hiding place to be used, if necessary, for emergency purposes.

31. THURSDAY. Pleasant. Morale in the workplace is likely to be high. A new colleague with a good sense of humor and a fresh outlook can be a tonic for everyone. Sagittarius singles may strike up a new romance with someone met through work. Starting off a relationship with professional interests in common is sure to be a plus. This is a good day for business get-togethers of all kinds. Being able to discuss your work with others in the same field can be enlightening. There could be good news on the financial front for your partner, perhaps a pay raise or a bonus. You are sure to benefit from their generosity. Make weekend plans tonight so that you are not disappointed.

AUGUST

1. FRIDAY. Demanding. If you are spending time with young children your reserves of patience are apt to be strained. Concentrate on striking the right balance between necessary discipline and gentleness. Keep in mind that losing your temper with youngsters is always counterproductive; you will only wind up becoming angry at yourself if you lash out at them. You need some adult company; invite a friend or neighbor to go out for lunch or dinner. If there is a problem on your mind which you find impossible to discuss with anyone close to you, consider the option of a counselor. Sagittarius workers may end the workweek feeling physically and emotionally drained. Make an extra effort to switch gears for the weekend.

2. SATURDAY. Mixed. Long-distance traveling is subject to delays. If you are leaving on vacation allow extra time; there could be road detours or traffic jams all along the way. Be sure that all your luggage is clearly labeled; there is a greater risk of it going astray. Take out insurance to guard against lost or stolen items. If you drive in town it may take a while to find a parking space. However, resist the temptation to park illegally; you could be fined or have your car towed away. Do not drive this evening if you know you are going to be drinking. Friends make the best company after dark.

3. SUNDAY. Variable. Entertaining guests at home can be fun. It may be difficult to break the ice at first with someone who is an acquaintance rather than a friend. As a Sagittarius you are probably an excellent host, enabling you to soon find a way of putting guests at their ease. If you are learning a new skill, avoid practice lessons with a loved one. Trying to impress them creates the classic scenario for an argument or, at the least, strained nerves. You may not be content to spend the entire day at home. This afternoon favors visiting a museum or art gallery or enjoying sporting activities of all kinds, either as a participant or a spectator. Be wary of getting too much sun.

4. MONDAY. Disquieting. The working week is unlikely to get off to a flying start. You may be suffering from Monday morning blues more than usual. Try to avoid crossing swords with a superior; a higher-up will not hesitate to pull rank on you in order to score points with their boss. The Sagittarius nature lends itself to impulsiveness, but keep repeating to yourself that this behavior is not always the wisest course of action. This is definitely not a time to walk out of a job unless you have definite alternatives already lined up. If you really want to change your job or your vocation, begin now to plan ahead. Avoid strenuous activities this evening; get to bed early.

5. TUESDAY. Productive. Career issues are dominant at the moment. This is an excellent time for sending off job applications if you are unemployed. Write to the companies you are interested in rather than waiting for them to advertise. Signing up with an employment agency could also be a good move; they may have several positions which would suit you. Any interview today is likely to go well. You might even be offered a job on the spot. Promotion prospects are good if you are satisfied in your current line of work. This can be an auspicious day for public speaking of all kinds. If your work involves dealing directly with the general public you should not have any trouble making a good impression. Humor can be a good tactic in all situations.

6. WEDNESDAY. Easygoing. Because you are unlikely to be under any significant pressure in your personal life, you can concentrate on your work interests. New business projects are well favored. This is an excellent time for a business merger, for taking on a new partner if you are self-employed, or for hiring temporary help. Being able to share responsibilities can make a big difference in the quality of your life. This is also a favorable time for contacting your parents, grandparents, or other relatives to arrange a family reunion. Check your calendar for forthcoming anniversaries or birthdays in your family circle.

7. THURSDAY. Buoyant. Conditions favor teamwork of all kinds. A brainstorming session can produce excellent ideas for a creative project you hope to start. The atmosphere in the workplace should be buoyant. If you are at home you should have ample free time for your own interests. Going to lunch with a friend can be a pleasant break. Make a point of reading the newspaper in order to catch up with events in the world around you. As a caring Sagittarius you may decide to lend support to a political or social reform campaign, perhaps by writing letters or taking part in a peaceful march or other demonstration. Your enthusiasm for humanitarian issues can have a strong impact on other people.

8. FRIDAY. Changeable.   This is a busy end to the workweek. Your services are apt to be in demand throughout the day. Be careful that your own work does not suffer in your eagerness to help someone else. It may prove impossible to tie up all of the loose ends of a business deal today. Although this can be frustrating, there is no point trying to force someone's hand; next week there is a better chance of getting a definite answer. Arrangements for this evening may fall through; have an alternative plan up your sleeve. The evening favors a group night out rather than a twosome. Try to find someone to introduce you to an intriguing newcomer.

9. SATURDAY. Difficult.   You might be tempted to pull out of an arrangement with a friend, but you risk doing so at heavy cost. Someone is relying on you far more than you realize. This is a time when it is important to honor each and every commitment you have made. Someone who challenges your principles could bring out your argumentative side. Count to ten before launching a verbal attack; there is a greater risk that you do not have all the facts. You are apt to regret being aggressive verbally and certainly physically. You may feel generally dissatisfied with your current situation. Enjoy your own company rather than joining in with others unwillingly.

10. SUNDAY. Deceptive.   It is unusual for anyone born under the sign of Sagittarius to suffer from pessimism. However, there is a risk that yesterday's difficult mood may continue into today. Take some time to work out exactly what it is that is getting you down. You may be able to trace your negative feelings back to a specific incident. Understanding the cause can help you deal with the problem in a constructive way. In the meantime you may still prefer to be left to your own devices. Do not allow yourself to be pushed into an outing or other social arrangement if you know that you will not enjoy yourself. An older relative can offer sound advice once you are willing to listen.

11. MONDAY. Sensitive. The working week gets off to a quiet start. Work which requires close concentration may demand most of your attention. This is a favorable time for meetings of a confidential nature. You should be able to get certain issues sorted out off the record, preventing a small problem from escalating into a large one. If you are involved in any type of litigation, this is a time for brain, not brawn. Negotiations of all kinds need to be handled with the greatest tact and delicacy. If you are contemplating initiating any course of legal action, be sure to seek professional advice first; you may change your mind when you find out how much court action will cost you in both time and money.

12. TUESDAY. Fair. For Sagittarius singles who are footloose and fancy-free this is a good time for considering work abroad. Seasonal work is favored. A job move of a more permanent nature could create some problems you have not anticipated. It is important to do all your homework before making any irrevocable decisions. In the workplace this is a good time for exerting the power of your personality if someone is attempting to block your forward progress. You may have more influence with certain superiors than you imagine. Recognize your own strengths rather than focusing on your weaknesses.

13. WEDNESDAY. Productive. If you are on your summer break you may feel like getting down to some work today. Make a start on a project which has to be ready later in the year. Now is a good time for ordering supplies, especially if you suspect prices will increase after the summer. Reading for pleasure as well as academic purposes is apt to appeal to you. If money is short there is probably no need to buy books; check out your local library instead. While you are there you might want to find out about evening classes to be offered in the fall. You might decide to sign up for a class you dropped in school, sensing that you will enjoy it more the second time around.

14. THURSDAY. Manageable. If you are unemployed there is a greater chance of being offered some temporary work today. You are likely to be paid with cash in hand. If you are finding it hard to make ends meet at the moment, help may be forthcoming from a relative or close friend. There is no need to feel embarrassed about accepting a loan or even a gift of money; you would do the same for them if the situation were reversed. If you know that you will not be able to pay all your creditors before the end of the month, now is the time to decide who gets what amount. Try to bring your household bills up to date so that you do not risk having your electricity or phone turned off.

15. FRIDAY. Rewarding. This should be a particularly lucrative day for Sagittarius people who work in sales. A customer who refused you an appointment in the past may now agree to see you; this could turn out to be a real feather in your cap. This is also a good time to apply for a promotion or a better paid job; you should at least end up on the short list. An employment agency can come up with some attractive propositions for you. Romance is in the air for Sagittarius singles. You may be attracted to someone you meet through work, but guard against playing it too cool. Someone may need encouragement; let your interest in them show.

16. SATURDAY. Variable. This is a good time for adding to a favored collection. Browse in secondhand stores; you may make quite a find. In looking around markets or antique shops there is a greater chance of coming upon a genuine bargain because the rarity of the item is not well known. Fresh flowers can brighten up your home. If you are entertaining, make a floral arrangement for the table. And flowers in a guest room are a thoughtful touch if you have friends staying overnight with you. There may be a phone call or a relayed message from someone in your past. You might not know at first if this is good or bad news; meeting face-to-face is the only way to find out for sure.

17. SUNDAY. Calm. This promises to be a lazy, pleasant day. If the weather is fine this is a good time for a barbeque; invite your neighbors to join in. Children can be especially pleasant company, guaranteed to break the ice with any stranger or new acquaintance. There may also be news of a birth or a baby on the way for someone close to you. This is a favorable day for celebrating any special occasion, especially a wedding anniversary or a new addition to the family circle. Indulge your extravagant side and buy some prime steaks or vintage champagne. A long telephone call to someone special can do a lot to keep your spirits soaring this evening.

18. MONDAY. Disquieting. Business transactions at a distance can be tricky to pull off. A language barrier may have to be overcome; employ the services of a top translator or interpreter. If you are sending important documents or artwork by mail, it would be wise to send them registered and pay for a return receipt. There is a greater risk of a package going astray which will be difficult to replace. Administrative errors may come to light at work. Be ready to assume the responsibility for any mistake which is clearly yours. Trying to pass the buck will almost certainly be noneffective. Domestic chores are likely to take up most of your time this evening. Stock up on groceries for the week ahead.

19. TUESDAY. Fair. Your trip to work is subject to delays this morning. Sagittarius commuters are advised to leave home earlier or later than usual in order to miss the morning chaos. Working from home is a clever option. Take extra care with written work, especially if it has to be endorsed by a superior. A higher-up is in the mood for splitting hairs. Sagittarius employers should make a point of checking out references before taking on a new staff member. Their work history may not be all that they claim. Charity work of all kinds is likely to be successful, especially if you are raising funds. An anonymous donation can be a most welcome surprise.

20. WEDNESDAY. Easygoing. A chance to make extra money could be in the cards. If you are self-employed you are more likely to get new work by referral from satisfied customers. A pay dispute could be settled, with back pay to come. This is a favorable time for buying new furniture. Take advantage of credit in the larger stores as long as it is interest-free. Brighten up your place of work with some plants or cheerful prints for the walls. Later in the day is a starred time for creative projects of all kinds, particularly sewing or writing. A new romance is likely to start off first as a friendship; be content to let the relationship grow at its own pace.

21. THURSDAY. Mixed. Guard against getting your priorities wrong. Sooner or later you have to face a problem and find a way to resolve it. Having it nag at your conscience or disturb your sleep is not a good option to choose. Instead, select a potentially worthwhile solution and give it a try. You will feel better for the effort, even if it is not totally successful. You may feel a little sluggish. It is time to commit to a regular exercise program in order to improve your energy and overall health. Doing a little but doing it often can be the most effective way to get fit. You might decide to take up a new sport which you can learn and enjoy together with your mate or partner.

22. FRIDAY. Disconcerting. Do not leave any valuables lying around in your workplace, especially if strangers often pass through. There is a greater risk of having money or personal belongings stolen or borrowed without your permission. Children can be the source of extra expense. Getting them ready for the new school term can make a bit dent in your bank balance. You may have to put off buying items which you need for yourself until a later date. In a personal relationship an old argument could flare up once again. You may be forced to realize that you have not yet resolved the basic issue. Underlying problems will remain hidden until you are both prepared to admit and to face your true grievances.

23. SATURDAY. Unsettling. Sagittarius people are known for honesty and directness. However, this is a time when you should keep in mind that not everyone takes your comments in the spirit you intend. Being too outspoken can offend or upset someone close to you. Your best approach is to think before you speak. Trying to explain what you really meant may make matters even worse. You have a tendency to blame yourself too much for problems in a close relationship. There is nothing to be gained from punishing yourself; try to be as forgiving of yourself as you are toward other people. Double-check time and place for a social arrangement; you may have your wires crossed.

24. SUNDAY. Variable. Even if you had a late night you should still feel good this morning. A health problem may now be responding to new or more intense treatment. You may decide to get some exercise, such as swimming or jogging. Getting out into the countryside or the nearest park can blow away the cobwebs from your mind. Make an extra effort to maintain your good mood later in the day. Your partner or another loved one may not share your high spirits, pouring cold water on your enthusiasm for an outing or a special project. It is not always necessary to seek approval from others or their companionship. You can be quite content on your own if you allow yourself to be.

25. MONDAY. Cautious. You may find yourself out of favor with a superior at work. If there appears to be no specific reason, try to let the bad atmosphere wash over you. However, be quick to realize the danger of being made a scapegoat for recent mistakes. You might have to stick up for yourself; colleagues are likely to lend their support as well. The day's schedule may not run according to plan. Appointments are apt to be canceled at short notice. If you are trying to conduct business by phone make sure that you are speaking to the real decision maker; someone could be wasting your valuable time. Stay home tonight even if a good friend invites you out.

26. TUESDAY. Pleasant. Your working relationships are now back on an even keel. Being at work can seem more like pleasure than duty. Your sense of humor should get you through any tricky moments. You might realize that you have been taking certain work matters too seriously. A more lighthearted approach can turn negotiations in your favor. For Sagittarius singles this is a time when a new romance can start quickly and easily. You may feel you have known a new love interest for much longer than you actually have. If you have been going through a stressful time in an ongoing relationship, the tide is likely to turn today. You may even want to plan a second honeymoon or a ceremony to renew your vows.

27. WEDNESDAY. Satisfactory. This is an excellent day for business meetings of all kinds. Agreements can be much easier to finalize than you anticipate. A contract signed at this time is unlikely to present any further problems. Consider inviting a potential customer or employee out to lunch. Getting to know them in a less formal setting than the office can be revealing. For Sagittarius employees this is a propitious time for talking to the boss about a pay raise or job transfer. If you can back up your claim with solid facts and reasons they may see that you have a valid point. Loved ones can be in a generous mood this evening.

28. THURSDAY. Slow. You may be tempted to give someone advice concerning a personal matter. However, it would be smart to keep your opinions to yourself unless you are asked for them directly. Someone may accuse you of interfering or even sermonizing. Sometimes you just have to watch others learn by their own mistakes, no matter how much you wish you could pass on the benefit of your own experience. This can be especially testing for Sagittarius parents of teenage children. Even with them, your best policy is simply to lend moral support while they work out a problem for themselves. Do not choose this evening to discuss money matters with your partner or to pay bills.

29. FRIDAY. Fair. If you are paid at the end of the month, find time today to work out next month's budget. Even if you normally are slapdash in the way you handle money, you should find that planning ahead is very helpful. Money may be going out faster than it is coming in at the moment. Come up with ways in which you can economize for the next few weeks; even small sacrifices can make a significant difference. This can be a lucky day for finding a last-minute bargain vacation in the sun. The Sagittarius itchy feet can be satisfied by a weekend break, perhaps to a distant city for some sightseeing and a change of culture and cuisine. Friends who live at a distance might be delighted to have you visit.

30. SATURDAY. Mixed. If you are thinking of returning to school this is a good time for applying. This may be purely for your own pleasure rather than being specifically related to work. As a Sagittarius you constantly need intellectual stimulus of some kind. If you are single this is not the time for beginning a relationship with someone who clearly does not share your views or outside interests. You are almost sure to become bored once the initial physical attraction has worn off. A certain friendship requires more effort on your part if you are going to remain close to one another. Do not make any definite social commitment without first consulting your mate or partner.

31. SUNDAY. Good. Parties of all kinds can be fun. Throw yourself into the spirit of the occasion. A formal occasion can be especially successful. A family get-together should go smoothly. A difficult relative should be more indulgent toward you. If you are planning a family outing be sure to choose a destination which is geared toward children. This is a good day for sports, whether you are a participant or spectator. Success is likely in both individual and team efforts. If you want to improve at a sport, this is a favorable time for some professional lessons. Learning a musical instrument can keep you engrossed for hours.

SEPTEMBER

1. MONDAY. Rewarding. This is likely to be a busy start to the week even though many Sagittarius workers have the day off. This morning can be a good time for a leisurely discussion with a loved one. This way the left hand will know what the right hand is doing. You may be called upon to drive a family member to a store or help in another way. If a neighbor or work colleague is moving, take it upon yourself to organize a collection for a going-away gift. You may be given some inside information concerning changes in the neighborhood. Do not be tempted to gossip; prove that your discretion can be relied upon. A night out with an old friend, or even an old flame, can bring back a lot of happy memories for you.

2. TUESDAY. Sensitive. Early in the day it will become obvious that a certain individual is in a difficult mood. Delay a planned conversation or request if you sense that the time is not right. Most Sagittarius people, as a fire sign, are blessed with excellent intuition. Make sure that you use yours today when it comes to making snap judgments. Personal insight could be more helpful than logic or reason untempered by feeling. Meetings of all kinds can be tricky. You might be outvoted on a certain issue which is close to your heart, but make sure that you at least have your say. Some personal hopes and wishes may take a long time in coming true; resolve to be optimistic as well as extra patient.

3. WEDNESDAY. Starred. This promises to be a productive day for you. It may even seem that you cannot put a foot wrong. If you work toward weekly targets you should be able to reach the goal today; you could even be set for a record week. Income for self-employed Sagittarius people is also likely to be higher than average. If you are unemployed, this is a good time to apply for state benefits. Any forms should be filled out in detail; ignore a question and you may delay the benefits due you. This can be a good time for lending support to a fund-raising event for a charity. Accept an invitation to a friend's gathering; you could meet someone special.

4. THURSDAY. Changeable. The morning is the more enjoyable part of the day. You may bump into someone you know while traveling to work. If you are using public transportation on a regular basis, now is a good time to invest in a season ticket or a weekly pass. Written work of all kinds should be straightforward even if there is a lot to get through. Be sure to make a backup copy of a document that you are creating; there is a greater danger of the original going astray. An older car may break down. Seriously consider whether it is worth spending any more money on repairs. If necessary, this is a good time to buy a current-model-year automobile at a reduced price.

5. FRIDAY. Deceptive. A relationship with someone special may not be working out the way you hope. Ask yourself if you have been too trusting or have expected too much too soon. There is a greater risk that you do not have all the facts about a certain situation. Someone may not be as independent as they have led you to believe; this could account for their frequent absences or unreliability. If you need to employ professional services of any kind, ask for a written estimate of costs; a verbal agreement is insufficient to guarantee the price. Shop around for a special purchase; prices and taxes may vary dramatically from one place to another.

6. SATURDAY. Uncertain. A quarrel or misunderstanding with a loved one this morning can get the day off to a stressful start. You might feel someone is making unreasonable demands on your time or affection. You are right not to respond to anything which smacks of emotional blackmail. In the long run you will gain more respect by sticking to your principles now rather than giving in just to keep the peace. Even if you have a busy schedule today, try to find time to visit a friend who is in a hospital or is convalescing at home. If you are mixing friends and workmates this evening, guard against talking shop; someone may end up feeling left out and uncomfortable.

7. SUNDAY. Unsettling. You may learn a lesson today about confiding in the wrong people. It may come to light that a certain individual has revealed what was supposed to be confidential information. Let your anger show rather than pretending that you do not care. The important lesson to be learned is not to trust this person again. Sagittarius singles need to guard against putting social activities on hold while waiting for the attentions of someone special. Do not sit around waiting for a telephone call; it might not come. Do not miss out on social opportunities which you would normally accept without a second thought.

8. MONDAY. Useful. This is an especially busy day for those who work in the caring professions, such as nursing or social work. You might have to put in a longer shift than usual, but the day is likely to have especially rewarding moments. This morning is the best time for clearing your desk of a backlog of minor matters put aside during busier times. Afterward, you can approach new projects with an uncluttered mind. If you work in a managerial capacity, very little time will be your own today. Expect to have to deal with a wide assortment of problems. A staff member may be dissuaded from quitting if you can support them through a difficult period in their personal life.

9. TUESDAY. Misleading. If you are trying to lose weight or give up an unhealthy habit this can be a difficult day for sticking to your resolve. Lunch with a friend or a business contact could put far too much temptation in your way. Promise yourself that you will start fresh tomorrow rather than abandoning your attempt altogether. Guard against raising your hopes too high with regard to a new job or a promotion. There is a greater risk of losing out to someone who has more experience or more personal pull. Remind yourself that this is not a reflection on your own abilities; there is no need to be downhearted. A friend may be too caught up with their current love life to find time for you; be patient for now.

10. WEDNESDAY. Pleasant. This can be a good day for shopping, especially for clothes or shoes. Take along a friend whose taste you admire. You may also find bargains if you are looking for jewelry or other accessories. You might decide to try out a new hairstyle or even change the color of your hair. Be sure to use a top-class beautician rather than experimenting on your own. This can also be a good day to shop for a gift for a friend; you are likely to find the ideal item. Someone who owes you money may repay you this afternoon. If you are looking for a part-time or evening job to boost your income you could hear of an opening by word of mouth. Cutting expenses could be more worthwhile than trying to work excessive hours.

11. THURSDAY. Calm. There should be a lull in business for you Sagittarius people who are self-employed. It is up to you to use your spare time constructively. For example, this is a good time to put your accounts in order. Make a point of sending out reminders for invoices which are overdue. Also bring your own household bills up to date. This evening favors inviting friends for a meal or accepting an invitation to have dinner at their house.

You are apt to be in the mood to spend time with those people with whom you are most comfortable. A new relationship can settle into a firm and faithful friendship, which could lead to love.

12. FRIDAY. Mixed. Bills which arrive in today's mail might not be quite as high as you had expected. However, some unforeseen expenses could soon deplete any spare cash. You may have to do some economizing as far as your social life is concerned. Start by opting out of a get-together at an expensive restaurant that you know is well above your current spending limit. Others are more likely to go along with your suggestions of less expensive socializing. Entertaining at home does not have to cost a lot if you use your imagination. Take your time when shopping in the supermarket; stock up on the special offers that you know you will use, and make a point of buying fruit and vegetables which are in season.

13. SATURDAY. Disconcerting. This morning is a good time for returning telephone calls. Someone may be puzzling over why you have failed to get in touch with them recently; assure them that the oversight was not intentional. Catch up with your personal correspondence as well. This is a good time for having your car serviced, especially if you are planning a long trip in the near future. Be wary of buying anything secondhand if your technical knowledge is somewhat sketchy. Seek an expert opinion rather than just trusting to luck. You may be asked to add your name to a neighborhood petition or financially support a candidate for local office. An unexpected telephone call could change your plans for this evening.

14. SUNDAY. Changeable. Someone close to you may embark upon a relationship which you find hard to understand or accept. Remind yourself how different things can look from an outsider's viewpoint. It is important to try to empathize with how they are feeling; guard against sitting in judgment. A relationship which has been struggling along for some time may come to a final end. You may have to accept that staying friends will be impossible. Your best approach is to wipe the slate clean. Try to learn from your mistakes without punishing yourself. A family member can come to your emotional rescue if you need a shoulder to cry on.

15. MONDAY. Variable. You are apt to be more sensitive to criticism than usual. At work, you should make an extra effort to hear someone out rather than flying off the handle in self-defense. You will make life much easier for yourself if you can admit you were wrong about a recent incident. A genuine apology should quickly clear the air and put you back in good standing with your pride intact. If you have some leave due you, this is a good time for taking an extra day so that you have a long weekend break. Some small decorating jobs at home can be easy to do yourself with the help of a good how-to manual.

16. TUESDAY. Frustrating. If you have been trying to sell an item or your house for some time without results, consider a new approach. This is a good time for advertising in a different publication or on your own rather than through an agent. In this way you could also save yourself an expensive fee. The offer of a new job or a promotion can create a dilemma for you. If more money means spending more time away from your family, you might decide it is a wrong move. First discussion the decision with your loved ones in order to get your priorities straight. You might even consider taking a drop in salary in order to get into a line of work that offers more job satisfaction.

17. WEDNESDAY. Good. This is a lucky day if you are taking a test of any kind. There is no reason you should not sail through once you have conquered your initial nervousness. If you have not yet learned a skill that most other people have acquired, especially involving computers, arrange for some lessons. Lessons could make the perfect gift for a younger relative who has just begun to show an interest in technology. A job which provides a company car should be worth applying for. Working with children can be special fun. If you have not had much prior experience with the younger set you should find that you are now comfortably in your stride. This evening is a good time for introducing a new friend to your family.

18. THURSDAY. Tricky. Sagittarius people who rely on creativity at work cannot expect to have a very productive day. There is a greater risk of a mental block when it comes to dreaming up ideas for a new project. You may decide to abandon certain work altogether once you realize that it is never going to take shape in the way you had hoped. Learning any new skill may seem like a hopeless task, but try not to lose patience with yourself; you will win through in the end. Young children can be difficult to deal with and may show you up in public. To diffuse the situation, stay as calm and low-key as possible.

19. FRIDAY. Fair. If you have a spare room in your home this could be a good time to consider taking in a boarder. The extra money could make the difference between scraping along and having cash to spare. Make your terms and conditions clear in advance, and be sure to ask for references. If you share with one or more roommates you might find yourself craving more privacy. Maybe the time has come to look for a place by yourself or just with one other person. This evening is a favorable time for a formal function, especially if a speaker will cap the event. The knowledge you gain could start you off in an exciting new career direction.

20. SATURDAY. Changeable.   Domestic chores may take up a good part of today. Keep in mind how much better you will feel once you have put your surroundings in order. There is no point putting off dull tasks, such as ironing or cleaning; they will only mount up to unmanageable proportions. There may be cause for concern over a pet's health. Seek the opinion of your vet if you are worried. Most Sagittarius people are animal lovers, but think twice about giving a home to a pet if you know that it would not fit in with your current lifestyle. You may bump into someone you would rather avoid at a social function this evening. If you cannot avoid talking with them, at least make the conversation brief.

21. SUNDAY. Cautious.   If there is any sort of building or decorating work going on at home you need to be extra alert. Sagittarius people are known for a tendency toward clumsiness. There is a greater risk of injuring yourself if you are not concentrating totally on what you are doing. The important person in your life may not be in your good graces. They may be preoccupied with their own thoughts, making you feel neglected or unappreciated. Guard against being too demanding or you could unintentionally create a hostile atmosphere. This is a good time for going off on your own or spending time with your own family or friends.

22. MONDAY. Unsettling.   In the workplace you should avoid making decisions on behalf of other people. Even if you feel sure of your judgment at the time, you may still find that it was wrong. You do not have to come up with immediate answers. First check out the facts to your own satisfaction. If you constantly have to deal with a lot of administrative work, this is a good time to reorganize your filing system. Being able to lay your hands on papers at a moment's notice can save you a lot of time and stress. Try not to take any work home with you this evening. Your partner or another family member may need your undivided attention to help sort out a personal problem.

23. TUESDAY. Disquieting. This is a good time for checking up on your tax situation, especially if you are self-employed. There is a chance that you have been paying too much or too little. If you have not yet had a reply from an insurance claim, now is the time to look into it. Do not be put off with lame excuses; insist on speaking to the person in charge. The sunny Sagittarius nature means that you are usually at ease in any social situation, even when you do not know a lot of people. However, at an event later in the day you could find yourself wishing that you had stayed home. There is probably no harm in making your excuses and leaving soon after you arrive.

24. WEDNESDAY. Profitable. In your business dealings guard against laying all your cards on the table at once. Keep an ace up your sleeve, especially if you are trying to stay one step ahead of your competitors. The element of surprise can work in your favor. If you are hoping to establish your own business, this is a favorable time for seeking advice from others who have already taken a similar step; you could benefit greatly from their experience. In your personal relationships you are finally learning lessons from the past. Take pride that you are not repeating the same mistakes that once caused you heartache or grief.

25. THURSDAY. Fair. Check your bank balance before writing a check; there may not be enough left in your account to cover it. You could find yourself in an embarrassing situation if a check bounces. If you suddenly realize that you have overstretched financially, contact your bank immediately to make necessary arrangements. There are times when a debt situation seems to be getting out of hand. Do not bury your head in the sand. Instead, seek some professional advice to help you regain control of your finances rather than having them control you. Going to the movies with friends can be a pleasant evening.

26. FRIDAY. Manageable. You need to spend at least part of the day preparing for the month ahead. If you are starting a new job or school course you may feel overwhelmed at first by all that is ahead of you. However, keep in mind that you will find your stride as you go along; no one expects you to know everything right away. A long-distance journey can take longer than you expect. Make sure that you have some work with you or a good book to help pass the time. A fellow passenger can be entertaining company once you get talking. Legal matters are subject to postponements and other frustrating delays. Be sure to keep copies of all correspondence; you may need it as proof later.

27. SATURDAY. Exciting. This is a good weekend for hosting overnight guests. Showing people around your town can be educational as well as fun for everyone. There may be contact from a person you met on vacation earlier in the year. If you would like to renew your acquaintance with someone you knew only briefly, drop them a line. Cultural activities of all kinds are favored, especially a visit to a museum or art exhibition. A lecture or workshop on a subject which interests you could be fascinating, giving you plenty to think about. The opera or a classical concert can suit your mood even if you have to go alone.

28. SUNDAY. Slow. Sagittarius salespeople and others who work on weekends are unlikely to feel motivated today. You may be suffering the effects of a late night. A superior may seem intent on throwing their weight around. Do your best not to get caught up in any sort of power battle; you are almost sure to come out the loser. Some friction with an older relative may cast a cloud over the day. Try to accept that many of your differences are probably due to the generation gap. Make allowances in the hope that they will show you the same courtesy in return. Getting to bed early could be a wise move.

29. MONDAY. Pleasant. This is an excellent start to the workweek for Sagittarius employees. Recognition for recent achievements can make you feel as if all your efforts have been worthwhile. An extra cash bonus could be coming your way as well. If you are self-employed with an expanding business, this is a favorable time to consider moving to a more prestigious address. You may also want to allocate more money to your advertising budget, especially when it comes to promoting your business image. Career changes made at this time are likely to be worthwhile; follow your instincts. A romance with someone at work needs to be kept under wraps for a while.

30. TUESDAY. Starred. If you are unemployed it may be worth buying out-of-town newspapers today. The help-wanted sections could offer several possibilities which are worth following up. A former colleague may also let you know about a vacancy which would suit you. Do not hesitate to let someone with influence pull strings on your behalf. Sometimes it is a question of who you know rather than what you know. A person close to you may go to a lot of trouble to let you know how much you matter to them. Savor the moment of feeling special. A display of love or loyalty can help put problems into their true perspective. Stay in touch with friends at a distance.

OCTOBER

1. WEDNESDAY. Exciting. This is a very promising start to the new month. Exciting opportunity is right around the corner. Arrange your day around at least one social engagement. Friends you have not seen for a long time could get in touch today. You are apt to be in demand socially and may have to choose among several invitations for the weekend. Teamwork of all kinds should be more successful than tackling a project on your own. Take advantage of an opportunity to get together with others who are in your line of work, maybe at a demonstration or at lunch. Exchanging ideas and information is sure to be stimulating. Choose a local restaurant if you are going out this evening; do not stray too far from home.

2. THURSDAY. Calm. You are unlikely to be under any great pressure on the job. If you often have to work at a break-neck pace, this should come as a welcome relief. You have a chance to get to know a certain colleague much better, which can benefit the quality of your working relationship. It is in the Sagittarius nature to think long and hard about the future. This is a time when you should concentrate on making firm plans rather than just building dreams. You can make your own wishes come true; you do not have to wait for others to open doors for you. Activities centering around a club or association can be enjoyable later in the day.

3. FRIDAY. Changeable. Although most work matters have gone smoothly during the past few days, the week is likely to end on a sour note. A last-minute crisis can put you under the intense pressure you had hoped to avoid. A tightly organized schedule is almost sure to unravel as unforeseen demands on your time throw you out of kilter. The best policy is to keep plans for the day as flexible as possible. Do not try to pack in too many appointments; some could easily wait until next week. Married Sagittarius people going through a restless period may have trouble resisting the temptation to stray. However, this is a time when even the smallest lie is almost sure to catch up with you.

4. SATURDAY. Variable. This is a good time for cleaning out closets, drawers, or the attic. Guard against being too ruthless when it comes to throwing things away; you may later regret tossing out certain items which have sentimental value. Sagittarius people embarking upon a new romance should steer clear of talking about past relationships. Keep in mind that what matters is the here and now. This is a time to leave old hurts or grievances in the dust where they belong so that you can concentrate on the future. Make an extra effort to be environmentally conscious. Recycle all that you can, and also use as many recycled products as possible.

5. SUNDAY. Excellent. A new romance could benefit if you spend some time as a twosome today rather than mixing with other friends or family members. As a Sagittarius you are naturally outgoing and friendly, but keep in mind that it is difficult to develop intimacy if you are always surrounded by other people. Find out about each other's interests. You may also naturally exchange life histories. This is a perfect day for a traditional Sunday brunch with your family or other loved ones. Conversation is almost sure to turn toward happy memories of the past. You may receive a gift of money or jewelry. A family heirloom could now be passed to you for safekeeping.

6. MONDAY. Dynamic. The working week starts off at full speed. It may be helpful to arrive at your place of work a little earlier than usual. If you make a point of prioritizing the day's tasks you could be surprised by how much you accomplish. This is a good time for investing in new office equipment or more up-to-date technology. An advertising or publicity campaign is likely to produce a better response than you expect. For Sagittarius students this can be a busy but stimulating day, especially working on a written report. An advanced class should live up to your expectations. Fellow students can soon become firm friends.

7. TUESDAY. Quiet. If you are at home you will probably enjoy your own company. You need some peace and quiet to think through a personal matter. If you have been at other people's beck and call lately, now is the time to put your own needs first. This may mean having to say no to certain demands or requests which are made of you at home or at work. You should be able to do this without upsetting anyone. Sagittarius people who have recently ended a love affair can now begin to enjoy a new sense of independence. Enjoy the positive side of being single for a while, such as being able to please yourself.

8. WEDNESDAY. Manageable. Do a favor if a friend seeks you out, even if it is somewhat inconvenient. Keep in mind the times they have come to your rescue in the past. A colleague values your advice regarding an important job now in the works and will give you credit for successful results. This is a good time for activities which involve the younger generation. A discussion with ample give-and-take can be more effective than a lecture when it comes to putting across your newest ideas or stimulating other people to give your views a fair hearing. A friend may offer to treat you to a night out if they know you are a little short of money; accept their generosity without embarrassment.

9. THURSDAY. Difficult. If you make any purchases be sure to hold on to your receipts. If you have to return something that is faulty you may be refused a refund without proof of purchase. Having to deal with red tape of any kind is frustrating but unavoidable if you are eventually going to win what is rightfully yours. Refuse to take no for an answer. In the workplace this is a day when personal differences may interfere with the job you are assigned to do. You may have kindled someone's professional jealousy, but do not be pushed into feeling responsible for their inadequacies or insecurities.

10. FRIDAY. Mixed. Do not shy away from taking on unexpected responsibilities at work. This is a time when you can impress the right person with your ability to cope, even with tasks which are totally new to you. New challenges should also bring you greater job satisfaction despite no immediate financial reward. Gaining experience counts for a lot right now. You may have the chance to set the record straight regarding a recent misunderstanding with a brother, sister, or other family member. A housebound neighbor would probably appreciate your offer to run some errands. Sagittarius singles may encounter a romantic opportunity through a chance conversation.

11. SATURDAY. Disconcerting. No matter how much a certain friend has upset you, refrain from talking about them behind their back. There is a greater risk that someone will repeat your words and maybe even twist your meaning or intent. Communication is the key to unraveling a personal problem. This can be difficult if someone simply refuses to talk to you; consider having them write down their complaints instead. This is a good time for keeping a personal diary, but make sure it is for your eyes only. Trying to organize a social outing can be a thankless task. Others may be unwilling to offer assistance of any kind; ask yourself if it is worth any more effort.

12. SUNDAY. Changeable. Plans for a quiet day at home may change when you get a better offer. Make sure that a sudden change in your own arrangements for the day does not inconvenience or upset someone close to you. If you are in the process of house hunting, this could be a fruitful day. If you find the right place, put in an offer as soon as possible; there is a greater risk that another purchaser could beat you to it. Certain decorating jobs could be more difficult than you anticipate. Guard against doing one job but creating another. Be careful about selecting a color scheme; you could make an expensive mistake.

13. MONDAY. Productive. This is an especially productive day for Sagittarius people who work from home. You should start the day with a clear head and plenty of enthusiasm. If you are unemployed, this is a good time for offering your services on a voluntary basis to a worthwhile cause. The work is likely to be stimulating and may even lead to a paid position. What started as a temporary job could now be offered to you as a permanent position. Luck is on your side if you are bidding for work. Offering extra services rather than a lower bid can help you win out over your competitors. Getting together with teammates after work could lead to being told some interesting inside information which may be of benefit to you.

14. TUESDAY. Good. Sagittarius creative types can look forward to an idea-filled day. You may produce what you consider to be the best work you have done in some time. If you work in the entertainment field, this is a starred time for an audition. There is a greater chance of being offered a lucrative contract. Theater and film jobs of all kinds are also well favored. A dress rehearsal is likely to be a roaring success, which is sure to boost your confidence. Sagittarius parents should make a point of encouraging a child's artistic, musical, or sports skills. These natural talents can be as important as academic achievements. Get to bed early tonight.

15. WEDNESDAY. Variable. You may be feeling the burden of sole responsibility for a work project or family matter. Try to arrange some time for yourself. You may want to hire a professional to do some gardening or redecorating around your home. This could be far easier than relying on busy friends to come to your rescue. Guard against expecting too much of other people. If someone lets you down, remind yourself that everyone is fallible. Others will respond more willingly to your needs if your

attitude is upbeat and appreciative. Accept your own portion of
the blame for an argument with your partner or another loved
one.

16. THURSDAY. Disquieting. You may not be in top form
physically. If you suspect that you are going down with a cold, it
would be smart to take a day off. No one will thank you for
spreading your germs. This is a day to avoid putting yourself
under unnecessary pressure. Illness can be a result of overwork
or mental anxiety. Keep in mind that you cannot expect your
body to endure a punishing routine without eventually rebelling.
This is a good time for making routine health appointments,
such as with the dentist or to have your eyes tested. Expect a
sudden change in plans this evening, which probably will not be
to your liking.

17. FRIDAY. Deceptive. This is a tiring end to the working
week. Even the simplest of tasks can be more time consuming
than you anticipate. Sagittarius powers of concentration may not
be at their best. A colleague can delay a work project, or they
may nag you for assistance even though you are snowed under
with your own work. Documents or contracts of all kinds need to
be scrutinized carefully. Do not sign any official paper without
fully understanding it. In your personal life this is a time when it
is impossible to get a straight answer to a serious question. Someone close to you is being secretive for reasons which are yet to be
revealed.

18. SATURDAY. Fair. Morning hours are likely to be the more
enjoyable part of the day. Household chores should not seem as
tedious as usual. You may actually enjoy sprucing up your home
and catching up with other domestic tasks. This is a good time for
practicing some yoga or meditation. Any form of relaxation can
be beneficial, especially if you had a busy week at work. If you
are playing a sport or doing any sort of strenuous activity, make
sure that you do not overdo; listen to your body. Your partner
may want to pursue individual interests later in the day; try not
to feel left out. A new love interest for Sagittarius singles will
probably develop slowly at first, then pick up steam.

19. SUNDAY. Happy. This is a starred day for visiting friends
or family members who live in another town. The trip may
already be overdue. Consider traveling by train or subway rather
than driving. In this way you can avoid traffic jams or road
repairs. Neither will you have to worry about driving when you

are exhausted. A change of scenery can do a lot to make your spirits soar. Your buoyant mood is sure to rub off on those around you. This is a special day for Sagittarius singles who are enjoying the first flush of a new romance. You may choose today to announce engagement or wedding plans. If you are meeting your partner's friends or family for the first time you can be sure of a warm welcome.

20. MONDAY. Uncertain. As much as you enjoy the company of your current colleagues, you may be ready to move on to new pastures. It may now be obvious to you that your current job is not your true vocation. However, which direction to take could still be doubtful. This is a good time for seeking some career guidance. You might choose the services of an astrologer or clairvoyant to gain fresh insights or a glimpse of future trends. If you are delegating work, make sure that you give detailed instructions. If you want a job done well, it may be best just to do it yourself. A certain individual can be more of a hindrance than a help despite their good intentions.

21. TUESDAY. Stressful. Someone who is not pulling his or her own weight may test your patience. There is a risk that their personal problems are interfering with their concentration or sapping their motivation. Your best approach is to show some kindness rather than laying down the law. Offer to take more difficult tasks off their hands for the time being. A child's difficult behavior should not be corrected too harshly. Keep in mind that they cannot always articulate their inner anxieties. A love affair may leave you feeling alternately stressed and happy. Do not allow anyone to have too much emotional power over you.

22. WEDNESDAY. Tricky. In your business dealings you should not be tempted to stoop to underhanded tactics of any kind. Keep on the right side of the law. Sagittarius entrepreneurs may decide to write off a certain project which is proving too costly. Beware of attempting to solve problems just by throwing money at them; you could end up losing money but making no progress. If you are taking out a loan, carefully consider how much you can afford to repay each month. The debt could become a millstone around your neck. Arguments over money are likely, especially where joint finances are concerned. Someone may not be playing fair and square with you.

23. THURSDAY. Mixed. You may find it difficult to complete written work. Make a point of taking regular breaks; in this way your creative urges are less likely to dry up altogether. An essay or important letter may need more research before you can hope to make a real start on the final version. Concentrate fully in meetings and even during casual conversations. There is a greater risk that you will miss a vital piece of information if you are not really paying attention. It may be too soon to take a skills test; fit in some extra lessons first. Steer clear of heated debates on religion or politics or any other controversial topic this evening. A good book can be the best company.

24. FRIDAY. Good. The end of the working week is a good time for a long-distance trip. You might be able to extend your travel over the weekend and mix business with pleasure. The notorious Sagittarius itchy feet could keep you jumping. Consider taking off for the weekend to visit friends in another part of the country. If finances allow, you might be tempted to spend the weekend in a distant city. Legal matters of all kinds can be brought to a successful conclusion. If you are involved in litigation of any kind, there is a greater possibility of settling out of court. Going out to the theater or the movies can be the perfect night for you and a loved one.

25. SATURDAY. Variable. Family duties have to come before pleasure. This may include a trip to visit in-laws or other older relatives. An older person who always seems to get on your nerves is unlikely to be any different today. Restrain yourself from being sarcastic or hurtful in return; this only makes matters worse. Criticisms which are clearly intended to hurt you should not go completely unchecked; stand up for yourself, but keep your cool. Later in the day is a good time for meeting with someone from your past. Reminiscing should bring back some pleasant memories even if you no longer have much in common with one another.

26. SUNDAY. Difficult. Lend your support to a charity fundraising function. You could have a fun time in the process. Do not insist on the company of someone who would rather stay home; they could end up being a wet blanket. Be prepared to enjoy your own company if others are busy or already committed elsewhere. Discussions regarding a sensitive subject could be unavoidable. Guard against being too strident in your views; you may unintentionally intimidate someone. You may wonder if you have done the right thing by trusting someone with a secret. This could be a reminder to you to be more cautious in the future.

27. MONDAY. Changeable. This promises to be a lucrative start to the week if you work on commission. A deal which has been in the pipeline for some time may now be signed and sealed. If your work involves serving the general public you could make more than usual. A cash bonus should be salted away rather than spent; you may regret frittering away money when you realize that it has left you short for other things. Someone at work may be difficult to please, and this could bring out the rebellious side of your Sagittarius nature. However, do not be blatantly disrespectful or sarcastic. It is probably in your own best interests to keep your negative opinions to yourself.

28. TUESDAY. Excellent. This is an excellent day for Sagittarius people who are politically active. Now is the time for intensive effort if there is an election coming up. A campaign can receive a boost by way of donations from new or existing supporters. You might decide to donate money to a favored political or medical cause, or to donate your time. In the workplace this is a favorable time for pooling ideas and resources. Teamwork of all kinds can be fun as well as very effective. A colleague can soon become a friend out of work as well. Seek out the company of someone you have known for a long time if you want unbiased advice on a personal matter.

29. WEDNESDAY. Demanding. It can be hard work being at home with children. This is a good time for joining forces with another parent and going out for at least part of the day. Guard against a feeling of isolation. If you are planning a party or outing, make sure that you invite a mix of people, including at least one newcomer. Try to avoid taking on any work which is creatively demanding. Your mental processes are not at their quickest when it comes to thinking up original ideas. Routine jobs can be boring but easier to complete. Make sure that you are not neglecting a close friend in favor of a romantic relationship.

30. THURSDAY. Deceptive. A friend may have a change of mind about a social arrangement which you already paid for, which could create some bad feeling. You may be able to sell a ticket to someone else in order to recoup the cost. Be wary in the future about laying out money for someone who is known to be unreliable. Be selective about the social invitations you accept at this time. You cannot afford to do everything you would like to do, so choose the best of the bunch. News of someone falling ill can be upsetting. Medical personnel may be unhelpful or just too busy to talk to you. Do not forget to make a promised call.

31. FRIDAY. Frustrating. If you recently made a fresh start in an old relationship you may now be feeling disheartened. There is a greater risk that the same old problems are again cropping up despite good intentions on both sides. You might just have to accept that you are fundamentally incompatible. The end of the month is a good time for fresh starts of all kinds. This might include clearing out some deadwood in your personal or work life. Do not feel guilty about breaking off contact with a person who does not value you or who is clearly using you. Do not fall into the trap of believing that you have to please all of the people all of the time.

NOVEMBER

1. SATURDAY. Successful. Although Sagittarius people are known for a tendency to live life at full tilt, this is a day when you should enjoy being able to slow down the pace. If you have a chance to sleep late, relish it. Catching up on sleep can make you feel a hundred times better, both physically and mentally. Later in the day you may want to browse around antique shops or secondhand stores, especially if you are looking for items which are purely ornamental rather than functional. A musical recording could be the perfect birthday gift for someone you know well. Create a romantic atmosphere if you are entertaining at home this evening.

2. SUNDAY. Variable. If you are harboring resentment after a recent argument with a loved one, now is the time to let it go. Make a point of being the first to back down and they will quickly follow suit. Keep in mind that few people can resist the persuasiveness of a sincere apology. You could be in the mood to get yourself in better shape, especially if you have been lax recently about diet and exercise. This is a good time to become a member of a health club. Paying a membership fee can help you stay motivated. It should be easier to lose weight at the moment. You may receive a sincere compliment about your personal appearance.

3. MONDAY. Calm. In the workplace you should find it easier to work alone rather than in a group. You have definite ideas when it comes to a certain project. If you must work as part of a team you may have to give in on certain priorities dear to you. If you are at home you might not feel the need to seek out company. Although Sagittarius people are usually outgoing and social, you still have a strong need for space of your own. This is a good time for sorting through your wardrobe. You might decide to throw out old garments which are now out of date, although some could be altered or dyed a more current color. Making your own clothes can be satisfying as well as economical.

4. TUESDAY. Pleasant. You are high in the popularity stakes at the moment. This is a day when others seem especially indulgent toward you and eager to be in your company. This is the perfect time for getting a new romance off the ground. Someone considerably older or younger than you can be the perfect lover. Take the initiative if you sense that someone is too shy to ask you out. There is no need to put on any airs with someone who has captured your interest; simply be yourself. Trust the power of your personality both in your personal life and in your business dealings. Hunches are likely to pay off. Listen to your intuition; it will not steer you wrong.

5. WEDNESDAY. Mixed. Unexpected bills, such as appliance or car repairs, could mean that you will have to dip into your savings. Consider opening a separate account to cover emergencies such as these; putting a little away each month can mean that you are never caught short. Be wary when it comes to keeping a secret that has been entrusted to you. Sagittarius often have a tendency to let the cat out of the bag unintentionally. If you would rather not have the responsibility of guarding someone's secret, do not hesitate to tell them so. Your loyalty could be taken for granted today, but at least this shows that you are very well regarded.

6. THURSDAY. Fair. You have a tendency to be scatter-brained today. Keep a tight hold on your wallet if you are out in a crowd. There is also a risk of leaving valuables in a restaurant or on a bus. Do not wear jewelry which has a loose clasp. Anything you lose is unlikely to be returned to you. Consider extending a home insurance policy to cover loss of valuables outside the home. Do not forget to repay someone from whom you recently borrowed money, even if it is a trivial amount. Plans for this evening may go awry due to travel complications. Keep your arrangements as open-ended and flexible as possible.

7. FRIDAY. Manageable. Administrative tasks may take up a lot of your time at work. Colleagues are willing to pitch in if they see you struggling. Conducting business over the telephone can be productive. Sagittarius sales representatives should concentrate on arranging appointments for next week. A superior may volunteer some constructive criticism concerning an assignment at work. You should be able to accept what is said without feeling attacked, then make improvements accordingly. Sagittarius singles may receive a last-minute social invitation this evening. At a get-together you could be introduced to someone you will want to see again.

8. SATURDAY. Changeable. Today's mail may at last bring a letter you have been waiting for. The earlier part of the day is the best time for a shopping trip, either to the supermarket or department store. There is a possibility of running into someone you once knew. An exchange of news and gossip over a cup of coffee can be fun. Personalized stationery can make the perfect gift for a friend's birthday or for someone who has recently moved to a new home. Minor friction with another household member could surface later in the day. Try not to let a squabble escalate into a more serious disagreement. Someone is not ready to hear your advice, so keep quiet for now.

9. SUNDAY. Good. This is a lucky day for house hunting, whether you are looking for a place to buy or rent. If your own house is on the market, you may find that a prospective purchaser simply knocks at the door. This is also a good day for beginning major decorating, such as stripping old wallpaper or paint. If you live in an older home you may uncover some original woodwork or even a closed-off fireplace. If you have a garden, do not put off clearing up the autumn debris. Entertaining at home is a relaxed way to spend the evening. You are sure to enjoy a sense of family togetherness.

10. MONDAY. Changeable. The working week gets off to a relatively easy start, but do not be lulled into a false sense of security. Pressure is apt to mount quickly as the day goes on, especially if a deadline is moved forward on short notice. Try not to waste time this morning; you could regret it when you end up having to miss your lunch break or having to put in overtime this evening. Sagittarius business people should be prepared for a few headaches when it comes to dealing with a budget. Someone is sure to oppose your priorities for allocating money. Children can tire you. An early night for everyone would be beneficial.

11. TUESDAY. Fair. Life may seem to be all work and no play at the moment. However, efforts on your part to cheer everyone up are sure to be worthwhile. Do not let your sense of humor desert you when faced with a tricky situation. Colleagues appreciate your ability to make them laugh at a difficult moment. Certain individuals who take themselves too seriously are likely to unbend in the face of some kindly teasing. Someone who knows that you can be relied upon to be totally honest may seek your opinion. The effects of exercise or dieting are likely to start being noticed. This can spur you on to greater efforts. You should be successful in a competitive sporting event later in the day, and you could win a wager.

12. WEDNESDAY. Deceptive. This is not a favorable day for financial transactions of any kind. Someone may not be able to fulfill a financial obligation, so be cautious. A get-rich-quick scheme may sound tantalizing on paper, but there is a greater risk of being conned or swindled by someone whose principles are nowhere near as high as yours. Someone who once offered you a loan may have forgotten all about it; it may be best not to remind them. If you need to borrow money, contact your bank; keep the arrangement professional. Socializing with a person who never pays their own way can be annoying; point out that you have limited reserves yourself.

13. THURSDAY. Changeable. Money spent on health products should be money well spent. Consider supplementing your diet with extra vitamins and minerals. Kicking a bad habit, such as smoking or biting your nails, can be difficult at any time. Now, however, you can tap into extra reserves of willpower, so give it your best shot. Avoid exaggerating a problem in order to win sympathy; you could produce the opposite effect. Trust those close to you to recognize your needs. Do not talk about a business deal until it is firmly in the bag. You want to avoid looking foolish should the transaction fall through at the last minute.

14. FRIDAY. Good. If you have been unemployed for a while, this is a day when the famous Jupiter luck is likely to turn in your favor. An offer of work now could rescue you from a financial predicament just in time. If you are looking for a roommate, someone you meet through work could be the ideal candidate. The end of the working week may bring news of changes within your department. Some of these may be unwelcome at first, but you should soon see the sense behind them. This is not a time for making waves, especially regarding decisions which have already been made official. You could be treated to a meal this evening, either out or at someone's home.

15. SATURDAY. Variable.   You may be going through a tempestuous time in your love life. Someone deliberately tests you because they are not yet sure of your sincerity. You are apt to find these sort of mind games annoying because, as a Sagittarius, you prefer to say what you think. However, go along for the time being in the interests of the courtship. A long-standing relationship can be put to the test at this time. If someone cannot or will not stick by you in a time of crisis, you may be better off alone. If you are hosting a party this evening, keep the number of guests to a sensible limit.

16. SUNDAY. Quiet.   Enjoy the company of someone who is very special in your life. Sagittarius people who recently split up with a partner may find that reconciliation is in the cards. However, first you need to get down to some serious talking; do not shy away from a heart-to-heart conversation. If you are contemplating becoming self-employed, someone may show an interest in going into partnership with you. Discuss business expectations from both sides to see if you seem professionally compatible. Sagittarius people who are unattached may receive a call from someone recently met. It is too soon to tell if this will turn into a full-fledged romance.

17. MONDAY. Fair.   It may concern you that the same problems in your personal life keep repeating themselves. An unconscious pattern of behavior from your early years could be the cause. This is a good time for reaching a clearer understanding of what you want and how you hope to get it. The most effective way could be through counseling or through reading relevant books. A support group for a specific issue could be educational as well as comforting. A child is looking to you for approval; be generous with your praise. Joint finances require some discussion, especially if you are attempting to provide for a child or an elderly family member.

18. TUESDAY. Easygoing.   This is a day when you should enjoy an inner sense of calm. Life is moving along in just the way that suits you. Any problem is easy to resolve as long as you create an atmosphere of peace and quiet for thinking it through in your own way. You are unlikely to need the advice or opinions of others; in fact, these are more likely to confuse you rather than help you. Put more trust in your own sense of what is good and bad, right and wrong. In the library you might choose books which discuss spiritualism or problem-solving techniques. You are ready to broaden your thinking regarding such subjects. Business transactions of all kinds should be straightforward and rewarding.

19. WEDNESDAY. Mixed.   If you are not getting the results or answers that you want, now is the time to put some pressure on. Sometimes you have to make a lot of noise if you want others to take you seriously. Computer errors could cause delays. Someone who is being evasive about an appointment needs to be pinned down or written off; do not let them waste any more of your valuable time. Aim to create the impression that they need you more than you need them, even if this is not strictly true; in this way they may become more cooperative. A lost object is likely to be at home but may not come to light for a while.

20. THURSDAY. Changeable.   If you usually spend the Christmas vacation at home you might be considering a change of plan for this year. With your Sagittarius love of travel, you do not need much encouragement to try new places. Drop by a travel agent to see what is being offered. Be prepared for your first choice to be already booked up. If you have children it may be helpful to choose a place which includes activities specifically for the younger set. You might decide to investigate the cultural attractions in your own area. Pick up leaflets advertising forthcoming concerts, plays, or exhibits.

21. FRIDAY. Disquieting.   An impending deadline can be a struggle at the moment. You may be in a panic about the amount of work you have to get through. Your best approach is to plan a work schedule for the rest of the month; this should give you a clearer idea of the way ahead. The negative side of the Sagittarius nature is to give up too easily once your initial enthusiasm has waned. However, this is not a time for taking any action on the spur of the moment. Keep in mind that anything worthwhile has its good and bad moments. You will savor your achievements all the more if they are hard won. Loved ones may seem unsympathetic but only because they are preoccupied.

22. SATURDAY. Variable.   As a person born under the sign of Sagittarius you need your freedom. At times this can mean that you seem aloof from family ties. And this can make it all the more difficult when a relative tries to pressure you into an arrangement which does not fit in with your personal life. It is important to aim for a compromise. If you do your best to meet people halfway you can avoid hurt feelings. This is a busy day, especially if you deal directly with the public. You are likely to be asked more questions than usual, but the potential new business should make the extra work worthwhile. You could be in for a pleasant surprise after dark.

23. SUNDAY. Confusing. If you have been lazy about keeping up with your correspondence lately, catch up today. Review the last letter you received so that you can remember what is going on in their life. Trying to sort out social arrangements may prove difficult at the moment. Be quick to sense if someone wants to pull out of a commitment even if they do not say why directly; they will be grateful to you for letting them off the hook. Advice from an older relative may border on interference in your affairs. Their way of thinking is apt to be at odds with your own. Your best approach is to hear them out before you go ahead and do what you want regardless.

24. MONDAY. Good. If you work in a managerial capacity this promises to be a productive day. Although you may have your favorites among your staff, your innate Sagittarius sense of fairness can be of great help in your judgments and decision making. This is a time when the good of the group as opposed to any individual has to be put first. Teamwork of all kinds is favored. This is a good time to sign up for a course to improve the skills you need at work. Extending your social circle is also important. It may seem that keeping up with all your friends is a full-time operation, but you secretly love being high in the popularity stakes.

25. TUESDAY. Unsettling. For Sagittarius business people this is a tricky time for entertaining clients. Stick to restaurants where you are known and where you can guarantee the quality of food and service. Someone is waiting to be impressed; make a greater effort to show your professionalism. Trying to raise money for a cause can be hard going. It may be difficult not to get angry by what appears to be meanness or selfishness. Keep in mind, however, that not everyone is as generous as you. Steer clear of social events which you know will be costly unless you can be sure of having a good time. You will resent spending money on an evening which falls flat.

26. WEDNESDAY. Unclear. If you are paid at the end of each month you may be at risk of running out of money before your paycheck is deposited in your account. This is not a good time for unauthorized borrowing. A purchase you try to make with a credit card could be refused. Keep charges to a minimum by staying away from a tempting sale. Money which is owed to you may be slow in coming through. Try not to spend in anticipation of it. Use only cash, or do not buy. An interview for a job or special assignment can be a stressful experience. Although you may feel that you have not put yourself across very well, you could still be in the running for the position.

27. THURSDAY. Demanding. Make an extra effort on this Thanksgiving to be fair as far as personal relationships are concerned. You may come across as coldhearted or uncaring if you do not offer the sympathy or interest that someone needs. It is up to you to tune in to their unspoken request and spot the signs. A who-cares attitude at home could get you in trouble. Even if you cannot get excited about your current company, it is in your own interests to at least go through the motions. Your Sagittarius nature will probably prevent you from sticking with a relationship which you do not believe in wholeheartedly. Now can be the time for a change even if this means less security or some temporary loneliness.

28. FRIDAY. Easygoing. You should welcome an easy end to the workweek. The pressure is off to such an extent that you may have to hunt around for things to do. There is a greater possibility of getting off early. Take advantage of any free time to do the shopping which normally takes up part of your weekend. In this way you create more time for your own outside interests or just to enjoy being lazy. This is a good day for a reunion with an old friend. You may also be able to breathe new life into a stale romance if you take the trouble to make your partner feel special. Intimate conversation can be satisfying.

29. SATURDAY. Mixed. You may start the day feeling weary, especially if you had an emotional night. Your mental and physical energy is likely to pick up in the course of the day. You may decide to get an early start on Christmas shopping, although you could find the stores crowded even beyond expectation. If you go out, get an early start. If shopping for clothes you should have a successful trip. You can make a little money go a long way. It may be less trouble to use public transportation rather than fighting for a parking space. If you are planning a party in the near future, your best policy is to invite your neighbors. Otherwise be sure to at least warn them in advance.

30. SUNDAY. Inactive. Be especially kind to yourself. There is no harm in putting off your least favored chores until another time. Indulge the fun-loving side of your personality. Games of all kinds can be pleasant, especially those which include all age groups. If you are playing cards for money you are apt to come out on top. This can also be a lucky time for making a friendly bet on a sporting event. If you are athletic, spend at least part of the day participating in your favorite sport, perhaps golf or tennis. Children may ask to invite friends over for the day; the more the merrier. Get to bed earlier than usual.

DECEMBER

1. MONDAY. Productive. This busy start to the working week is a good time for dealing with the backlog of paperwork. Written work of all kinds can be easier than usual. You should be able to dash off letters or a report at an impressive speed. You may be offered a financial advance or prepayment; be sure the particulars are written down to avoid future uncertainty. The beginning of the month is a favorable time for putting your personal finances in order. It could be helpful to plan a detailed budget for the forthcoming Christmas expenses, especially gifts and entertaining.

2. TUESDAY. Manageable. Make a greater effort to pace yourself throughout the day. You could find yourself slowing down before lunchtime if you get too early a start or push yourself too hard. A sense of urgency about certain tasks may be probably misguided; try to take the pressure off yourself. Sagittarius people can often be clumsy, but this is a day when you are distinctly accident-prone. Slow down; being in a hurry could result in a fall. Take extra care if using sharp instruments of any kind. Steer clear of strenuous or dangerous sports. A child may need extra attention this evening just when you feel least like giving of yourself.

3. WEDNESDAY. Unsettling. The generous Sagittarius nature can sometimes work against you. This is a time when you need to guard against devoting too much of your energy to other people's problems. Someone who takes it for granted that you are always ready, willing, and able to act as counselor needs to be kept at arm's length for a while. You are apt to be especially sensitive today, probably due to lack of a good night's sleep. You might overreact to comments which are not intended to be hurtful. Try to maintain your sense of humor when someone teases you. A misunderstanding with your partner could result in tears but can also be quickly resolved.

4. THURSDAY. Fair. Expect a difficult start to the day. Early morning travel can be disrupted by traffic delays or train cancellations. If you have appointments to keep, be sure to have some spare cash ready in case you need to take a cab. This may be the only way in which you can guarantee to arrive on time. Take extra care with your personal appearance if you are going on an interview or are dealing with important customers. Do not underestimate the importance of making a good first impression. If you are shopping for clothes, look for those which could easily double up for both business and casual wear. Opt for colors which are best for you even if not in current fashion.

5. FRIDAY. Good. Receiving a holiday card today will take you by surprise. As a Sagittarius you are unlikely to be so well organized that you have even bought your cards. This can be a good time to at least make a list of the people to whom you will send greetings. Make a separate list for gift buying. You might decide to make some purchases from a charity as a way of making a donation. This should be an easy end to the workweek as far as your job is concerned. There may be time to talk about subjects other than those which are work related. A night out can be both fun and relaxing.

6. SATURDAY. Disquieting. Household chores are likely to be more tedious than usual, but certain tasks cannot be put off any longer. If you find yourself cleaning up after other family members, you could end up seething with resentment. Do not maintain a martyred silence; let your annoyance be known, even if this creates some friction. If you rent rather than own your home, there is a greater risk of a rent increase. If you feel that the increase is excessive, consider lodging a formal protest. Do not allow yourself to be exploited. It is vital to know exactly what your rights are, then insist on them. Friends make good company at a Sagittarius birthday party.

7. SUNDAY. Pleasant. Do not wander far from home. You can relax best staying in the comfort of your own four walls. Playing host to friends or family members can be enjoyable. This is a good time for cooking a traditional dinner, including dessert. A family gathering is likely to be especially successful. Someone who often rubs you the wrong way may be making a greater effort to be sociable. If you go out, enjoy browsing in a shopping mall. You could pick up all sorts of good-quality bargains. This is also a good time for stocking up on fruit and vegetables as an antidote to all the sweets available around the holiday period.

8. MONDAY. Deceptive. It can be hard to make up your mind today, mostly due to fear of making the wrong decision. This fear is not completely ungrounded. There is a greater likelihood that you are not in full possession of the pertinent facts. Follow your good Sagittarius instincts; they can be as good a guide as anything else. Listen analytically and ask for further explanations of anything that is unclear; this could prevent you from jumping to the wrong conclusions. Money which was supposed to arrive by mail or be paid direct into your account may not materialize, forcing you to juggle other expenses or ask a relative for a loan.

9. TUESDAY. Rewarding. If you are approaching your busiest time of year at work, consider boosting your advertising. This is a good time for obtaining professional advice from an outside agency or consultant. Their marketing ideas can be worth paying for even if they make a big hole in your budget in the short term. This is a favorable day for shopping for presents for the children in your family, although you may end up spending more than you intend. An active social life can be fun at the moment but may also be stretching your finances to an uncomfortable limit. Exercise some moderation by eating dinner at home or watching videos instead of going to the movies.

10. WEDNESDAY. Variable. This can be a difficult time if you are involved in research of any kind. Obtaining information and analyzing results can be more time consuming than you bargain for. Buy only necessary books; check out others from the library. You could end up spending a lot on items which are nonessential. It goes against your Sagittarius expansiveness to limit your spending. However, you could come up with considerable savings if you buy necessities only; luxuries can wait until another time. Avoid rich food this evening; a simple but nutritious meal is best and keeps you on your health program.

11. THURSDAY. Mixed. In the workplace you could be loaded down with all sorts of odd jobs which you find boring or difficult. Someone in authority may not realize just how much they are delegating to you at the moment. Point out that you have only one pair of hands. This can be a good time for taking on temporary staff to help you through until the new year. Any health problem at this time is apt to be connected to self-indulgence or excessiveness of some kind. Avoid putting in over-time. Get some physical exercise in order to give your system the boost it needs. A good night's sleep can also work wonders for your physical and mental well-being.

12. FRIDAY. Changeable. The Sagittarius nature lends itself to impatience. You usually want to take action immediately, and you expect others to produce instant results as well. However, this is a time to guard against putting too much pressure on a colleague. Keep in mind that everyone has their own individual way of pro-ceeding. Let others work at their own pace. Sagittarius singles could be the object of attention at the moment. Although you might not think a potential suitor is your type, if you make an effort to get to know them you could be pleasantly surprised. Do not miss out on opportunities by making too many presupposi-tions or sticking to preconceived ideas.

13. SATURDAY. Satisfactory. The person who is most impor-tant in your life is making greater efforts to meet your emotion-al needs at the moment. You are more likely to get your way when it comes to little things as well as major issues. A new romance can be surprisingly pleasant; you could find that you have more and more in common. A holiday card from someone special can lift your spirits. This is a favorable time for planning ahead with regard to upcoming social events. Book tickets now for a concert or a theatrical performance. For Sagittarius parents it may be wise to make baby-sitting arrangements, too. Throwing a party can be the ideal way in which to get to know someone on a more intimate level.

14. SUNDAY. Disconcerting. There may be some arguments concerning your plans for the upcoming holidays. If you are mar-ried, your spouse may have different preferences, and it may seem they are making an unnecessary fuss. It is important to try to reach a compromise rather than just demanding your own wants regardless. If you are single you are unlikely to lack for social invitations, although deciding which to accept can present you with a dilemma. Later in the day is a good time for writing greeting cards or returning personal telephone calls from last week. Also be sure to pay bills that are due.

15. MONDAY. Slow. You are apt to be preoccupied with a personal matter. This can interfere with your concentration at work; you will probably end up clock watching. This is unlikely to be a productive day. Even though you start out this morning with good intentions, it may prove impossible to complete certain tasks. Your creative powers are unlikely to be at their best. A relationship which seems increasingly complicated could get you down. Although you hate to admit defeat, this may be a time when you have to accept that there are no easy solutions. Someone is intent on curbing your freedom, not knowing that this can be the quickest way to alienate you.

16. TUESDAY. Misleading. Money concerns may be uppermost in your mind. If you have a large family to buy holiday presents for, try to agree on a price limit. If you are finding it hard to make ends meet, it may be difficult not to worry. However, your optimistic Sagittarius nature does not allow you to stay down for long. This is not a good time for taking out a loan; you may overcommit yourself on repayments. It may be smarter to sell a stock or cash in a bond to tide you over until the new year. Stock up at a sale on wrapping paper, ribbon, and other seasonal trimmings, including decorations for the tree.

17. WEDNESDAY. Changeable. If you have cards or parcels to be sent, make a point of mailing them without delay. They should still arrive in time. Expect long lines in the post office or bank. It is not too late to make last-minute travel arrangements to spend the upcoming holidays away from home, perhaps abroad. Do not forget to cancel the newspaper or other home deliveries if you are going to be away. This is a busy day for Sagittarius people who work in the entertainment field. There may be extra bookings for musicians or performers. A theatrical performance this evening can be fun for adults and children.

18. THURSDAY. Variable. Cards or packages that arrive in today's mail may include some that are unexpected. Both long and short distance journeys are unlikely to be trouble-free today. Allow extra time for reaching your destination. Sagittarius people who deal directly with the public can expect a frantically busy day. A special promotion can bring in customers in droves. If you are shopping you could come across some good ideas for trims and presents. Books or records can be a sound option for teenagers or for an older relative who seems to have everything. If you decide to spend money which you received for your birthday, make sure you spend it on yourself.

19. FRIDAY. Disquieting. This is likely to be a hectic end to the working week. The pressure is still on despite the festive atmosphere that is building. Work has to come before pleasure. Even though you try hard to wrap up your current projects today, you probably cannot bring everything up to date or to a satisfactory conclusion. If this is your last working day before the Christmas break, you may have to put some matters on ice until the new year. Contain your natural exuberance at an office party at least until your superiors have left. Someone who does not share your sense of fun should be given a wide berth.

20. SATURDAY. Unsettling. The last shopping weekend before the big day is the time to hunt for last-minute gifts. Something you have ordered may not arrive; have an alternative up your sleeve. This is a notoriously bad time for break-ins or theft; make sure that you do not leave valuables in your car or your home unlocked. Keep money in a safe place; do not make it easy for someone to pick your pocket in the shopping crowds. Some family squabbles seem inevitable at the moment, but take these in stride. Make allowances for someone who is under a lot of strain in their work or personal life. Be generous in giving to a worthwhile charity.

21. SUNDAY. Fair. This morning is likely to be the most peaceful part of the day. You may choose to spend the morning in bed, either sleeping or reading. Make the most of having some time to yourself. You may be drawn into social arrangements later in the day even though you had intended to stay home. If you have guests arriving this afternoon, try to do as much preparation in advance as possible. It may be more enjoyable to eat out rather than going to the bother of cooking at home, especially if you have to cater to a large number of guests and varying tastes. A telephone call can bring an exciting invitation. Accept even if you know you will be expected to bring a gift.

22. MONDAY. Demanding. If you have to be at work there is little hope of any quiet or easy interludes. You may have to cover for colleagues who have already started their holiday vacation. Make sure to write down telephone messages and document any decisions made in their absence. A certain individual may expect too much of you at this time. Politely refuse to take on any additional responsibilities in the workplace. Putting in extra hours at work on short notice is unlikely to go over well with your loved ones. Children should be given priority when it comes to allocating your time and attention; work can wait.

23. TUESDAY. Enjoyable. This is a day when the festive spirit really comes into its own. Pressure is likely to lift in the workplace, giving way to a lot of good humor and joviality. This is the ideal time for a leisurely lunch with colleagues or business associates; you may not return to the office. If you are at home today, friends or family members are apt to drop in unannounced. Have plenty of food and drink on hand; they will appreciate your hospitality. Seeing old friends can be heartwarming. This evening is a good time for a social gathering at home. Have some extra gifts on hand, such as calendars or books, in case you receive a surprise present.

24. WEDNESDAY. Mixed. Sagittarius business people who are working right up until the last moment should have a productive morning. Aim to clear your desk by lunchtime. Last-minute shopping might take longer than you anticipate, so allow yourself as much time as possible. A bonus in this month's pay may not be as much as you expect, but every extra dollar will help with your Hanukkah or Christmas expenses. If you are traveling out of town, expect to run into heavy traffic. Leave as early in the day as possible. If picking up out-of-town guests, expect delays in their arrival time.

25. THURSDAY. MERRY CHRISTMAS! If you are hosting at home for your family, the day could start earlier than you would like. Young children will probably not allow you to sleep late. The day is apt to start off in a chaotic fashion. Your best plan of action is to keep your timetable flexible so that you feel more relaxed and able to enjoy the occasion. A gift from someone special may overwhelm you; you may be rewarded for your own generosity in the past. Telephone calls from absent loved ones should make you happy but also nostalgic. You are almost sure to overdo food and drink, but enjoy indulgence for its own sake and do not even think of dieting now.

26. FRIDAY. Fair. A lazy start to the day is indicated for most Sagittarius people. You may choose not to get out of bed until lunchtime or even later. Yesterday's leftovers can be used imaginatively to provide a meal, but you will be less inclined to eat or drink too much today. Opt for some outdoor physical exercise if you feel sluggish. This is a good day for visiting members of your family who did not share yesterday with you. A late exchange of gifts could include jewelry or money. An invitation to a social gathering, perhaps at a neighbor's, is sure to be enjoyable later. Parties too far away may not appeal to you.

27. SATURDAY. Manageable. Young children need extra attention. Some boredom may be setting in now that the excitement of new gifts has subsided. Make a point of playing a new game with them; also try to include them in your own social arrangements. A trip to a shopping mall can be rewarding if you want to hunt for bargains and discounts in stores which have already started their sales. A new romance which has been interrupted by the festivities can be picked up from where you left off. Expect a telephone call early in the day; absence may have made the heart grow fonder. Sporting events of all kinds can be fun, whether you are a spectator or a participant.

28. SUNDAY. Good. If you have to return to work tomorrow, make the most of this final day of leisure. You may be content to spend the day reading a book or relaxing in front of the television. Or you could be busy on the telephone, both making and receiving calls. Later on you are apt to be in a more outgoing mood. Others are likely to respond willingly to your suggestions for an informal get-together. There should be no shortage of guests if you prefer to entertain in the comfort of your own home. A neighbor who may have spent much of the vacation alone would probably be most grateful for an invitation to join in on your festivities.

29. MONDAY. Demanding. A spot check of your finances may cast a momentary cloud over the day. There is a greater chance that you have already spent far more than you had intended. However, there is no point in becoming too anxious. Keep in mind that you can always make renewed efforts at economizing once the festivities have drawn to a close. Children's outings can be especially expensive; set limits before going out with them. If you are weight-conscious, you may find that a few extra pounds are showing up on the scale. This is a good day for sticking to a careful diet in order to quickly get back in shape. If you have young children, confirm baby-sitting arrangements if you will be out late on New Year's Eve.

30. TUESDAY. Deceptive. If you are back at work you may be surprised at how much there is to do. Dealing with correspondence or other administrative matters can keep you busy. It would be wise to delay any projects which require close attention to detail; your powers of concentration may not be up to the task. Public transportation can be erratic. It may be easier to stock up with provisions from stores which are within walking distance of your home. Do not risk illegal parking; you could be fined or have your car towed away. Last-minute changes to plans for tomorrow night are possible. Someone who keeps changing their mind can be annoying, but go along with them.

31. WEDNESDAY. Exciting. This is a very special day of the year for Sagittarius people. Having a naturally optimistic and forward-looking nature, you are always inspired by the prospect of a new beginning. Anticipating what the future may bring lifts your spirits. Others will delight in your cheerful company. Take time to reflect on the past year. It can be encouraging to remind yourself of your important achievements, both in your professional and personal life. You may have a choice of invitations for this evening. A local party or your own gathering at home is likely to be best for ushering in the New Year with friends and family members.

NOVEMBER

1. FRIDAY. Changeable. Moodiness and a wish to escape from reality could get the better of you. You may be tempted to ignore your problems, but sticking your head in the sand is rarely a solution to problems. It is wiser to stay fully alert, and watch your back where colleagues are concerned. If you are offered an appealing solution to a financial problem, sleep on it overnight; appearances can be deceptive. You may find it difficult to discuss matters which involve you personally. Make an effort to understand the other person's point of view as well as your own motives. Results should be pleasing for those who work alone, especially Sagittarius artists, designers, or researchers.

2. SATURDAY. Good. Your plans should go smoothly, enabling you to deal with things you were not able to cope with last month. Make inquiries about the plans you want to launch next year. At the library or bookshop you can read up on your latest interest or hobby. A meeting with an older friend could make you aware of how much potential you still have to fulfill. Sagittarius parents might like a day alone together as a special treat. Ask in-laws or a close friend to help out with the kids; they will probably be delighted. A sports or country club could be the ideal place to enjoy healthy activity followed by socializing.

3. SUNDAY. Uncertain. Thoughts about the past and plans for the future fill your mind. Although you feel optimistic and energetic, think seriously about some of your relationships, particularly with people in authority. Try not to become angry and thwarted if other people refuse to go along with your wishes. Avoid power struggles and deep-seated disagreements. If you engage in any type of ruthless behavior, the fallout could be very destructive. Try to put the finishing touches on a deal that has been dragging on. Buying or selling a car or a house should not prove too difficult. Sagittarius retirees might receive an unexpected financial bonus, perhaps a pension increase.

226 / DAILY FORECAST—SAGITTARIUS—1996

4. MONDAY. Difficult. Keep a tight rein on your emotions as new worries combine with the tensions from yesterday. Your need to succeed at all costs can give rise to jealous feelings toward colleagues and anger toward your boss. It could feel like a replay from childhood, filling you with infantile rage. Go out of your way to avoid quarrelsome people and negative thinkers. You are unlikely to work well with other people today, so focus any burst of energy on an individual project. If it is impossible to keep your anger under control, write about it in a letter you never send, or get out of the office for a tough workout in the gym. Sagittarius drivers should be especially careful and alert.

5. TUESDAY. Rewarding. If you are employed outside the home you can expect an easy working day. Self-employed Sagittarius could be offered some well-paid work. Someone influential is about to give you a helping hand up the career ladder. You are now sufficiently secure financially to buy an item for which you have been saving. Make sure, however, that you do not go over your budget. A realistic approach to future career or travel plans can make most things possible. Thinking of others comes naturally to you; charity work or a visit to a hospitalized friend adds to your own sense of well-being. A casual meal with friends could round off a perfect day.

6. WEDNESDAY. Easygoing. If you have an idea which needs support from other people, today could be the ideal opportunity for winning their approval. Be sure that all of the details have been carefully researched and are accurately presented; a slipshod project does not impress. Your relaxed attitude and willingness to consider all views encourage people to trust your judgment. The reputation of creative Sagittarius craftspeople can be enhanced by recently completed work. If you have been thinking of learning to play a musical instrument, do not wait; make inquiries about a suitable teacher today. Enjoying a film or concert is the perfect way to spend the evening.

7. THURSDAY. Fair. Sudden changes in your routine are likely. You might be pushed into a thorough housecleaning by the imminent arrival of an unexpected guest. Or you may decide to tidy up a spare room or the garage which has become a jumbled storage area. A female friend may become the sudden focus of your attention. Seek the company of friends or colleagues who share your aims in life. Keep a minor difference of opinion in proportion, and do not automatically doubt yourself. It is important to stick to your ideals and gain respect for your integrity. If a family member begins to get on your nerves, curl up on the sofa and lose yourself in a good detective novel.

8. FRIDAY. Tricky.   All money matters should be approached with extreme care. Although Sagittarius people enjoy making bold decisions, do not give in to such temptation today. Give any new business enterprise careful consideration, and be sure to read all the fine print. Friends or a charity organization could seek your help for a joint endeavor. Although their request is flattering, find out in advance exactly what is required of you. Misunderstandings can cause future pain and anger, and it is not always possible to iron out problems at a later date. Keep personal spending to a minimum. Avoid being tempted to gamble; the fastest horse in the world can still break a leg.

9. SATURDAY. Mixed.   You may find it difficult to choose between several enticing invitations. If you squeeze in more activities than is sensible, you could end up exhausted. If you are on a diet you could be tempted to break your regime. It is important to remember that drinking and driving do not mix. You might decide to play the big spender and invite a group of friends to an expensive restaurant. And you are going to be tempted to spend far more than you can afford on clothes. A check of your bank balance could be a somber moment of reckoning. Make time for a hobby or creative pursuit; a new approach to an old problem might be the answer you have been seeking.

10. SUNDAY. Promising.   The New Moon brings a new way of looking at things. Time spent on your own gives you a chance to think about positive changes you can make in your life. Out of the blue could come an offer of help which improves your chances for financial security. People considered lucky are often those who recognize an opportunity when it is offered; be sure to jump at your chance today. Your personal relationships are sure to bring a feeling of warmth and contentment, increasing your sense of well-being. Show your appreciation to a loved one with a gift or loving gesture. A get-together with old friends with whom you can relax and reminisce is a pleasant way to spend the evening.

11. MONDAY. Starred.   This is a wonderful day for all creative endeavors. If you have recently felt blocked or uninspired, exciting new ideas and a release of your particular talent are likely. This inspiration can help you complete a book or article, or a painting or design. If you enjoy dancing, you should be able to perform with abandon. Any of these activities can also produce some financial reward. You should now feel that your abilities are appreciated and that your dreams can become reality. The evening brings a need for entertainment with a new or different group of people. You might find yourself in an intensely passionate emotional situation.

12. TUESDAY. Unsettling. The responsibilities and routine of your life may weigh you down, bringing a strong urge to break free. Try to take a long-term view of the situation. Sagittarius people hate feeling slighted or trapped. A surge of energy and determination to do things your way could create problems at work. Avoid being too outspoken with colleagues; you are probably unaware of the hurt it causes. If you receive a tongue lashing from a superior you may feel unjustly criticized. Allow plenty of time for what needs to be done; rushing can lead to a minor accident. Exercise is an ideal way to use up surplus energy; judo, wrestling, aerobics, or a run in the park can do the trick.

13. WEDNESDAY. Disquieting. It is possible that nothing works out as you hoped today, which can leave you feeling depressed. An unexpectedly large bill may arrive, causing worry about how you will pay it. Your holiday plans may have to be changed for reasons beyond your control. Children in your care might become unruly and disobedient, unwilling to obey your simplest wishes. You may be expected to shine at an evening social occasion, but feel shy and ill at ease. Try not to feel lonely or to fear that you no longer know how to relate. This is merely a passing phase, so do not let it get you down. A loved one can restore your self-confidence through their belief in you.

14. THURSDAY. Productive. This is the day to really get things done outside the home. You should be bursting with energy and an infectious can-do approach. In striving to get ahead in the world, build on your ideas and go for it. You could make significant money and a significant impact. Your optimism and good humor encourage other people to work well with you; a great deal can be achieved. Jump at any offer which requires your leadership; you are likely to carry it off with ease. This is an excellent opportunity to prove what you can do in a sports competition. You have a good chance of winning. An evening spent with relatives could go well, with no tension or unspoken criticism.

15. FRIDAY. Fair. You could find your greatest satisfaction from work today. Try not to stick to your usual routine, but allow time for some solo brainstorming. Approach every topic with an open mind. You may be amazed and excited with some of the ideas you come up with. Talk to your employer about new plans; you are sure to present them clearly and find them well received. If you are joining friends for an evening out, be certain the financial arrangements are clear beforehand. Otherwise you can be left to pay the bill for everyone. You may be accused of being overly possessive. Be realistic about a love relationship or you will tend to feel left out.

16. SATURDAY. Variable. Chance encounters may get you involved in gossip. Anything you say may get back to the person involved, with possible unpleasant consequences. A close relative could upset you by bringing up some forgotten issue from the past. Or you may discover a family secret from which you have been excluded. A friend can help you put the matter into perspective. Time spent with neighbors can be stressful. If you feel strongly about the topic of conversation you may be tempted to try to influence their thinking. Although your opinions are important, it is not helpful to tread on people's toes; you may be shocked by the response if you overstep your bounds.

17. SUNDAY. Excellent. This is a great day for putting plans into action; make the most of it. A visit to a friend should prove enjoyable, or you may decide to make a long-hoped-for trip to your hometown. You could receive a proposal from someone you idolize. It is important, however, to keep a realistic view of the relationship. Realize that the person you have put on a pedestal is only human. A social occasion with people who share your special interests could make you feel like the star of the night. People tend to seek your company, and your head could be easily turned. You may even receive a prestigious invitation beyond your wildest dreams.

18. MONDAY. Disconcerting. You may feel that you are being manipulated into a situation which was not of your choosing. This could bring to the surface old buried feelings of jealousy and rage. Being able to recall the initial childhood situations which made you feel so thwarted will help you deal with these unpleasant emotions. At work you are likely to feel that everyone is getting on your case, which can make you feel anxious and irritable. It is wise to avoid speaking your mind unless an important issue is at stake. So much negative energy may make you careless and accident-prone. Take great care when driving or using any type of sharp instrument.

19. TUESDAY. Routine. Family life flows easily today, filling you with warm feelings of affection and a sense of well-being. You are likely to find your loved one particularly responsive to your moods and wishes. If home is where the heart is, you probably want to escape from the outside world. Relax with family members or old friends with whom you have an easy relationship. Socializing gives you the opportunity to realize what you really value in life. A shopping trip is a good idea to choose together the next big household purchase. Sagittarius people who work in public relations or sales can confidently make ambitious plans.

20. WEDNESDAY. Fair. You may feel surprisingly lonely and depressed, sensing that you are not getting the support that you need. Analyze exactly what the problem is; then you can make any necessary changes. Sagittarius parents should resist being overprotective toward a child until you have a better perspective about the situation. A friend may come up with a plan to help you deal with your restless feelings. Or you might be offered a change of direction in an unexpected letter or phone call. If you are engaged in research, or work in a technical field, you could come up with an exciting idea. Try to communicate it to others; you will be relieved at how lucid and convincing you are.

21. THURSDAY. Misleading. Keep your feet on the ground or you could badly misjudge a situation. Work may seem rather unappealing. Overconfidence can cause you to neglect the details. If you are attending an important meeting, it might be wise to get someone else to check the fine print beforehand. Sagittarius people with strong religious or philosophical views might be tempted to force them down other people's throats. An exchange of views is interesting, but always respect differences of opinion. Sagittarius romantics and lovers may decide to make a grand gesture. Be sure a gift is appropriate to the occasion, or the recipient could feel embarrassed by your generosity.

22. FRIDAY. Disquieting. A strong urge to be free from responsibility is at odds with tasks that have to be completed today. This can make you tense and on edge, ready to snap off the head of the first person who crosses your path. You probably want to take center stage at work and will feel frustrated if this is denied you. In the long run it is better to settle down quietly to work that needs concentration and accuracy. The satisfaction of work well done should calm you down. Try to get away early for some time on your own. Pay attention to your personal needs, and sort out your priorities. If you are not happy you will not be a pleasant or welcome companion.

23. SATURDAY. Exciting. Your mind may be working over-time, filled with exciting and unusual ideas. Any new projects you undertake are likely to do well, particularly if you work in an artistic or creative field. Your confidence can be an inspiration to others who might want to work with you. If your own career is going well, make time to advise a friend who is currently unem-ployed. Providing them with a list of contacts may be helpful. If you are still bursting with energy later in the day, a session at the gym would put you in tiptop condition. Accept an unexpected invitation this evening; it could lead to meeting someone who introduces you to a completely new way of looking at things.

24. SUNDAY. Challenging. The Full Moon is likely to produce some excellent results if your work is of an artistic or creative nature. If you make handicrafts, you could find a financially worthwhile outlet for your work. Close relationships have an especially intense quality, particularly with women. You may decide that some serious talking needs to be done. Business or partnership matters might need your attention, and the time spent should pay dividends. If you feel pressured to act against your will, bring the matter out into the open. Doing so will clear the air and might patch up a situation that is in danger of break-ing down. Be sure to avoid people who are less than honest.

25. MONDAY. Unsettling. Although you have tried to fit in with the wishes of your partner, you may still have been accused of selfishness. The current demands being made upon you may make you feel emotionally suffocated. Whatever triggers the ten-sion tends to set the mood today. Work is unlikely to provide a safe haven. If you decide to go all out to achieve a particular aim, you could find yourself in conflict with colleagues. They may think you are attempting to claim all the glory. Try not to see crit-icism where none was intended. It is better to analyze what has really upset you, then state your case calmly. Flying off the han-dle can put you at a disadvantage, and you could end up the loser.

26. TUESDAY. Routine. This is a day for coasting along and paying attention to your own and your loved one's needs. All relationships require give-and-take, but it is important to get the balance right. You will enjoy an evening out. Book a table at your favorite restaurant; good food and wine make for contentment. If you are feeling restless, make some plans to change your usual routine. A weekend away may be fun. Sagittarius people need some promise of excitement. Time spent with a business col-league could be useful. A day without distractions provides the opportunity to attend to minor matters.

27. WEDNESDAY. Pleasant. An invitation to a special cele-bration could be delivered to you, making you feel that you have arrived socially. Sagittarius homeowners may decide it is time for some redecorating. Buy some magazines to get you started with ideas. Order paint samples and fabric swatches. You are likely to enjoy the planning almost as much as the end result. You could be advised of a legacy, perhaps even an old family property left to you in the will of a distant relative. Happy moments with your family are likely to be a source of particular pleasure. A request for help from a loved one should receive your instant attention. Satisfaction comes from being able to lend a hand.

28. THURSDAY. Variable. An abundance of energy helps you achieve your goals this Thanksgiving. Although you get along well with others, a leadership role suits you best. Being in charge gives you the opportunity to impress your family and friends. An underlying feeling of restlessness could make you dig in your heels if anyone tries to clip your wings. Be wary when dealing with financial matters, especially if a loved one is involved. Some-one could put up a powerful argument to persuade you to part with some of your hard-earned savings. Although you do not want money to rule your life, it is important to have a realistic understanding of its importance.

29. FRIDAY. Mixed. Sagittarius business people who stay alert should be able to take advantage of excellent opportunities today. Minor problems are unlikely to bother you and can be taken in stride. Arrange to spend a little time alone in order to give seri-ous thought to your long-term goals. Some type of formal study could be the answer, broadening your mind and offering new pos-sibilities. An older person might come up with some helpful insights. Although serious changes may not be necessary at pres-ent, over a period of time your approach to life has changed. You may now find that your previous concerns have been replaced by new ones. This is inevitable and should not be fought.

30. SATURDAY. Emotive. The weekend allows ample time for a full social calendar, but it could lead to complicated personal entanglements. A party can present all sorts of problems. It is advisable not to get into a situation where you might make a fool of yourself. Sagittarius singles may find they have attracted the wrong person, who is then difficult to fend off. If you are tempt-ed to become involved in a clandestine relationship, carefully consider what is at risk. A chance meeting with a previous roman-tic partner is likely to revive old memories and a longing for what seemed gone forever. Your need for excitement could be met by a new friend from overseas or from a background very different from your own.

DECEMBER

1. SUNDAY. Good. The phone keeps you busy today with news and gossip from friends and family. You will enjoy the chance to talk about what is happening in your own life. A neighbor could pop in for a chat and add to your feeling of popularity. If you have the time for letter writing, remember that faraway relatives are always thrilled to hear from you. You may be invited to join a group of younger friends who are helping less fortunate people. Volunteer work gives you the opportunity to consider your own good fortune, and it could encourage you to help by giving your time as well as money. An environmental project or a youth group for disadvantaged kids can be rewarding.

2. MONDAY. Disquieting. This is not an easy day for dealing with people. A major argument over a minor matter could erupt. The issue under discussion may not be the real problem. You are apt to be unaware of how much pressure you are putting on your partner in an effort to get your own way. It is helpful if you are clear in your own mind what you want, which makes you more open about your real needs. At work it is important to proceed carefully. An envious colleague could overreact to a trivial misjudgment on your part, blowing it out of all proportion. This could leave you feeling misjudged and exhausted. Separate home and office life or both could get out of hand.

3. TUESDAY. Variable. Try not to let an issue from the past bring up old feelings of irritation. The day has a lot to offer. Business dealings of all kinds are likely to meet with success. You could put a new sales drive into action, or complete a pending legal matter. Make sure that the boss knows of your plans. If approached by a family friend for advice, do not allow your past personal experience to cloud your judgment. Sagittarius people who love sports are apt to be on a winning streak, with boundless energy and good fortune on your side. You should have a wonderful evening if it is spent with the person of your dreams.

4. WEDNESDAY. Demanding. Take a different approach to your work. Consider new ideas seriously; concentration and hard work enable you to put them to practical use. Sagittarius people with an interest in science or technology could solve a problem that has been perplexing for some time. Unfortunately you may find it difficult to communicate your enthusiasm to others. Their less than positive response could make you feel criticized and depressed. Wait until you are less excited and therefore able to state your views more clearly. Try to avoid important business transactions today. Your motives are likely to be misconstrued or twisted by competitors out to undermine you.

5. THURSDAY. Starred. You can take on the world today, and chances are good that you will win. Life could feel like one great social whirl. Your can-do sense of optimism enables you to win over your sternest critics. You should also receive pleasing support from a friend. If it is your birthday, a surprise party may be arranged in your honor. The evening presents a choice of entertainment, with friends playing an important role in your plans. An invitation to a new club could highlight your activities. Tonight is a starred time for lovers to be together. Warm feelings and happy moments can provide good memories in days to come.

6. FRIDAY. Deceptive. You could feel discontented with your lot. Sentimental memories about a past attachment can tempt you to idealize what was a less than perfect relationship. Valuing what you have at present is a more helpful way of dealing with insecurities and moodiness. An escape into drink or drugs is certainly not the answer to this problem. Time spent with caring friends can make you feel much better about your life. A friend may help you deal with some of your unanswered questions. Important decisions about property or finanancial matters should not be made now. Your judgment could let you down and give you cause for regrets in the new year.

7. SATURDAY. Productive. Your down-to-earth approach leads to an easy atmosphere with those around you. An unsatisfactory relationship could be coming to an end, but it is likely to bring a sense of relief. A commercial venture of some type may come your way. If you have done the ground work, a quick response could bring you financial gains. Find time to deal with bills that have been gathering dust. Write a long, chatty letter to a close friend in whom you can really confide. Shopping with a neighbor could provide a pleasant interlude. You could have fun socially, with several inviting options from which to choose this evening.

8. SUNDAY. Stimulating. Sagittarius people who are in a relationship may be overtaken by warm surges of affection. Your partner is likely to greatly appreciate breakfast in bed. If a minor irritation should surface, you will be in the right frame of mind to deal with it. Time spent at home could be enjoyed in a creative way. You might decide to redesign a disappointing area of the garden or refinish a stained piece of furniture. A concert or exhibition with friends is the perfect way to spend the afternoon. If you are going to a party this evening, your warmth and vitality could make everyone flock to your side. A romance that begins today is sure to get off to a good start.

9. MONDAY. Fortunate. This is a good day for satisfying your own needs while keeping those around you happy. An unexpected meeting with an old friend may cause you to reconsider some of your aims. A change of direction could bring a new dimension to your life. Sagittarius technicians are likely to work with precision and skill, perhaps bringing an opportunity for promotion. Legal matters or foreign investments made today can work out to your advantage. A gamble on the stock market may also pay off. Put aside time for the special person in your life; together you are sure to enjoy feelings of contentment. If you are unattached, make plans to be with friends. The evening favors fun.

10. TUESDAY. Changeable. Today's New Moon brings challenges and tensions in your place of work. Your plans may not meet with the uncritical approval you had anticipated. If your restless Sagittarius energy is denied an outlet you could feel angry and frustrated. Consider whether you are really being outmaneuvered and obstructed in your aims. Your no-nonsense approach and blunt comments might have inadvertently hurt the feelings of a colleague. Or you may have overstepped the boundary between achieving your own desire for success and treading on someone else's toes. An evening of quiet reflection could help you get the situation into better perspective.

11. WEDNESDAY. Mixed. A quick-witted response to a business opportunity could lead to an unexpected windfall. If you are self-employed you may come up with an idea for turning a hobby into a money-earner. Personal relationships should be handled with care; an unguarded remark could be blown out of proportion. Sagittarius people who care for children could find them aggravating today. They will be under your feet, needing constant attention. If you are not alert, a treasured item could be broken by small, inquisitive fingers. Healthy outdoor exercise and an early bedtime should put you in much better spirits tomorrow and better able to cope.

12. THURSDAY. Good. Get things done. Spend time with people you care about. The easy, relaxed attitude at work provides a positive environment for action. And the friendly atmosphere helps you take a leading role in whatever you hope to achieve. A generous gesture by a friend can add to your feeling of well-being. Home life should be a source of contentment, bringing an awareness of your present good fortune. Entertaining at home is likely to be a pleasure. Invite some close friends home for a relaxed dinner with good food and thoughtful conversation. A colleague with problems will appreciate being asked to join you, even if it is a last-minute invitation.

13. FRIDAY. Challenging. If you are superstitious, be wary today. Difficulties that arise at work may cause you to suspect someone is trying to get the better of you. A decision you made some time ago may not have proved as successful as you had hoped. Calmly explain the reasons which motivated you. If they are still valid, the discussion can clear the air. Family commitments take priority. A visit from a relative can encourage some long overdue household repairs. Sagittarius parents can enjoy helping youngsters bake their favorite cookies for the occasion. A certain song can bring back memories that make you want to revisit a place of sentimental attachment.

14. SATURDAY. Fortunate. You need to take stock of your life. Changing your approach could broaden your horizons and lead to an interest in something new. Make sure, however, that you do not get too carried away with your ideas. If exploration, adventure, and excitement are high on your list of priorities, a travel agent could provide you with some great ideas. Vacation plans give you something to look forward to. A relative may offer some helpful advice. New friends tend to recharge your batteries, so think about ways to enlarge your social circle. Personal relationships are running smoothly; a close companion can make you feel good about yourself.

15. SUNDAY. Disquieting. Your need for solitude could be misinterpreted. Sagittarius people of all ages need time for quiet reflection away from the hurly-burly of daily life. However, this may force a confrontation, which can shock you by the intensity of the emotions it brings to the surface. Do not feel guilty about a genuine desire to consider your future direction; an honest reappraisal is appropriate. Problems do not go away when they are ignored. Although this might seem like a crisis, it could prove a blessing. If you are at last forced to make decisions and choices, the crisis will have been worthwhile. A break from the past is one possibility. You must choose your own path.

16. MONDAY. Useful. Sagittarius business people should be able now to complete a deal which has been in the pipeline for some time. This presents a good excuse for a celebration. If you have an idea for a new project, you can count on judging today's situation accurately and on realistically assessing any possible problems. If you are thinking of moving, this is a good day to put your home on the market. A quick sale is likely. Shopping for household furniture should be successful; you can find what you need with relative ease. A visit from a friend may prompt you to take out the family photo album. Talking about the past could bring back memories of happy times spent together.

17. TUESDAY. Fair. The highlight of the day could be a birthday party. You are likely to enjoy the preparations as much as the event. Putting up some fancy decorations can add to the occasion. Make sure that you have enough adult help if the party is for children. Your feelings may get the better of you, bringing sentimental tears to your eyes. A new romance is a strong possibility for Sagittarius singles. Be sure to look your best all day. A chance meeting could lead to an encounter which releases powerful emotions on both sides. Although you may be willing to make compromises, it is unwise to become too obsessed.

18. WEDNESDAY. Manageable. Do not let doubts about your abilities get the better of you. If a creative activity is not working out well, it might simply require a slightly different approach. This is a passing mood; try to put it in perspective. If you are involved with children, make this a day of fun. Set serious topics aside and plan to do something which will entertain or amuse them. If you are beginning a new course of study you should be able to grasp the basic concepts with ease. A new romance in your life is apt to bring a sparkle to your eye. Socially you should feel you can do no wrong. Your current popularity is bound to feel exhilarating.

19. THURSDAY. Deceptive. Too much socializing yesterday could mean a hangover this morning. Take things slow and easy, and do not let your feelings get the better of you. Sudden changes at work are putting you under intense pressure. A sense that you are being taken advantage of may tempt you to overreact, causing an unpleasant scene which you are apt to regret. You may be taking too personally what is merely a suggestion. Feelings of insecurity about a relationship could make you uneasy; talking with your partner could clear the air and reassure you. Spend the evening with interesting friends; you are unlikely to be in the mood to put up with bores.

20. FRIDAY. Calm. This quiet day, without pressure, gives you time to take stock of your life. Occasionally it is helpful to analyze which aspects of your work and relationships bring you the greatest contentment. Make the most of this lull in normal activity by dealing with outstanding household or office matters. A coat of paint or a new desk or filing cabinet might seem minor but can make all the difference to your working environment. Ask your mate or steady date for ideas on the ideal way to welcome in the New Year. A few days of careful eating before the festive season is a wise precaution to keep you from breaking the scales next month. If you still have gifts to buy, stop at a department store this evening.

21. SATURDAY. Good. The last weekend before the big day requires considerable organization. If you make lists and plan activities like a military operation you are less likely to forget something important. The last of the gifts should be bought and wrapped. The evening could be spent decorating your home and Christmas tree. If you are going to spend time with family or friends, check your travel arrangements. Fortunately your energy level is high. Try to get as much done as possible while you still have the strength and stamina. As a warmhearted Sagittarius person you may know of someone who will be alone or in an institution for the holidays. A gesture from you could make all the difference.

22. SUNDAY. Difficult. Tension tends to run high today, creating a difficult atmosphere. You could feel that your partner is disregarding your wishes and paying scant attention to your needs. It is vital to resolve differences without forcing a confrontation, which can open old wounds and leave you feeling even worse. You probably both have grievances. Try to understand each other's point of view. If you are in a new romance, thoughts of separation may fill you with dread. However, your loved one is likely to feel claustrophobic and trapped if you appear too possessive. Show that you care, but allow things to take their natural course.

23. MONDAY. Quiet. It should be easy to work well with other people. As part of a team your own input can be positive, and you are likely to take seriously the ideas and suggestions of your colleagues. Enjoy the warm companionship of a joint effort, which can produce results far exceeding those that are possible when you work alone. Close companions are the focus of your attention this evening. You may be in demand for advice and sympathy. Your support can help identify the problem, which can then be more easily solved. A relaxed dinner for two at your favorite neighborhood restaurant is the ideal setting for a real heart-to-heart talk.

24. TUESDAY. Disconcerting. Today's Full Moon puts family relationships under the microscope. A wounding exchange of words at breakfast can leave you feeling isolated and depressed. Sagittarius parents may have a lot of trouble understanding their children or communicating with them. It should help to remember that a minor quarrel is not the end of the world; your friends and neighbors are probably dealing with similar tensions. Sagittarius people engaged in a legal battle may have to decide whether property or relationships are more important. If you have been raising funds for a charity or local hospital, you could receive a windfall that helps you meet your target.

25. WEDNESDAY. MERRY CHRISTMAS! This promises to be a day of constant activity for you, especially if you are with family or close friends. If you are hosting the festivities you may worry that you have not bought sufficient food and drink. And afterward you might wonder whether the effort and expense were really worthwhile. Your Scrooge-like mood may result from tensions that seem to surface when everyone gets together. Unfortunately, reunions can reactivate old rivalries and grudges. Try to avoid this by planning the day carefully; a long walk after dinner and games for all age groups can keep people from getting in each other's hair. Sagittarius spending the day away from home might end up having a memorable encounter.

26. THURSDAY. Mixed. Make time alone your priority today. Responsibilities feel like a burden, and an appeal to your better nature can have the opposite effect. Most people occasionally need space and the chance to consider their aims and priorities, so do not feel guilty. A new activity could engage your interest and offer a solution to your present boredom. An older person may give you the support and encouragement you need. You could be approached with a scheme to make a fast buck. It is difficult to know whether it is realistic; you might be taken for a ride. Investigate thoroughly before you commit yourself.

27. FRIDAY. Fine.   Your need for solitude continues. If you are able to take the day off from work, prepare a lunch and go off on your own for a while. If this is not possible, take a break in the middle of the day to visit an art gallery or the library. Time spent in quiet reflection may help you solve personal problems which have been troubling you recently. The release of inner tension should give you back your old self-confidence and sociability. A romantic evening with your soulmate might suddenly seem like a great idea. This gives you the opportunity to talk about your deepest feelings and clear the air.

28. SATURDAY. Tranquil.   Few demands give you time to think about your future aims. Consider carefully the New Year's resolutions which you hope to achieve. If you are unemployed or frustrated in your present work, you might decide on a new plan of action. A specialized training course could give you the edge on other job applicants. For the young at heart, a move overseas could be the answer to itchy feet. Talk to friends who might like to join you in a travel adventure. Sagittarius sports lovers may feel like some exercise; find a game to use up some of your energy. A foreign film this evening sets the seal on a pleasant day.

29. SUNDAY. Disquieting.   Rumors at work could make you uneasy. You may decide to deal with the matter unofficially. An invitation to a close colleague can bring some unpleasant facts out into the open. Perhaps someone you trusted has not been as loyal as you thought, which can make you angry and insecure. Maybe you are unaware that your will to succeed has ruffled a few feathers, and jealousy is at the core of a current problem. Do not be tempted to rush in and confront your adversaries; doing so could give them satisfaction if they think you are hurt. Guard against blowing the situation out of all proportion. It is better to talk things over with an ally and make clever plans to outwit your opponents.

30. MONDAY. Variable.   Financial matters occupy your thoughts. You could clinch an important deal. Success is likely for the quick-witted who instinctively know when to buy and when to sell. A brainstorming session with colleagues could produce some wonderful ideas. A public speaking engagement is possible. You should have no real cause for concern if you have prepared your talk well in advance. You might even receive more compliments than you anticipated. Do not neglect your appearance; a good-fitting outfit and a manicure can add to your self-confidence. If the evening calls for a celebration, do not overdo the champagne.

31. TUESDAY. Fair. Your work could present minor problems. A colleague may step out of line and publicly criticize your efforts. This can be upsetting but is not worth an argument. If you treat the incident with apparent indifference your rival could seem rather small-minded. Sagittarius people who work in the world of film, art, or dance will have the creative inspiration which can sometimes be elusive. After a season of giving to others, you should treat yourself to a beautiful item for your home such as a limited edition print or sculpture. Spend New Year's Eve with people you care about, especially a group of friends who make you feel good about yourself.

Having A Good Psychic Is Like Having A Guardian Angel!

Love, Romance, Money & Success
May Be In Your Stars...

Get A **FREE** Sample Psychic Reading Today!!!

1-800-799-6582

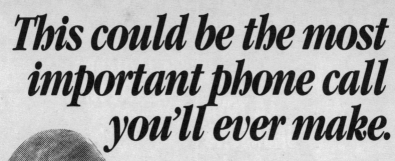

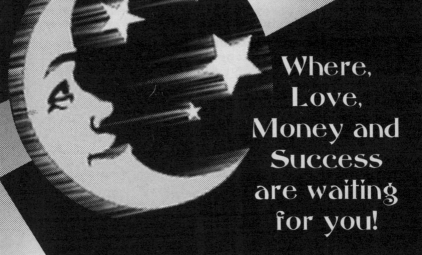

Who is Maria Duval?

◇ She holds the highest honorary awards and degrees.

◇ She has been making accurate and verifiable predictions for the past 23 years in at least:
- 2,391 television shows • 8,407 radio broadcasts

◇ Her achievements have been described in no less than 707 major newspaper articles.

◇ She has been able to predict:
- the rate of the dollar and the stock-market index
- major newspaper headlines

◇ She regularly works with doctors and the police. She has been able to telepathically locate at least 19 missing persons ... she has never failed.

◇ Every experiment conducted on Maria Duval by the greatest scientific authorities has confirmed her exceptional ability to see into the future.

◇ International celebrities come from around the world to consult her.

...ithin 4 days, Maria Duval will give you her precious ...ersonal lucky talisman *for free.*

...a second personal ...ree gift from ...laria Duval

The precious lucky talisman ...ove that Maria Duval offers ...ou is too large to wear. She ...ggests you always leave it at ...ome to protect you (and those ...ou love) from bad luck, and to ...tract good luck and success.

If you send the original coupon ...ithin 48 hours, Maria Duval will ...so give you a second, smaller, ...rsonal talisman that she asks you ...ways to wear or keep near you (in ...few days, you will understand ...hy).

Important

...his offer of free help will ...onclude once we have enough ...articipants for this study. To ...e sure you can participate, ...espond *right now*, while you ...ave this right in your hands. ...hat way, you won't forget and ...ater regret having missed Maria ...Duval's free offer of help.

Confidential Coupon For [Free] Help From Maria Duval*

Mail the original of this coupon today to:
Maria Duval c/o National Parapsychology Center, 435 West , 44th Street, New York, NY 10036-4402

YES I want to take advantage of the *free* help offered by Maria Duval. It is clearly understood this offer *is absolutely free and commits me to nothing—not now, and not later.*

☐ **IMPORTANT:** On a separate sheet I am listing *in a few words* (in capitals):
a) my greatest wish (one single wish)+
b) the question that disturbs me most at this time (one single question)
In return, and without charge, Maria Duval agrees to answer me and to send me a detailed study (of at least 15 pages) concerning me personally and my future. She also agrees to send me my personal lucky numbers.

☐ Don't forget to include my precious lucky talisman offered without charge by Maria Duval (I am responding within 4 days).

☐ I am responding *within 48 hours*. Maria Duval also offers me without charge a second personal talisman that I agree to keep near me.

☐ * I am enclosing only seven 32¢ stamps (or $2) to help defray first-class shipping and handling costs.

IMPORTANT
Honestly answer the following *confidential* questionnaire

1. Do you have any financial problems? ☐ YES ☐ NO
How much money do you urgently need? $ _____

2. Are you unlucky (do you feel like you're born under a bad star)? ☐ YES ☐ NO

3. Are you working? ☐ YES ☐ NO
Are you retired? ☐ YES ☐ NO

4. Are you married or do you have a spouse? ☐ YES ☐ NO

5. Are there major problems in your love or family life? ☐ YES ☐ NO

6. Do you feel lonely or misunderstood? ☐ YES ☐ NO

7. Do you feel as if a spell has been cast on you, or like someone has thrown bad luck your way? ☐ YES ☐ NO

☐ Ms. First name _____ Last name _____
☐ Miss
☐ Mrs. Number and Street _____

Town _____ State ____ Zip Code _____

[Important:] Date of Birth: |__|__|__| 1 9 |__|__| Hour of birth |__|__| ☐ a.m.
Month Day Year Hour/minute ☐ p.m

Age: I am _____ years old and I confirm my zodiac sign is: _____

Place of birth: Town: _____ State _____ Country: _____
AOFL